# Progress to Advanced Mathematics

*Mary Teresa Fyfe*
*Andrew Jobbings*
*Kitty Kilday*
*Mary Read*

Arbelos
?

Shipley, United Kingdom

Progress to Advanced Mathematics

Copyright © A K Jobbings 2011

Published by Arbelos.

PO Box 203, Shipley, BD17 5WT, United Kingdom
http://www.arbelos.co.uk

First published 2011.

Cover illustration and typographic design by Andrew Jobbings.
Typeset with LaTeX.

Printed in the UK for Arbelos by The Charlesworth Group, Wakefield.
http://www.charlesworth.com

ISBN 978-0-9555477-3-7

# Contents

# Preface

We have written this book in response to the experience of teachers who are familiar with the difficulties students face as they make the transition from GCSE, or equivalent, to AS Level, A Level and other advanced mathematics examinations. *Progress to Advanced Mathematics* aims to make the transition smoother and more motivating. We designed the sister book *Progress to Higher Mathematics* with a similar purpose for the Scottish system, and we have been encouraged by the reception it has received.

Students will find this book helps to build their confidence by ensuring they have a good grounding in fundamental material before starting advanced topics. In particular, the book will help to develop the fluency in algebra necessary for success in later work.

*Progress to Advanced Mathematics* provides a series of exercises which can be used either before embarking on sixth form studies or throughout the teaching of the course as introductory material before each topic. Proficiency in algebra is emphasised, but the basics of graphs, coordinate geometry and trigonometry are also covered.

Sometimes a technique studied earlier is needed in a slightly different form in advanced work. For example, though GCSE students will have solved simple linear equations, they may not have solved equations that have decimal coefficients. In order to provide practice in such techniques, we have included questions of an appropriate type in the exercises.

We have designed the material to suit students with any starting level of competence, from basic to well beyond GCSE. The range of exercises should enable students of all abilities to practise the techniques essential to improving their performance in an advanced course. Each section has clearly defined learning outcomes, allowing exercises to be used individually or as part of a complete unit.

Within each exercise the questions are carefully graded. In addition, foundation questions are indicated by an anchor symbol ⚓ and extension questions are indicated by a snowflake symbol ❄. Each chapter ends with a miscellaneous exercise, to provide consolidation as well as helping to identify areas where further practice is needed.

We would like to thank all those who have given us advice and encouragement during the preparation of this book. In particular we would like to thank Vesna Kadelburg for several helpful discussions. Pupils and colleagues, past and present, have always been an inspiration—usually unknowingly—and we hope that this book helps future generations enjoy teaching and learning mathematics.

# 1 Basic algebra

## 1.1 Simplifying expressions

The following exercise will help you to practise:

❑ simplifying an expression involving multiplication

### Exercise 1.1a

**1** Simplify:

    (a) $t \times 7$      (b) $s \times s$      (c) $g \times 5g$      (d) $m \times m \times m$

    (e) $t \times 5 \times t$      (f) $5\beta \times 3\beta$      (g) $6a^2 \times 2$      (h) $2q^2 \times 4q$

**2** Simplify:

    (a) $x \times y$      (b) $\alpha \times \beta$      (c) $3r \times 2s$      (d) $6z \times 2t$

    (e) $4n \times 2m$      (f) $2p \times 3 \times 5q$      (g) $3 \times 4t \times 2t$      (h) $\omega \times 2\pi \times 4$

**3** Simplify:

    (a) $3pq \times 4$      (b) $3 \times 2tz$      (c) $\alpha \times \alpha\beta$      (d) $3hk \times 4hk$

    (e) $6\pi\omega \times 2\omega$      (f) $5 \times 2pq \times 3p$      (g) $vw \times 3w \times v$      (h) $2cd \times cd$

**4** Simplify:

    (a) $p^2 \times pq$      (b) $6hk \times 2k^2$      (c) $f^2g \times fg^2$      (d) $x^3 \times \pi y$

    (e) $2pq \times 3p^2q^2$      (f) $2\alpha^2\beta \times 3\alpha\beta$      (g) $5a \times 2b \times ab$      (h) $2\theta t \times 3 \times t^2$

**5** Simplify:

    (a) $(2x)^2$      (b) $(3y)^2$      (c) $(5\omega)^2$      (d) $(pq)^3$

    (e) $(rs)^2$      (f) $(2cd)^2$      (g) $(3\alpha\beta^2)^2$      (h) $(3a^2b^2)^2$

**6** Simplify:

    (a) $3.2\omega \times 5\omega$      (b) $5.4t \times 10r$      (c) $(0.5m)^2$

    (d) $40t \times 0.3t^2$      (e) $4m \times 0.5n \times 0.1m$      (f) $0.1\alpha \times 0.2\alpha$

    (g) $2\pi rs \times 4.5rt$      (h) $60de^2 \times 0.4d$      (i) $7\pi p^2 \times 1.2pq$

7. Simplify:

(a) $\frac{1}{2}x \times 4y$

(b) $10 \times \frac{3}{5}t$

(c) $\frac{3}{4}\mu \times 24$

(d) $\frac{1}{2}x \times 10 \times \frac{4}{5}y$

(e) $6x^2 \times \frac{1}{12}xy$

(f) $\frac{1}{2}\beta \times \frac{1}{2}\beta^2$

(g) $\frac{1}{5}pq \times \frac{1}{2}p \times 40q$

(h) $\frac{5}{7}y^2 \times 21z \times \frac{3}{5}y$

(i) $\left(\frac{1}{10}s^2\right)^2$

(j) $\left(\frac{2}{3}k\right)^2 \times 9$

(k) $\left(\frac{1}{2}d\right)^3$

(l) $9t \times \left(\frac{1}{3}t\right)^3$

---

The following exercise will help you to practise:

❏ simplifying an expression by collecting like terms together

---

## Exercise 1.1b

1. By collecting like terms together, simplify:

(a) $5x + 4x + 6x$

(b) $\pi - 4\pi + 2\pi$

(c) $5e - 6e - e$

(d) $6\alpha - 2\alpha + 4\alpha - 7\alpha$

(e) $6h + 2h - 5h - 3h$

(f) $\beta - 7\beta + 2\beta$

2. By collecting like terms together, simplify:

(a) $5x + 6 - 2x - 3$

(b) $10p - 4p - 6 - 3$

(c) $7c + 3 + 4c - 2$

(d) $2\pi + 4 - 5\pi - 1$

(e) $4mn + 3 - 3mn - m$

(f) $\alpha\beta - 5 - \alpha\beta + 3$

(g) $5 + 6xy - 3 - 2yx$

(h) $10 - \beta\gamma - \beta\gamma - 2$

(i) $5pq + pq - 7 - 4qp$

3. By collecting like terms together, simplify:

(a) $6x + 2y - 4x + 3y$

(b) $b - 2a + 5b - 4a$

(c) $r + 2pq - 2r + 5pq$

(d) $6h + 5g - 2h - 3g$

(e) $7\pi + t + \pi - 2t$

(f) $\alpha - 3\beta + 4\beta + 5\alpha$

(g) $10s + 4st + 2t - ts$

(h) $6cd + 3c - 2d - 6dc$

(i) $5m - 2nm + 3m - 3mn$

4. By collecting like terms together, simplify:

(a) $3x^2 + 4x - x + 2x^2$

(b) $2 - 3x^2 + 5 - 3x^2$

(c) $5y^2 + 6y - 2y + 3$

(d) $5t - 4t^2 + t - t^2$

(e) $3 - 3\beta - \beta^2 - 4 + 2\beta + \beta^2$

(f) $3s^2 + s^3 - 4s^2 + s^3$

5. By collecting like terms together, simplify:

(a) $6y + y - 4 - 2$

(b) $6r + 5q - q + 3r$

(c) $4m^2 + 2m - 2m^2 + 5m$

(d) $6 - 2n^2 - 3 - 5n^2$

(e) $x^3 - 4x^2 - 3x^3 + x^2$

(f) $7\lambda + 2e - 5e + \lambda$

**6** By collecting like terms together, simplify:

(a) $f^2 + 6 - 4f - 3$

(b) $3t^2 - 5t + 4 + 2t^2 - 4t + 3$

(c) $8 + 6s - s^3 + 2 + 2s^2 - s^3$

(d) $10x^2 + 4x - 3 - 5x + 2$

(e) $4 - 6t + 3t + t^2 - 7$

(f) $y - 5y + 6y^2 - 4 + y$

❄ **7** By collecting like terms together, simplify:

(a) $3.2y + 5.7y - y$

(b) $6.8t + 1.2t - 8t$

(c) $1.6uv + 5.4 - uv - 6.1$

(d) $4.2\alpha - 3.1\beta + 3\beta + 6\alpha$

(e) $5.6 - 1.2\sigma^2 + 4.8 - \sigma^2$

(f) $7.4 - 1.2z - z^2 - 0.8 + 0.8z + 1.4z^2$

(g) $0.4e^2 + 3.4e^3 - 0.7e^2 + e^3$

(h) $4.8 + 6.2m^2 - 0.9 - 5.7m^2$

❄ **8** By collecting like terms together, simplify:

(a) $\frac{1}{2}q + \frac{1}{2}q - \frac{1}{6}q$

(b) $\frac{3}{4}\pi + \frac{1}{3}\pi - \pi$

(c) $a - \frac{1}{6} - \frac{2}{3}a + \frac{5}{6}$

(d) $\frac{1}{2}\theta + \frac{1}{3}\theta - \frac{1}{4}\theta - \frac{1}{6}\theta$

(e) $\frac{2}{3}\pi + \frac{1}{6}t - \frac{1}{4}\pi - \frac{1}{3}t$

(f) $\frac{5}{7}r - \frac{1}{10}s - \frac{1}{100}s - \frac{1}{2}r$

(g) $\frac{2}{5}\omega^3 - \frac{1}{3}\omega - \frac{1}{10}\omega^3 + \frac{1}{6}\omega$

(h) $1 - \frac{2}{5}x - \frac{7}{10}x^2 - \frac{1}{6} + \frac{2}{9}x + \frac{1}{6}x^2$

## 1.2 Expanding brackets

The following exercise will help you to practise:
  ❑ expanding single brackets and simplifying

### Exercise 1.2a

⚓ 1  Expand the brackets:

  (a) $2(x - y)$  (b) $3(2\lambda + 5)$  (c) $6(5y - 4)$
  (d) $3(2a + 3b - 4c)$  (e) $2(\pi - 2x + x^2)$  (f) $5(t^3 - 2t^2 + 4t - 5)$

⚓ 2  Expand the brackets:

  (a) $-2(x + y)$  (b) $-5(a - b)$  (c) $-(2\alpha - 3\beta)$
  (d) $-4(a - 3b + 4c)$  (e) $-\pi(x^2 - 4x)$  (f) $-5(1 - 2t - t^2)$

3  Expand and simplify:

  (a) $4(x - y) + 3(x + y)$  (b) $5(a + 2b) - 3(2a - 3b)$
  (c) $3(t - 1) - (5 - 2t)$  (d) $2(3 - \pi) + 4(3\pi + 5)$
  (e) $3(m^2 - 4m) + 2(1 - 2m + 4m^2)$  (f) $3(n^3 - n^2 + 3n - 5) - (n^3 + 3n - 4)$

4  Expand and simplify:

  (a) $3(2\omega + 7) + 4(\omega - 3) + 8$  (b) $6(2y - 3) - 2(3y - 12) - 4(2y + 3)$
  (c) $5(3u + 2v) + 2(w - 2v) - (w - u)$  (d) $3(z + 2t) + 6q - 4(q - 2z) - t$
  (e) $2(5 - w) + 4(m - t) - 4m + 3$  (f) $x - 4y + 3(y - 2x) + 10$

⚓ 5  Expand the brackets:

  (a) $x(x - 2)$  (b) $e(2e - 5)$  (c) $3h(4h - 2)$
  (d) $-3\omega(2\omega + 3)$  (e) $-2x(1 - 2x + x^2)$  (f) $5p(p^3 - 2p^2 + 4p - 5)$

6  Expand and simplify:

  (a) $4 - 2(x + 3)$  (b) $6 - 2(4 - 2\mu)$  (c) $10 + 2(4z - 2)$
  (d) $3p - p(p + 2)$  (e) $h - 2h(5 + h)$  (f) $\beta^2 - 2\beta^2(\beta + 4)$

7  Expand and simplify:

  (a) $2p(p - 5) + 3p$  (b) $2t + t(3t^2 - 1)$  (c) $a(b + a^2) - b^2$
  (d) $x(3x + 4y) - xy$  (e) $3m(4 - n) + m^2$  (f) $z^2 - z(1 - z)$

8 | Expand and simplify:

(a) $x(3x - 2) + 5x(x - 2)$

(b) $a(a - 4) - (3a + 1)$

(c) $2n(3 + m) - 5m(m - 2n)$

(d) $\alpha(4\alpha - 5) + (\alpha + 7)$

(e) $\beta(\beta - 5) + 2\beta(1 - 2\beta + \beta^2)$

(f) $k(k^3 - k^2 + 4k + 1) - (5 - 3k + 2k^2)$

❄ 9 | Expand and simplify:

(a) $1.6(2y - 5)$

(b) $-0.4(10 + 2x)$

(c) $5.6(2y + 3z) - (3.4z - 12.6y)$

(d) $0.4\alpha(10\alpha^3 - 20\alpha^2 + 400\alpha - 50)$

(e) $0.3t(5 - 4t) + 0.2(t^2 - 2t)$

(f) $2k(0.4k^2 - 0.55k) - 0.7k^2(3k - 20)$

❄ 10 | Expand the brackets:

(a) $\frac{1}{2}(6s + 4t)$

(b) $\frac{1}{3}\left(\frac{1}{2}a^2 - \frac{1}{4}a\right)$

(c) $12\left(\frac{1}{3} - \frac{1}{4}c + \frac{1}{6}c^2\right)$

(d) $\frac{2}{3}\left(6q^3 - 12q^2 + 21q - 15\right)$

(e) $\frac{1}{3}\left(\frac{3}{7} - \frac{6}{7}e\right)$

(f) $-\frac{3}{4}\left(\frac{1}{3}z + \frac{1}{6}t\right)$

❄ 11 | Expand and simplify:

(a) $\frac{1}{3}(\sigma - 1) - \frac{1}{3}(5 - 2\sigma)$

(b) $\frac{1}{2}\left(t^3 - t^2 + 3t - 5\right) - \left(t^3 + 3t - 4\right)$

(c) $z - \frac{5}{6}z(4 - z)$

(d) $m^2 - \frac{1}{3}m^2(m + 4)$

The following exercise will help you to practise:

❏ expanding double brackets and simplifying

## Exercise 1.2b

1 | Expand and simplify:

(a) $(x + 1)(x + 3)$

(b) $(3m + 7)(4m + 1)$

(c) $(9t + 2)(2t + 3)$

(d) $(2 + n)(3 + n)$

(e) $(4 + z)(1 + 2z)$

(f) $(6 + 5s)(2 + 3s)$

2 | Expand and simplify:

(a) $(x - 1)(x - 4)$

(b) $(5e - 2)(3e - 2)$

(c) $(b - 1)(5b - 3)$

(d) $(1 - z)(2 - z)$

(e) $(3 - 2t)(1 - 3t)$

(f) $(2 - 5n)(5 - 2n)$

3 | Expand and simplify:

(a) $(x + 2)(x - 3)$

(b) $(p - 4)(p + 4)$

(c) $(7 - q)(6 + q)$

(d) $(3 - 5n)(3 + 5n)$

(e) $(2 + z)(z - 1)$

(f) $(2h - 3)(4 + 3h)$

4 | Expand and simplify:

(a) $(5x + 1)(x - 3)$      (b) $(4m - 5)(3m + 1)$      (c) $(2k - 1)(2k + 1)$

(d) $(4p + 1)(2p - 3)$      (e) $(6m - 5)(2m + 3)$      (f) $(7 - 5\beta)(2\beta - 3)$

(g) $(2 - 9n)(9n + 2)$      (h) $(1 - p)(3 - 2p)$      (i) $(5 + 2y)(1 - y)$

5 | Expand and simplify:

(a) $(x + 3)^2$      (b) $(y - 4)^2$      (c) $(2a + 1)^2$      (d) $(3x - 2)^2$

(e) $(5m + 4)^2$      (f) $(2t - 7)^2$      (g) $(3 - t)^2$      (h) $(10 - 3m)^2$

6 | Expand:

(a) $(x + 3)(y + 2)$      (b) $(t - 4)(s + 2)$      (c) $(z - 1)(y - 3)$

(d) $(5 + r)(4 - w)$      (e) $(2q - 3)(4p + 3)$      (f) $(1 - d)(2 - c)$

7 | Expand and simplify:

(a) $(x + y)(x - 3y)$      (b) $(5\lambda - 2)^2$      (c) $(4p - q)(3p + 2q)$

(d) $(\alpha + 1)(\alpha - 4)$      (e) $(4 - t)(5 - 2t)$      (f) $(3c - 2d)^2$

(g) $(4 - \omega)(5 + 3\omega)$      (h) $2(n + 3)^2$      (i) $4(s - 3)(s + 3)$

8 | Expand and simplify:

(a) $(n - 1)^2 + (n + 2)^2$      (b) $(4y + 3)(y - 1) - 5(y - 2)$

(c) $m^2 + 2m - (m + 2)(2m - 3)$      (d) $(\lambda - 2)(\lambda + 3) - (\lambda + 1)^2$

(e) $(\alpha - 1)(\alpha^2 + \alpha + 1) + \alpha^3 + 1$      (f) $2(s - 3)^2 - 3(s + 2)^2$

❄ 9 | Expand and simplify:

(a) $(x + 1)(x^2 + 2x + 1)$      (b) $(2p - 5)(p^2 - 2p - 1)$

(c) $(3y - 1)(y^2 + 3y + 1)$      (d) $(1 + t)(5 - 2t + t^2)$

❄ 10 | Expand and simplify:

(a) $(a + b + 2)(a - b + 1)$      (b) $(p - q + r)(p + q + r)$

(c) $(x + 3 - y)(y + 2 + x)$      (d) $(r - 2s + 3t)^2$

❄ 11 | Expand and simplify:

(a) $(n + 3)^3$      (b) $(\gamma - 2)^3$      (c) $(4 - q)^3$

(d) $(2s - 1)^3$      (e) $(3e + 2)^3$      (f) $(p - 2q)^3$

# 1.3 Factorising by finding a common factor

The following exercise will help you to practise:

❑ factorising an expression by finding a common factor

❑ recognising that $(a - b)$ and $(b - a)$ are related: $(b - a) = -(a - b)$

**Exercise 1.3**

⌱ **1** By finding a common factor, factorise:

(a) $3x + 3y$      (b) $5z - 5t$      (c) $3\theta + 9$

(d) $24 - 6k$      (e) $\pi + \pi t$      (f) $15y - 10$

(g) $15t + 10r - 25s$      (h) $50m - 30z + 40x$      (i) $24x + 30y - 42z$

**2** By finding a common factor, factorise:

(a) $x^2 + 5x$      (b) $n^2 - 2n$      (c) $\pi t - t^2$

(d) $p^2 + 7p$      (e) $pq + 2q$      (f) $4r + rs$

(g) $qt + qr + qs - 6q$      (h) $vz + vw - v^2$      (i) $sx - rx + 3x^2 - x^3$

**3** By finding a common factor, factorise:

(a) $2x^2 - 6x$      (b) $4y^2 - 4y$      (c) $6m - 3m^2$

(d) $12\alpha - 6\alpha^2$      (e) $6n^2 + 15n$      (f) $15q^2 - 18q$

(g) $8\omega^2 + 12\omega$      (h) $6\beta - 4\beta^2 + 20\beta^3$      (i) $25s^3 + 15s - 10s^2$

**4** By finding a common factor, factorise:

(a) $p^2q + q$      (b) $3rs^2 + s$      (c) $5\pi r^2 - 10r^2$

(d) $3rt^3 + 6r^2t - 3rt$      (e) $3\alpha\beta - 2\beta^3$      (f) $5cd + 6c^2d^2$

(g) $2s^3 + s^2$      (h) $5ab^2 + a^2b^2 + a^2b$      (i) $ar + ar^2 + ar^3$

**5** By finding a common factor, factorise:

(a) $2(x + 3) + z(x + 3)$      (b) $m(m - 1) + n(m - 1)$

(c) $r(t + 1) - 4(t + 1)$      (d) $q(r + 2s) + (r + 2s)$

(e) $(2x + 1) + 3x^2(2x + 1)$      (f) $5k(k - 2) - (k - 2)$

❄ **6** By finding a common factor, factorise:

(a) $5(x - 2) + z(2 - x)$

(b) $k(m - 1) + n(1 - m)$

(c) $r(2q - 3) + p(3 - 2q)$

(d) $2(m - 3) - m(3 - m)$

(e) $p(t - 1) - 3(1 - t)$

(f) $2(x - 4)^2 + 3(4 - x)$

(g) $p(q - 1) + (1 - q)^2$

(h) $k(7m - 1)^2 + r(1 - 7m)$

❄ **7** Factorise:

(a) $3(x + 4)^2 + z(x + 4)$

(b) $a(b - 1) + b(b - 1)^2$

(c) $t(7p - 1)^2 + r(7p - 1)$

(d) $x^2(x + 3) - x(x + 3)$

(e) $x(y + 1)^2 - z(y + 1)^3$

(f) $r(t + 1)^3 - 4r(t + 1)^2$

❄ **8** Factorise:

(a) $\sin x \cos x + \cos x$

(b) $3 \cos A \tan A - \tan A$

(c) $6 \cos \alpha - 10 \sin \alpha \cos \alpha$

(d) $5 \tan^2 t + 5 \tan t$

(e) $\cos^2 C - 3 \cos C$

(f) $\cos \theta \tan \theta + \sin \theta \tan \theta$

# 1.4 Factorising quadratic expressions

The following exercise will help you to practise:

❑ factorising a difference of two squares using $a^2 - b^2 \equiv (a - b)(a + b)$

### Exercise 1.4a

1. Factorise:
   - (a) $x^2 - y^2$
   - (b) $p^2 - 9$
   - (c) $t^2 - 25$
   - (d) $q^2 - 16$
   - (e) $b^2 - \frac{1}{4}$
   - (f) $49 - x^2$
   - (g) $\frac{4}{9} - \alpha^2$
   - (h) $c^2 - 36$

2. Factorise:
   - (a) $4x^2 - 9$
   - (b) $25m^2 - 49$
   - (c) $1 - 9t^2$
   - (d) $9 - 16\beta^2$
   - (e) $p^2 - 4q^2$
   - (f) $49k^2 - 25m^2$
   - (g) $9z^2 - 4x^2$
   - (h) $100 - 81t^2$
   - (i) $0.04b^2 - a^2$
   - (j) $\frac{c^2}{4} - \frac{d^2}{25}$
   - (k) $\frac{y^2}{49} - 1$
   - (l) $\frac{r^2}{9} - \frac{t^2}{16}$

3. By first finding a common factor, factorise completely:
   - (a) $2x^2 - 8$
   - (b) $3t^2 - 75$
   - (c) $12 - 3m^2$
   - (d) $45y^2 - 5$
   - (e) $\pi q^2 - \pi p^2$
   - (f) $cd^2 - ce^2$
   - (g) $x^2z - 16z$
   - (h) $4a^2b - 9b$
   - (i) $25km^2 - 4kt^2$
   - (j) $\frac{1}{9}\pi y^2 - \pi z^2$
   - (k) $4y^3 - 36y$
   - (l) $\frac{1}{3}st^2 - \frac{1}{3}s^3$

❄ 4. Factorise completely:
   - (a) $z^4 - 1$
   - (b) $4t^3 - t$
   - (c) $1 - p^4$
   - (d) $ar^2 - ar^4$

The following exercise will help you to practise:

❑ factorising a 'trinomial' quadratic expression into two brackets

❑ factorising a quadratic expression by first finding a common factor

### Exercise 1.4b

1. Factorise:
   - (a) $x^2 + 6x + 5$
   - (b) $y^2 + 4y + 3$
   - (c) $m^2 + 8m + 7$
   - (d) $t^2 + 5t + 6$
   - (e) $b^2 + 6b + 8$
   - (f) $e^2 + 8e + 12$

**2** Factorise:

(a) $p^2 - 3p + 2$      (b) $x^2 - 2x + 1$      (c) $q^2 - 7q + 12$

(d) $z^2 - 10z + 16$      (e) $y^2 - 11y + 24$      (f) $n^2 - 16n + 15$

**3** Factorise:

(a) $x^2 + x - 2$      (b) $t^2 + 4t - 5$      (c) $c^2 - 2c - 3$

(d) $p^2 - p - 6$      (e) $z^2 + 3z - 4$      (f) $r^2 + 4r - 12$

(g) $a^2 - 6a - 16$      (h) $e^2 - 5e - 24$      (i) $h^2 - 11h - 12$

**4** Factorise:

(a) $2x^2 + 7x + 5$      (b) $5y^2 + 8y + 3$      (c) $3m^2 + 10m + 7$

(d) $5n^2 - 6n + 1$      (e) $5q^2 - 7q + 2$      (f) $2z^2 - z - 6$

(g) $14a^2 + 25a + 6$      (h) $12e^2 - 25e + 12$      (i) $8w^2 + 13w - 6$

**5** Factorise:

(a) $1 + 3x + 2x^2$      (b) $1 + 6m + 5m^2$      (c) $4 + 5c + c^2$

(d) $10 + 7z + z^2$      (e) $12 + 7a + a^2$      (f) $6 + 5x + x^2$

(g) $5 - 6b + b^2$      (h) $6 + 13s + 6s^2$      (i) $2 - 19\beta + 9\beta^2$

**6** Factorise:

(a) $1 + x - 2x^2$      (b) $1 - 2y - 3y^2$      (c) $1 + t - 6t^2$

(d) $8 + 2t - t^2$      (e) $6 + 5m - m^2$      (f) $24 - 5w - w^2$

(g) $3 + y - 2y^2$      (h) $12 - 17n - 5n^2$      (i) $8 + 10p - 3p^2$

**7** Factorise:

(a) $x^2 - 12 + 4x$      (b) $3t^2 + 4 - 7t$      (c) $5m - 3 + 2m^2$

(d) $13\omega + 15\omega^2 + 2$      (e) $2 - z^2 - z$      (f) $15 + g^2 - 8g$

(g) $1 + 2c^2 - 3c$      (h) $9 - 8s^2 + 6s$      (i) $-5 + 6r^2 - r$

**8** By first finding a common factor, factorise completely:

(a) $2x^2 + 8x + 6$      (b) $5e^2 + 10e - 15$      (c) $3m^2 - 21m + 30$

(d) $4\alpha^2 + 24\alpha - 28$      (e) $xy^2 + xy - 6x$      (f) $0.3pq^2 - 1.5pq - 1.8p$

❄ **9** Factorise:

(a) $2p^2 - 3pq - 2q^2$      (b) $5t^2 + 24rt - 5r^2$      (c) $3x^2 + 8xy - 3y^2$

(d) $2a^2 + ab - 10b^2$      (e) $5w^2 + 8wx - 4x^2$      (f) $3k^2 + 14km - 5m^2$

❄ 10  Factorise:

(a)  $\tan^2 \beta + 2\tan\beta - 3$

(b)  $\sin^2 B - \sin B - 6$

(c)  $\tan^2 \theta - 7\tan\theta + 10$

(d)  $2\tan^2 \lambda + \tan\lambda - 1$

(e)  $6\sin^2 P - \sin P - 2$

(f)  $10\sin^2 \phi + 7\sin\phi - 3$

(g)  $5\cos^2 X - 7\cos X + 2$

(h)  $5\tan^2 C + 32\tan C + 12$

## 1.5 Substituting into expressions

The following exercise will help you to practise:
- ❏ substituting values into an expression

*You should be able to do most of the questions in Exercise 1.5 without a calculator.*

### Exercise 1.5

**1** When $x = 3$, $y = -2$ and $z = -1$, evaluate:

   (a) $x + y$        (b) $10 - y$       (c) $z - x$        (d) $y + z$

   (e) $x + y - z$     (f) $z - y - x$     (g) $y - z + x$     (h) $x + y + z$

**2** When $p = -5$, $q = 4$ and $r = -3$, evaluate:

   (a) $3q$           (b) $5r$          (c) $pq$          (d) $3pr$

   (e) $pqr$         (f) $p - 2q$     (g) $3p + q$     (h) $rq - pq$

**3** When $t = 2$, $m = -3$ and $k = -4$, evaluate:

   (a) $-t^3$         (b) $2m^2$       (c) $(3t)^2 - m^2$     (d) $(-2t)^2$

   (e) $(tm)^2$      (f) $tm^2$       (g) $-k^2 m$        (h) $kmt^2$

**4** When $x = 3$, $y = -1$ and $z = -4$, evaluate:

   (a) $\dfrac{x}{y}$        (b) $\dfrac{-2z}{y}$      (c) $\dfrac{xz}{-2y}$      (d) $\dfrac{x + z}{y + z}$

   (e) $\dfrac{3x}{2z + y}$    (f) $\dfrac{x^2 - y}{x + z}$    (g) $\dfrac{-x^2}{y^2}$      (h) $\dfrac{x - 2y}{3z - 2y}$

**5** When $a = 5$, $b = -6$, $c = 3$ and $d = -1$, evaluate:

   (a) $\sqrt{a + d}$     (b) $\sqrt{c^2 - a}$     (c) $\sqrt{2d - bc}$     (d) $-\sqrt{2a - b}$

   (e) $-\sqrt{abd + 2c}$    (f) $\sqrt{\dfrac{bc}{2d}}$     (g) $\sqrt{\dfrac{a + 4d}{3c}}$     (h) $-\sqrt{\dfrac{b + 2c}{a}}$

❄ **6** When $a = 1.2$, $b = -3.5$, $c = 0.4$ and $d = 4$, evaluate:

   (a) $b - a$       (b) $bd - 10c$    (c) $\dfrac{ad}{c}$        (d) $\dfrac{b}{d}$

   (e) $2c^2$         (f) $\dfrac{a}{c}$         (g) $b - d$       (h) $(5a)^2$

❄ **7** When $p = \frac{1}{3}$, $q = \frac{1}{4}$ and $r = \frac{3}{5}$, evaluate:

(a) $pq$       (b) $r - q$       (c) $pr^2$       (d) $2p^2$

(e) $\sqrt{q}$       (f) $\dfrac{q}{p}$       (g) $\dfrac{r}{p+q}$       (h) $\dfrac{q}{r} - p$

❄ **8** When $P = 13.2$, $R = 10.6$, $m = 3$, $a = -0.7$, $t = 5$, $g = 9.8$, $h = 5.8$, $u = 6.7$ and $v = -12.2$, evaluate:

(a) $P + 2R - mg$       (b) $\frac{1}{2}mv^2 - \frac{1}{2}mu^2$       (c) $mgh$

(d) $u + at$       (e) $ut + \frac{1}{2}at^2$       (f) $u^2 + 2gh$

(g) $P \cos 30°$       (h) $R \sin 30°$       (i) $mg \cos 50°$

## 1.6 Miscellaneous questions

### Exercise 1.6

1. Simplify:
    (a) $q \times q \times 3$
    (b) $mn \times m \times mn$
    (c) $0.3ab \times 5a^2b$
    (d) $4s - 6s - 3s$
    (e) $4h - 5 - 4h + 5$
    (f) $g^2 + 4 - 2g^2 - 5$
    (g) $1.9(10t - 40)$
    (h) $10 + 8(6\pi - 1)$
    (i) $4q(q + 2) - (1 - q^2)$

2. Simplify:
    (a) $(2c + 7)(c - 3)$
    (b) $(2w + 3)(4 - 5w)$
    (c) $(4x - 3)^2$
    (d) $(k - 2)(m + 1)$
    (e) $3(2t - 3)^2 + 2(t - 1)(t + 1)$
    (f) $(f + 3)^3$
    (g) $\left(\frac{1}{2}x + 2\right)^2$
    (h) $n\left(\frac{1}{3}n - \frac{1}{3}\right) + \frac{1}{2}n\left(n - \frac{1}{3}\right)$

3. Find expressions, in a form without brackets, for the perimeter and the area of the rectangle:

    (a)
    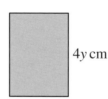
    $3x$ cm
    $2x$ cm

    (b)
    $4y$ cm
    $3x$ cm

    (c)
    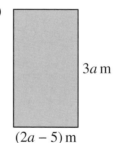
    $3a$ m
    $(2a - 5)$ m

4. Find expressions, in a form without brackets, for the perimeter and the area of the shape:

    (a)
    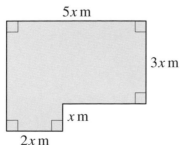
    $5x$ m
    $3x$ m
    $x$ m
    $2x$ m

    (b)
    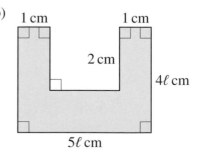
    1 cm    1 cm
    2 cm
    $4\ell$ cm
    $5\ell$ cm

**5** The diagram shows a square with a semicircle attached to each side.

Find and simplify expressions for the perimeter and the area of the whole shape.

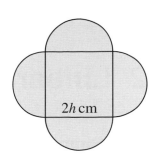

$2h$ cm

**6** The diagram shows a rectangle with a semicircle attached to each shorter side.

Find and simplify expressions for the perimeter and the area of the whole shape.

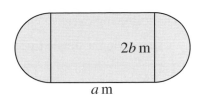

$2b$ m

$a$ m

**7** Factorise completely:

(a) $3p^2 + 6p + 3$

(b) $\pi r^2 - \pi$

(c) $10m^2 + 5m - 5$

(d) $8\mu^2 - 50$

(e) $6t^2 - 4t - 2$

(f) $0.6b^2 + 0.3b$

(g) $9 + 6a + a^2$

(h) $2y^2 - 5y - 3$

(i) $t^2 - \frac{1}{9}s^2$

(j) $12 - 3k^2$

(k) $p(q - 1) + 5(q - 1)$

(l) $t^2(t + 1) - t(t + 1) + 3(t + 1)$

**8** Factorise completely:

(a) $4x^2 - 1$

(b) $4x^2 + 4$

(c) $4x^2 + 4x$

(d) $4x^2 - 4$

(e) $3y^2 + 3$

(f) $3y^2 - 3$

(g) $3y^2 - 3y$

(h) $3y^2 - 3y^3$

**9** Factorise completely:

(a) $3\tan\phi + 4\tan^2\phi$

(b) $3\sin^3 x + 5\sin^2 x - 7\sin x$

(c) $\cos^2 t - 3\cos t + 2$

(d) $3\sin^2\alpha - 2\sin\alpha - 5$

**10** When $k = -3$, $m = 2$ and $z = 5$, evaluate:

(a) $kmz$

(b) $k - zm^2$

(c) $z(m - k)$

(d) $5k^2 - 3m^3$

(e) $\sqrt{2z + 3m}$

(f) $\dfrac{4z}{m}$

(g) $\dfrac{k^2}{m - z}$

(h) $\sqrt{\dfrac{2(k + m)}{k - z}}$

# 2 Linear equations

## 2.1 Simple linear equations

The following exercise will help you to practise:

❑ solving a simple linear equation

**Exercise 2.1**

⚓ 1  Solve the equation:

    (a) $8a = 72$                        (b) $5b = 2$

    (c) $1 + 12d = 29$              (d) $10f - 3 = -34$

    (e) $3m = m + 2$              (f) $14t = -12 + 11t$

    (g) $5e - 13 = 3e$             (h) $3f + 5 = f$

⚓ 2  Solve the equation:

    (a) $-6 = 36q$                  (b) $12 - 8r = r$

    (c) $1 - 3\mu = 7\mu$               (d) $7T = 13T - 5$

    (e) $10 + v = 3v$               (f) $w = 32 + 5w$

    (g) $6\theta - 2 = 9\theta$             (h) $8u + 7 = 10u$

⚓ 3  Solve the equation:

    (a) $6g + 20 = g$              (b) $2 - 5P = 7P$

    (c) $5 - 2y = 6y$              (d) $5\alpha = 3 - \alpha$

    (e) $4n = 30 - n$              (f) $8 - X = 5X$

    (g) $2k = 60 - 3k$            (h) $3 - 4\rho = 8\rho$

4  Solve the equation:

    (a) $8n - 2 = 3n + 8$        (b) $3r - 5 = r - 17$

    (c) $4t - 7 = t + 32$         (d) $5u - 1 = 3u + 7$

    (e) $1 + 5\lambda = 7\lambda - 2$       (f) $2W = 5W - 3$

    (g) $4 + 7\beta = 10\beta + 2$     (h) $4 + 3e = 3 + 14e$

5 | Solve the equation:

    (a) $3(4 - n) = 5(3 - n)$              (b) $7(2a + 9) = 3(1 - 2a)$

    (c) $5 + 3(4b - 7) = 7(b - 3)$      (d) $\frac{1}{2}(p + 2) = \frac{1}{4}(p - 1)$

    (e) $6(k - 0.1) + 0.2 = 5(k + 0.3)$   (f) $3(x + 2) - 2(3x - 4) = -10$

    (g) $5(3y - 2) = 23 - 6(7 - 2y)$    (h) $2(5z + 1) - 4(3z + 2) = 5 + 8(z + 3)$

    (i) $t(t + 2) = (t + 5)(t - 2)$       (j) $(2w + 1)(3w - 1) = (w + 1)(6w - 7)$

6 | Solve the equation for the term in the box:

    (a) $4 \sin x + 3 = 7 \sin x$           $\boxed{\sin x}$

    (b) $4 + 2 \tan x = 9$              $\boxed{\tan x}$

    (c) $1 - \cos x = 0.624$          $\boxed{\cos x}$

    (d) $1.2 + 3 \tan x = 2.73$        $\boxed{\tan x}$

    (e) $3 - 2 \sin x = 1.846$         $\boxed{\sin x}$

    (f) $4 \cos x + 1.415 = 2.741 - 9 \cos x$   $\boxed{\cos x}$

## 2.2  Linear equations with fractions

The following exercise will help you to practise:

❏ solving a linear equation with fractions, by multiplying every term by the same value

**Exercise 2.2**

**1** Solve the equation:

(a) $\frac{1}{2}a = 3$

(b) $\frac{x}{4} = 2$

(c) $\frac{2}{5}p = -4$

(d) $\frac{3t}{4} = 7$

(e) $-\frac{1}{3}z = \frac{2}{7}$

(f) $0.8t = 4$

(g) $1.5a = 6$

(h) $\frac{2}{3} = 4 - \frac{1}{6}k$

(i) $\frac{f}{3} + 1 = \frac{5}{3}$

**2** Solve the equation:

(a) $\frac{1}{2}r - \frac{2}{3} = r$

(b) $p - \frac{2}{3} = \frac{1}{4}p$

(c) $F + \dfrac{1}{2} = \dfrac{F}{3}$

(d) $\dfrac{g}{2} - 4 = \dfrac{g}{3}$

(e) $\frac{1}{8}d + \frac{1}{4} = \frac{1}{2}d$

**3** Solve the equation:

(a) $\frac{5}{3} + \alpha = \frac{1}{3} - \alpha$

(b) $1\frac{2}{3} + 8j = 5 - \frac{1}{3}j$

(c) $\frac{1}{3}e + \frac{2}{3} = \frac{1}{4}e - \frac{5}{6}$

(d) $\frac{3}{8}v - \frac{1}{4} = \frac{1}{2} + \frac{1}{4}v$

(e) $1.2b - 3.6 = 4.8b + 7.2$

(f) $5.2 - 0.5t = 4.6 - 0.25t$

**4** Solve the equation:

(a) $\frac{2}{5}(s - 2) = s$

(b) $\dfrac{t - 1}{7} = \dfrac{t + 1}{5}$

(c) $\dfrac{2a - 3}{6} = \dfrac{3a + 1}{4}$

(d) $\frac{3}{4}p = 0.25p - 2.3$

(e) $\frac{1}{2}(3r + 1) = \frac{1}{4}(1 - 4r)$

(f) $\dfrac{2 + 0.5f}{8} = \dfrac{3 + 0.2f}{4}$

**5** Solve the equation:

(a) $\dfrac{3p}{5} - 2 = \dfrac{p}{3} + \dfrac{2}{5}$

(b) $\dfrac{q - 2}{4} = \dfrac{q - 4}{5}$

(c) $\dfrac{x + 2}{4} - x = -4$

(d) $\dfrac{y + 1}{5} + \dfrac{2y + 3}{7} = y - 4$

## 2.3   Linear inequalities

The following exercise will help you to practise:

❏ solving a linear inequality

### Exercise 2.3

**1** Find all integers from 0 to 10 which satisfy:

(a) $4a < 8$      (b) $5s > -5$      (c) $8f \leq 56$      (d) $7u \geq 40$

(e) $\frac{1}{2}p < 3$      (f) $\frac{3}{4}x \geq 4$      (g) $0.4r < 2$      (h) $1.5t \leq 6$

(i) $-6c > -6$      (j) $-5y \geq 10$      (k) $2 < c \leq 6$      (l) $n < 2$ or $n > 6$

**2** Find all integers from 0 to 10 which satisfy:

(a) $1 + x > 7$      (b) $10 - u > 6$      (c) $3c + 2 \leq 20$

(d) $6n - 4 < 8n - 15$      (e) $1 + 0.5t \geq 5 + 0.1t$      (f) $\frac{3}{4}s + 3 > \frac{1}{3}s + 4$

**3** Solve the inequality:

(a) $5c - 8 < c + 4$      (b) $\frac{5}{6}x + 1 > \frac{1}{3}x - 2$      (c) $\dfrac{d + 1}{4} > d - 5$

(d) $0.6f - 3 \leq 0.4f - 5$      (e) $\dfrac{t}{5} + 9 < t + 10$      (f) $1 - 8e < 2e - 5$

(g) $1 + \frac{2}{3}g \geq \frac{1}{4}g - 2$

**4** Solve the compound inequality:

(a) $-2 < x + 3 < 7$      (b) $0 \leq 3c + 6 \leq 30$      (c) $-9 < \frac{4}{5}t - 1 < 3$

## 2.4   Simultaneous linear equations

The following exercise will help you to practise:

❏ solving a pair of simultaneous linear equations

### Exercise 2.4

**1**  Solve the simultaneous equations:

(a)  $3x + y = 10$
  $x - y = 2$

(b)  $a + b = 5$
  $2a - b = 7$

(c)  $12p + 5q = 50$
  $9p - 5q = 55$

(d)  $4y + 3z = 6$
  $8y - 3z = 12$

(e)  $6g - h = -9$
  $6g + 5h = -27$

(f)  $x + y = 2$
  $2x - y = 7$

**2**  Solve the simultaneous equations:

(a)  $x - 2y = 6$
  $3x - 2y = 14$

(b)  $2a + 3b = 15$
  $a + 3b = 15$

(c)  $5p - 2q = 2$
  $p - 2q = 0$

(d)  $8\theta + \phi = 2$
  $3\theta + \phi = 1$

(e)  $\frac{3}{4}x - \frac{1}{2}y = 11$
  $\frac{1}{4}x - \frac{1}{2}y = 5$

(f)  $5a + 9b = -1$
  $a + 9b = 1$

**3**  Solve the simultaneous equations:

(a)  $3m + 4n = 11$
  $m + 2n = 3$

(b)  $5a - 4d = 19$
  $a + 3d = 0$

(c)  $4f - 2g = -7$
  $9f + g = -2$

(d)  $\frac{1}{2}x - y = 3$
  $x - \frac{1}{2}y = 9$

(e)  $\frac{1}{4}r + s = -1$
  $r - \frac{3}{4}s = 15$

(f)  $h + k = 5$
  $\frac{2}{3}h + \frac{1}{2}k = 2$

**4**  Solve the simultaneous equations:

(a)  $6\alpha - 7\beta = 5$
  $7\alpha + 6\beta = 20$

(b)  $7a - 5d = 20$
  $5a + 3d = 11$

(c)  $7s + 3t = 1.3$
  $3s + 5t = 1.3$

(d)  $7h + 6w = 0.6$
  $5h - 8w = 3.5$

(e)  $6p - 5q = -14$
  $4p - 3q = -10$

(f)  $3c + 5d = -9$
  $5c + 3d = -15$

**5**  Solve the simultaneous equations:

(a)  $0.2x - 0.3y = 7$
  $0.5x + 0.3y = 7$

(b)  $p + 2q = 3$
  $0.5p + q = 1.5$

(c)  $5k - 0.5l = 17$
  $0.5k + 2l = 14$

(d)  $0.2\eta + 0.1\lambda = 0.7$
  $0.3\eta + 0.5\lambda = 2.45$

(e)  $a + 1.2b = 85$
  $1.2a - b = -20$

(f)  $0.11w + 0.48z = 7$
  $0.13w - 0.16z = 1$

**6** Solve the simultaneous equations:

(a) $y = 2x + 3$
$y = x + 4$

(b) $y = x - 5$
$y = 2x - 7$

(c) $b = 3a - 12$
$b = -a$

(d) $d = \frac{1}{2}c + \frac{1}{3}$
$\frac{1}{2}d = \frac{1}{6}c + \frac{1}{2}$

(e) $3n = 2m - 7$
$n = m - 5$

(f) $\frac{1}{3}t = \frac{1}{5}s + 3$
$\frac{1}{2}t = s + 1$

**7** Solve the simultaneous equations:

(a) $u + 2j + 1 = 0$
$u = 2 - j$

(b) $3e - 5f - 22 = 0$
$e = f + 4$

(c) $2\sigma - \tau - 4 = 0$
$\frac{1}{2}\tau + 2 = \sigma$

(d) $\frac{1}{3}k - \frac{1}{2}m - 1 = 0$
$2m + 1 = k$

(e) $0 = 0.2r + 0.1t - 3.6$
$t = 2.5r$

(f) $0 = 4A + 7B - 48$
$B = 10 + A$

**8** Solve the simultaneous equations:

(a) $x + y + 3 = 0$
$x + 3y - 5 = 0$

(b) $2u - v - 4 = 0$
$u + 4v - 11 = 0$

(c) $2a + 3b - 8 = 0$
$5a + 7b - 21 = 0$

(d) $7p - 5q + 1 = 0$
$4p - 3q = 0$

(e) $\frac{1}{2}m + \frac{1}{5}n - 4 = 0$
$\frac{2}{3}m - \frac{1}{2}n + \frac{7}{3} = 0$

(f) $0.2d + 2e - 1 = 0$
$d - 6e - 1.8 = 0$

**9** Solve the simultaneous equations:

(a) $3x + 2y = 14$
$x - y = 8$

(b) $y = 2x - 7$
$x - 5y + 1 = 0$

(c) $t = 2s + 7$
$\frac{1}{3}s + \frac{1}{2}t = \frac{5}{6}$

(d) $a + b + 6 = 0$
$2a + 5b = 0$

(e) $3e + 2f = 6$
$f = e + 3$

(f) $u = 3v + 7$
$u + 3v = 1$

(g) $p + q = 5$
$p - 4q = 5$

(h) $a + b = 0$
$a = b + 6$

(i) $5\phi - \theta = \pi$
$\theta = 2\phi + 2\pi$

(j) $\alpha = \frac{1}{4}\beta - \frac{\pi}{3}$
$\alpha = \frac{1}{2}\beta$

## 2.5 Miscellaneous questions

> *Where necessary, give answers to 2 decimal places.*

### Exercise 2.5

1. Solve the equation:
   (a) $2x + 5 = x - 4$
   (b) $\frac{2}{3}d = 30$
   (c) $t(t + 2) = (t + 5)(t - 2)$
   (d) $\frac{3}{5}(2e + 1) = \frac{1}{4}(5e + 1)$
   (e) $(2w + 1)(3w - 1) = (w + 1)(6w - 7)$

2. Solve the inequality:
   (a) $6 + 2a < 5$
   (b) $0.5f - 1 \geq 0.2f + 5$

3. Find the integer values of $n$ for which $-3 \leq 3n + 1 < 7$.

4. Solve the simultaneous equations:
   (a) $2a + b = 11$
      $3a - 5b = 10$
   (b) $T - 200 = 350a$
      $800 - T = 50a$
   (c) $3u + 8v = 16$
      $5u - 6v = 46$
   (d) $2k = h - 5$
      $k = h - 2$
   (e) $y = 6 - x$
      $\frac{1}{6}y = \frac{1}{2}x + \frac{1}{3}$
   (f) $p + q - 6 = 0$
      $4p - 2q + 1 = 0$
   (g) $t = 2s + 9$
      $t = 14 - s$
   (h) $3a + 4b - 1.9 = 0$
      $7a - 9b + 2.9 = 0$
   (i) $0 = 4g - h + 1.2$
      $g = 0.1h + 0.3$
   (j) $3P - 2Q + 0.2 = 0$
      $1 - 0.4Q = P$

✳ 5. Solve:
   (a) $\dfrac{x + 1}{4} - \dfrac{x + 3}{5} = 1$
   (b) $18m - T = 0.4$
      $T - 9m = 1.4$
   (c) $0.2\lambda + 1.5\mu = -1.2$
      $0.6\lambda + 0.2\mu = 0.7$
   (d) $0.6u + 0.5v = 3.8$
      $v - 0.5u = 0.8$
   (e) $40\mu + 30 \sin 30° = 25 \cos 30°$
   (f) $3.2(45 + y) + 6.2y = 4.8(45 - y)$
   (g) $R = 490 + P \sin 30°$
      $P \cos 30° = 0.6R$

# 3 Coordinates

## 3.1 Coordinates

The following exercise will help you to practise:

❏ working with coordinates and using the associated vocabulary

❏ relating points and an equation, using

> the equation of a curve (or straight line) is the connection between the $y$- and $x$-coordinates of any point on the curve

**Exercise 3.1**

**1**   $P(8,4)$   $Q(3,6)$   $R(-1,6)$   $S(0,0)$
$T(1,4)$   $U(-2,-6)$   $V(-4,-1)$   $W(-10,-5)$

From the above list of coordinates name the points for which:

(a) the $y$-coordinate is 3 more than the $x$-coordinate

(b) the $y$-coordinate is 2 times the $x$-coordinate

(c) the $y$-coordinate is half the $x$-coordinate

(d) the $y$-coordinate is 5 minus the $x$-coordinate

**2**   For which of the following points is the $y$-coordinate equal to twice the $x$-coordinate plus 1?
$P(2,5)$   $Q(-2,3)$   $R(-2,-3)$   $S(0,1)$

**3**   For which of the following points is the $x$-coordinate plus the $y$-coordinate equal to 7?
$K(2,5)$   $L(-1,8)$   $M(6,1)$   $N(-4,3)$

> In the following questions '$x$-coordinate' is abbreviated to $x$ and
> '$y$-coordinate' is abbreviated to $y$.

**4**   Which of the following points satisfy the equation $y = 3x - 4$?
$A(2,2)$   $B(-1,7)$   $C(-2,-10)$   $D(4,8)$

⌁ 5 Which of the following points satisfy the equation $x + y = 10$?

$A\,(12, -2)$  $B\,(1, 7)$  $C\,(-2, -10)$  $D\,(14, -6)$

⌁ 6 Which of the following points satisfy the equation $2x - y = 10$?

$K\,(6, 2)$  $L\,(-1, -12)$  $M(3, 4)$  $N\,(0, -10)$

⌁ 7 Which of the following points satisfy the equation $y = x^2 + 7$?

$A\,(3, 14)$  $B\,(-2, 3)$  $C\,(0, 7)$  $D\,(-5, 32)$

8 The diagram shows the curve with equation $y = 2x^2$.

State the coordinates of $P$ and $Q$.

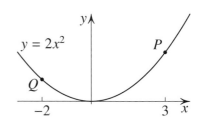

9 The diagram shows the curve with equation $xy = 4$.

State the coordinates of $A$ and $B$.

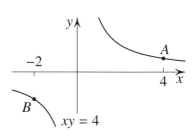

10 The diagram shows the curve with equation $x^2 + y^2 = 25$.

State the coordinates of $K$ and $L$.

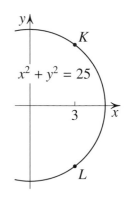

11 The diagram shows the curve with equation $y = x^3 + 4$.

(a) The point $P\,(3, s)$ lies on the curve. Find the value of $s$.

(b) The point $Q\,(t, -4)$ lies on the curve. Find the value of $t$.

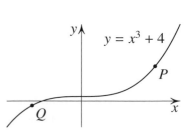

**12** The point $(3, q)$ lies on the curve with equation $y = x^2 - 8$.
Find the value of $q$.

**13** The point $(8, n)$ lies on the curve with equation $x^2 + y^2 = 100$.
Find the two possible values of $n$.

**14** The point $(t, 13)$ lies on the curve with equation $y = 4x^2 - 3$.
Find the possible values of $t$.

**15** The point $(k, k)$ lies on the curve with equation $xy = 9$.
Find the possible values of $k$.

## 3.2 The midpoint of a line segment

The following exercise will help you to practise:

❏ using the fact that the midpoint of a line segment is

$$\text{(mean } x\text{-coordinate, mean } y\text{-coordinate)} \;\; or \;\; \left(\tfrac{1}{2}(x_1 + x_2), \tfrac{1}{2}(y_1 + y_2)\right)$$

### Exercise 3.2

1 Find the midpoint of the line joining:

   (a) $(2, 8)$ to $(14, 4)$      (b) $(6, 0)$ to $(8, 4)$      (c) $(5, -1)$ to $(-9, 3)$

   (d) $(-6, 13)$ to $(8, -7)$      (e) $(-1, -5)$ to $(-7, -3)$      (f) $(-4, 3)$ to $(-9, -3)$

2 Point $M(3, 7)$ is the midpoint of the line joining $A(2, 8)$ and $B$.
Find the coordinates of $B$.

3 Point $K(-4, 5)$ is the midpoint of the line joining $L(1, 3)$ and $M$.
Find the coordinates of $M$.

4 Point $T(-6, 3)$ is the midpoint of the line joining $R$ and $S(2, 8)$.
Find the coordinates of $R$.

5 The parallelogram $PQRS$ has vertices $P(1, 5)$, $Q(10, -2)$, $R(7, -3)$ and $S(-2, 4)$.
Find the coordinates of the point of intersection of the diagonals of $PQRS$.

6 The point $M(5, -1)$ is the centre of the square $ABCD$ and $A$ is the point $(-2, 3)$.
Find the coordinates of $C$.

7 Find the coordinates of the midpoint of the line joining $(2a, 5b)$ to $(6a, -b)$.

8 Find the coordinates of the midpoint of the line joining $(4p - 2, 6 - 4p)$ to $(2, 6p - 6)$.

## 3.3 The length of a line segment

The following exercise will help you to practise:

❏ finding the length of a line segment *either* by drawing an appropriate right-angled triangle *or* by using the fact that the length is

$$\sqrt{(\text{change in } x)^2 + (\text{change in } y)^2} \quad or \quad \sqrt{(x_2 - x_1)^2 + (y_2 - y_1)^2}$$

### Exercise 3.3

**1** Write down the length of the line joining:

(a) $(3, 7)$ to $(3, 12)$      (b) $(-2, 4)$ to $(8, 4)$      (c) $(5, 10)$ to $(-2, 10)$

(d) $(-4, -7)$ to $(-4, -2)$      (e) $(0, 7)$ to $(0, -2)$      (f) $(-5, 0)$ to $(-12, 0)$

**2** Calculate the length of the line joining:

(a) $(4, 2)$ to $(7, 6)$      (b) $(1, 8)$ to $(6, 20)$      (c) $(-5, 3)$ to $(0, 15)$

(d) $(3, -6)$ to $(2, 1)$      (e) $(-4, 2)$ to $(-1, 5)$      (f) $(-3, -5)$ to $(-7, -2)$

**3** Triangle $PQR$ has vertices $P(-5, -1)$, $Q(1, 5)$ and $R(4, -4)$.

Prove that the triangle is isosceles.

**❄ 4** The length of the line joining $A(1, 6)$ and $B(a, 9)$ is 5.

Calculate the two possible values of $a$.

**❄ 5** The points $P$ and $Q$ have coordinates $(-3, 4)$ and $(3, -2)$.

The point $R$ lies on the line $y = 1$ and the length of $PR$ is half the length of $PQ$.

Find the coordinates of the two possible positions of $R$.

**❄ 6** The point $(x, y)$ is equidistant from the points $(0, 0)$ and $(5, 6)$.

Find the equation connecting $x$ and $y$.

**❄ 7** The distance between the points $(t, 0)$ and $(0, t)$ is equal to the distance between the points $(2, 3)$ and $(-1, 2)$.

Find the possible values of $t$.

**❄ 8** The point $(x, y)$ is twice as far from the origin as it is from the point $(-2, -3)$.

Find the equation connecting $x$ and $y$.

## 3.4 Straight lines parallel to the axes

The following exercise will help you to practise:

❑ using the fact that the equation of a straight line parallel to the $y$-axis has the form $x = k$

❑ using the fact that the equation of a straight line parallel to the $x$-axis has the form $y = \ell$

### Exercise 3.4

↕ 1  A straight line has equation $y = 4$.

    (a) Write down the coordinates of three points which lie on the line.

    (b) Sketch the line $y = 4$.

↕ 2  A straight line has equation $x = -2$.

    (a) Write down the coordinates of three points which lie on the line.

    (b) Sketch the line $x = -2$.

↕ 3  Sketch the straight line with equation:

    (a) $y = 2$         (b) $x = -4$         (c) $y = -5$         (d) $x = 3$

↕ 4  Find the equation of each of the straight lines shown in the diagram.

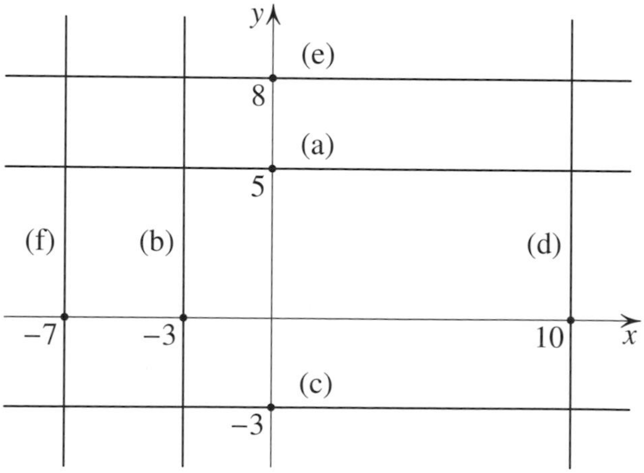

5  A rectangle has vertices $A\,(-6, 3)$, $B\,(4, 3)$, $C\,(4, -3)$ and $D\,(-6, -3)$.

    Write down the equations of the sides $AB$, $BC$, $CD$ and $DA$.

6   A rhombus has vertices $A(-2,5)$, $B(-8,1)$, $C(-2,-3)$ and $D(4,1)$.

Write down the equations of the diagonals $AC$ and $BD$.

7   The kite $KLMN$ has axis of symmetry $KM$. Three of the vertices are $K(-2,3)$, $L(3,7)$ and $M(10,3)$.

    (a) State the coordinates of N.

    (b) Write down the equations of the diagonals $KM$ and $LN$.

8   The points $A(-4,-3)$ and $C(8,-3)$ are two vertices of the square $ABCD$.

Write down the equations of the diagonals $AC$ and $BD$.

9   Write down the equation of the straight line:

    (a) through the point $(2,3)$ which is parallel to the $x$-axis

    (b) through the point $(1,4)$ which is perpendicular to the $y$-axis

    (c) through the point $(2,5)$ which is parallel to $x=3$

    (d) through the point $(7,1)$ which is perpendicular to $x=-1$

    (e) through the point $(3,4)$ which is parallel to $y=7$

10   A median of a triangle is a straight line joining a vertex to the midpoint of the opposite side.

Triangle $ABC$ has vertices $A(7,4)$, $B(1,6)$ and $C(1,2)$. Find the equation of the median $AM$, where $M$ is the midpoint of $BC$.

11   The diagonals of a rhombus have equations $x=-2$ and $y=5$.
The points $(0,5)$ and $(-2,8)$ are vertices of the rhombus.

    (a) Write down the coordinates of the point of intersection of these diagonals.

    (b) Write down the coordinates of the other two vertices.

12   The diagram shows the first few of a sequence of kites, placed together and extending to the right. The kites are labelled consecutively $A, a, B, b, \ldots$.

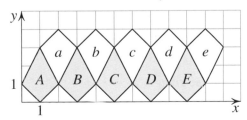

    (a) Write down the equations of the diagonals of the kites labelled $E$ and $e$.

    (b) Write down the equations of the diagonals of the kites that will appear later in the sequence with labels $G$ and $j$.

## 3.5 Areas

> The following exercise will help you to practise:
>
> ❑ finding the area of a shape defined by the coordinates of the vertices

**Exercise 3.5**

1. Triangle *ABC* has vertices *A* (3, 10), *B* (3, 3) and *C* (7, 3).

   Calculate the area of the triangle.

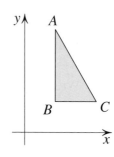

2. Triangle *RST* has vertices *R* (−2, 5), *S* (3, 5) and *T* (3, 1).

   Calculate the area of the triangle.

3. The diagram shows isosceles triangle *KLM*.
   The point *L* is (−1, 3) and *K* is (4, 7).

   Calculate the area of the triangle.

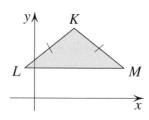

4. Triangle *ABC* is isosceles with *CA* = *CB*.
   The point *B* is (−6, 2) and *C* is (7, 4.5).

   Calculate the area of the triangle.

5. The diagram shows triangle *XYZ* with vertices
   *X* (−6, 3), *Y* (4, 3) and *Z* (−2, −3).

   Calculate the area of the triangle.

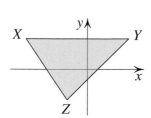

6. Calculate the area of triangle *PQR* with vertices *P* (3, 12), *Q* (3, −5) and *R* (−5, 0).

**7** Triangle $EFG$ has vertices $E\,(-5,2)$, $F\,(3,2)$ and $G\,(-5,k)$.
The area of the triangle is 12.

Calculate the value of $k$.

**8** Trapezium $ABCD$ has vertices $A\,(-6,5)$, $B\,(-6,-3)$, $C\,(10,-3)$ and $D\,(2,5)$.

Calculate the area of the trapezium.

**9** Three vertices of the rhombus $UVWX$ are $U\,(5,7)$, $W\,(5,-1)$ and $X\,(12,3)$.

Calculate the area of the rhombus.

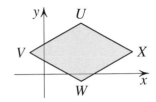

**10** The line $PR$ is a line of symmetry of the kite $PQRS$.
Three of the vertices of the kite are $P\,(-2,6)$, $Q\,(3,-5)$ and $R\,(-2,-8)$.

(a) State the coordinates of the point $S$.

(b) Calculate the area of the kite.

**11** The points $A\,(4,-3)$ and $C\,(4,7)$ are two vertices of the square $ABCD$.

(a) State the coordinates of the points $B$ and $D$.

(b) Calculate the area of the square.

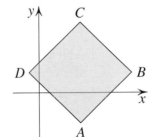

**12** The diagram shows a shape formed from a square and an isosceles triangle. The point $T$ is $(2,-4)$ and $Q$ is $(5,6)$.

Calculate the area of the shape.

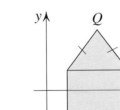

**13** The vertices of the triangle $KLM$ are $K\,(3,2)$, $L\,(7,5)$ and $M\,(10,4)$.

Calculate the area of the triangle.

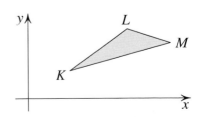

## 3.6  Circles

The following exercise will help you to practise:

- ❏ using circle diagrams plotted in the coordinate plane
- ❏ using diameter and tangent properties of a circle
- ❏ calculating the distance between circles

**Exercise 3.6**

1. The line joining $(-4, 8)$ and $(2, 16)$ is the diameter of a circle.

   (a) Write down the coordinates of the centre of the circle.

   (b) Calculate the length of the radius of the circle.

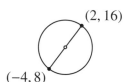

2. A square is formed from the lines with equations $x = 6$, $x = 2$, $y = -3$, $y = 1$.

   (a) Write down the coordinates of the centre of the largest circle which can be drawn inside the square.

   (b) Calculate the length of the radius of the circle which passes through all the vertices of the square.

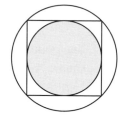

3. A circle has centre $(2, 6)$ and one end of a diameter $PQ$ of the circle is the point $P(4, 10)$.

   Find the coordinates of $Q$.

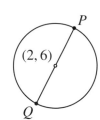

4. A circle has centre at the origin and radius of length 5.

   For each of the points $A(2, 3)$, $B(-3, 4)$, $C(5, 5)$, $D(-1, 7)$ and $E(1, -4)$, determine whether the point lies inside, outside or on the circle.

5. A circle has radius of length 2 and touches both the $x$-axis and the $y$-axis.

   Write down the coordinates of the centre of each possible such circle.

6. A circle touches the $y$-axis and two diameters of the circle lie along the lines $y = 7$ and $y = x$.

   Write down the coordinates of the centre and the length of the radius of the circle.

7 │ The diagram shows sixteen touching circles placed around the origin.

Each circle has radius of length 2 and the circle labelled $\mathcal{A}$ has centre $(2, 2)$.

Write down the coordinates of the centres of the circles labelled $\mathcal{B}, C, \mathcal{D}$ and $\mathcal{E}$.

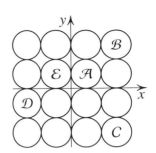

8 │ The diagram shows a repeating pattern of squares and rectangles.

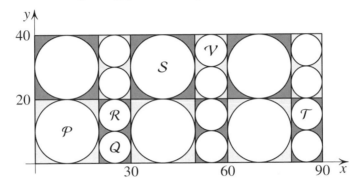

Each square has sides of length 20 and contains one circle of radius of length 10.
Each rectangle measures 10 by 20 and contains two circles with radius of length 5.
The circle labelled $\mathcal{P}$ has centre $(10, 10)$, circle $Q$ has centre $(25, 5)$ and circle $\mathcal{R}$ has centre $(25, 15)$.

Write down the coordinates of the centres of the circles labelled $S, \mathcal{T}$ and $\mathcal{V}$.

9 │ The diagram shows a rectangle whose sides have equations $y = 0$, $x = 16$, $y = 10$ and $x = 0$.

Four touching circles fit exactly inside the rectangle.

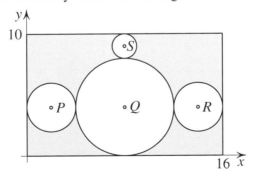

The circle centre $Q(8, 4)$ has radius of length 4.
The circles with centres $P$ and $R$ are congruent.

(a) Find the lengths of the radii of the circles with centres $P$, $R$ and $S$.

(b) Find the coordinates of $P$, $R$ and $S$.

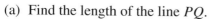

**10** A circle $C_1$ has centre $P(2, 3)$ and radius of length 5.
A second circle $C_2$ has centre $Q(-4, -5)$ and radius of length 2.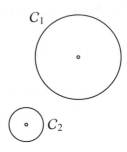

    (a) Find the length of the line $PQ$.

    (b) Find the shortest distance between the two circles.

**11** The circle $C_3$ has centre $(-1, 8)$ and radius of length 1.
The circle $C_4$ has centre $(2, 4)$ and radius of length 3.

    Calculate the shortest distance between $C_3$ and $C_4$.

**12** Circle $C_1$ has centre $(4, 2)$ and radius of length 4
Circle $C_2$ has centre $(-1, -10)$ and radius of length 9.

    Show that $C_1$ and $C_2$ touch.

**13** Circle $C_3$ has centre $(0, 10)$ and radius of length 14
Circle $C_4$ has centre $(7, -14)$ and radius of length 11.

    Show that $C_3$ and $C_4$ touch.

**14** A circle has centre $(0, 4)$ and the lines $y = x$ and $y = -x$ are tangents of the circle.

    Calculate the length of the radius of the circle.

**15** A diameter of the circle $C_1$ joins $(1, 5)$ to $(-7, 9)$.
Another circle $C_2$ has centre $(5, 11)$.
The point $A(4, 13)$ lies on the circumference of $C_2$.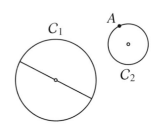

    Calculate the shortest distance between $C_1$ and $C_2$.

## 3.7 Miscellaneous questions

### Exercise 3.7

1. A straight line has equation $2x + 4y = 30$.

   (a) The point $(3, p)$ lies on the line. Find the value of $p$.

   (b) The point $(q, 8)$ lies on the line. Find the value of $q$.

2. The diagram shows the curve with equation $y = 3x^2 + 2$.

   Find the coordinates of $P$ and of $Q$.

   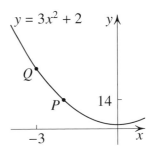

3. The point with coordinates $(m, 2m)$ lies on the line with equation $y = 3x + 4$.

   Find the value of $m$.

4. Calculate the midpoint of the straight line joining $(12, -4)$ and $(-2, 6)$.

5. What is the distance between the points $(4, -3)$ and $(-2, 5)$?

6. The point $P$ is $(3, -1)$ and $Q$ is $(-4, 5)$.

   (a) Calculate the length of $PQ$.

   (b) Find the coordinates of the midpoint of the line segment $PQ$.

7. The points $M$ and $N$ have coordinates $M(7, -2)$ and $N(-3, -2)$.

   (a) State the length of $MN$.

   (b) State the equation of the straight line $MN$.

   (c) Find the equation of the line which passes through the midpoint of $MN$ and is perpendicular to $MN$.

8. The points $A(-3, -7)$ and $B(0, 2)$ are vertices of an isosceles triangle with $AB = AC$.

   (a) If $C$ is the point $(k, 2)$ state the value of $k$.

   (b) If $C$ is the point $(0, m)$ state the value of $m$.

   (c) For each of the two positions of $C$ given in (a) and (b) state the equation of the axis of symmetry of the triangle.

9 Calculate the area of triangle $PQR$ with vertices $P(-7, -5)$, $Q(2, -5)$ and $R(2, 2)$.

10 Triangle $XYZ$ has vertices $X(3, -3)$, $Y(-3, -5)$ and $Z(-3, m)$.

The area of the triangle is 21.

Calculate the value of $m$.

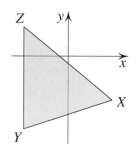

11 The diagram shows a shape of height 18 formed from two touching circles.

The line joining the centres is parallel to the $y$-axis.

The larger circle has centre $(4, 2)$ and radius of length 7.

Calculate the coordinates of the centre and the length of the radius of the smaller circle.

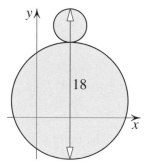

12 The diagram shows a rectangle $PQRS$ with $P(-2, -1)$, $Q(-2, 3)$ and $R(-4, 3)$.

   (a) State the coordinates of the point $S$.

   (b) State the equations of $PQ$ and $QR$.

   (c) Find the coordinates of the centre and the length of the radius of the circle passing through the vertices of the rectangle.

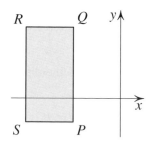

13 Two concentric circles have centre $(7, -2)$.

The length of the radius of the larger circle is three times the length of the radius of the smaller circle.

The larger circle passes through the point $(16, 10)$.

Calculate the length of the radius of the smaller circle.

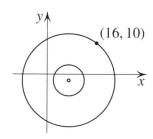

❄ 14 Two circles touch internally at the point $(-5, 2)$.

The smaller circle has centre $(0, -10)$ and passes through the centre of the larger circle.

Find the coordinates of the centre and the length of the radius of the larger circle.

# 4 Triangles

## 4.1 Sine, cosine and tangent

The following exercise will help you to practise:

❏ using sine, cosine or tangent in a right-angled triangle

*Where necessary, give answers to 3 significant figures.*

**Exercise 4.1a**

⚓ 1 Calculate the size of the angle marked ✲ in the triangle:

(a)

R, 8 cm, P, 10 cm, Q

(b)

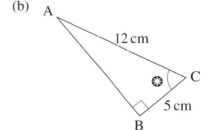

A, 12 cm, C, 5 cm, B

(c)

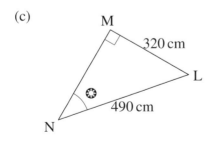

M, 320 cm, L, 490 cm, N

(d)

Y, 1.8 mm, Z, 2.6 mm, X

(e)

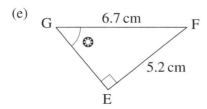

G, 6.7 cm, F, 5.2 cm, E

(f)

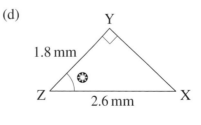
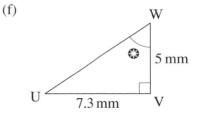

W, 5 mm, U, 7.3 mm, V

**2** Calculate the length of the side marked •—• in the triangle:

(a)

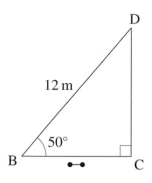

(b)

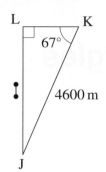

(c)

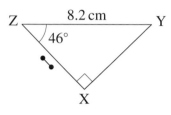

(d)

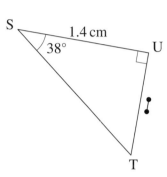

(e)

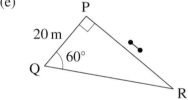

(f)

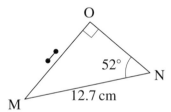

**3** Calculate the length of the side marked •—• in the triangle:

(a)

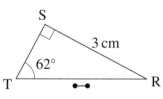

(b)

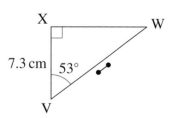

(c)

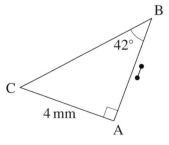

(d)

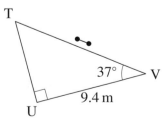

(e)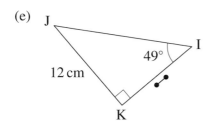

(f)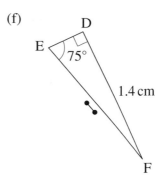

**4** Calculate the value of $x$ in the triangle:

(a)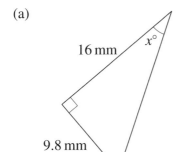

(b)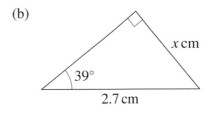

(c)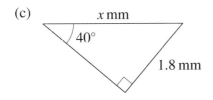

(d)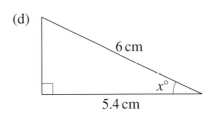

(e)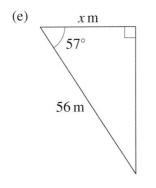

(f)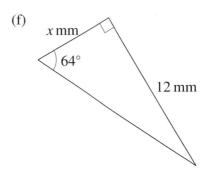

**5** The diagram shows a rectangle *PQRS*.
Calculate the size of angle *PRQ*.

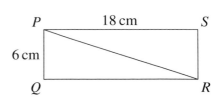

**6** The diagram shows a trapezium *KLMN*.
Calculate the length of *KN*.

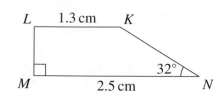

**7** Calculate the value of *x* in the diagram:

(a)

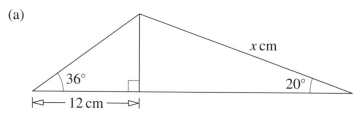

(b)

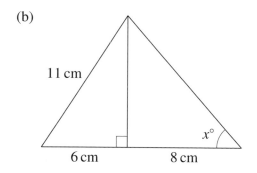

(c)

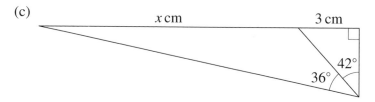

(d)

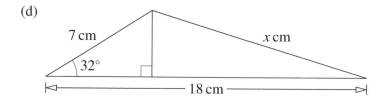

**8** The diagram shows a rectangle *KLMN*.

Find an expression for the perimeter length
of the rectangle in terms of *x* and *d*.

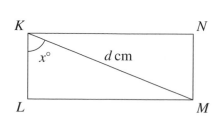

**9** Find an expression for $x$ in the triangle:

(a)
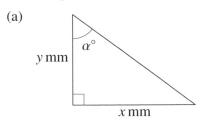

(b)
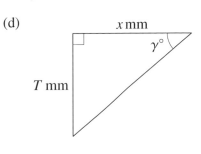

(c)
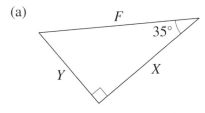

(d)
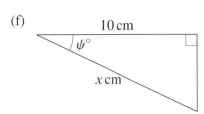

(e)
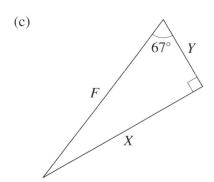

(f)
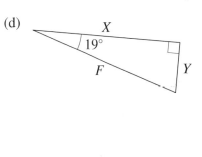

❄ **10** Find expressions for $X$ and for $Y$ in terms of $F$ in the diagram:

(a)
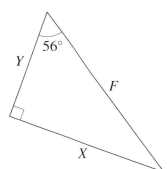

(b)

(c)

(d)

The following exercise will help you to practise:

❑ dividing an isosceles triangle into two right-angled triangles

*Where necessary, give answers to 3 significant figures.*

## Exercise 4.1b

**1** The diagram shows an isosceles triangle *ABC* with *AB* = *AC*.

Calculate the size of angle *BAC*.

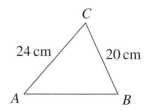

**2** The diagram shows a pentagon formed from a rectangle and an isosceles triangle.

Calculate the length of the perimeter of the pentagon.

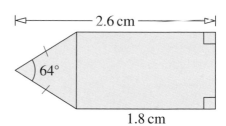

**3** A golfer putts a ball from point *A* towards a hole *H*, 17 metres from *A*. Although he putts a distance of 17 metres, he is 3° off the correct direction, so the ball ends at the point *B*. The diagram shows the situation seen from above.

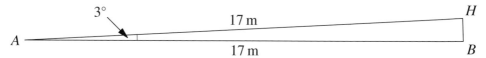

How far away from the hole does the ball stop?

[Give your answer correct to the nearest centimetre.]

**4** All five vertices of a regular pentagon are on the circumference of a circle of radius 9 cm.

Calculate the length of a side of the pentagon.

❄ **5** The diagram shows an isosceles triangle *PQR* with *QP* = *RP*.

Find an expression for the perimeter length of the triangle in terms of *ℓ* and *θ*.

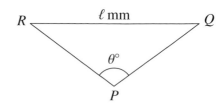

## 4.2 The sine rule

The following exercise will help you to practise:

❏ using the sine rule

$$\frac{a}{\sin A} = \frac{b}{\sin B} = \frac{c}{\sin C} \quad or \quad \frac{\sin A}{a} = \frac{\sin B}{b} = \frac{\sin C}{c}$$

Where necessary, give answers to 3 significant figures.

**Exercise 4.2**

1 Find the length of the side marked •—• in the diagram:

(a)
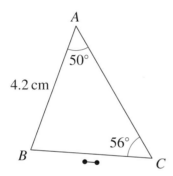

(b)
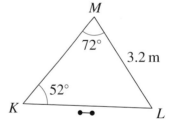

(c)
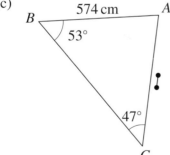

(d)
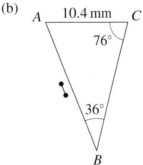

(e)
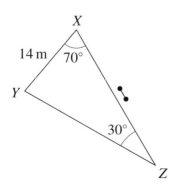

(f)
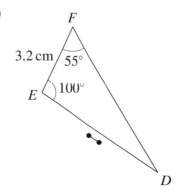

**2** Find the size of the angle marked ✪ in the diagram:

(a)

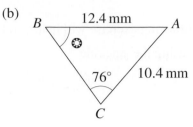

A

5 cm

56°

B

6 cm

C

(b)

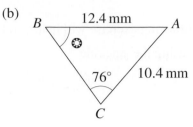

B    12.4 mm    A

✪

76°    10.4 mm

C

(c)

B

6.5 cm

C

5 cm    ✪

80°

A

(d)

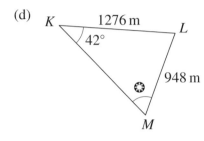

K    1276 m    L

42°

✪    948 m

M

(e)

X

15 m

Y    ✪    68°

15.6 m    Z

(f)

E

F    70°

5.9 cm

3.8 cm    ✪

G

**3** With the notation in the diagram, prove that $\sin \theta = \frac{1}{4}$.

b cm    2b cm

30°    θ°

**4** Calculate the value of $x$ in the diagram.

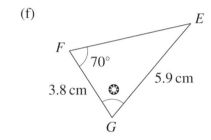

x cm

40°

8 cm  24°

97°    65°

**5** With the notation in the diagram, prove that

$$x = \frac{k \sin(90 + \beta)}{\sin \alpha}.$$

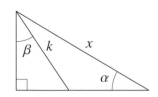

β    k    x

α

## 4.3 The cosine rule

The following exercise will help you to practise:

❏ using the cosine rule

$$a^2 = b^2 + c^2 - 2bc\cos A \quad or \quad \cos A = \frac{b^2 + c^2 - a^2}{2bc}$$

*Where necessary, give answers to 3 significant figures.*

### Exercise 4.3

**1** Find the length of the side marked •—• in the diagram:

(a)

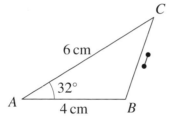

(b)

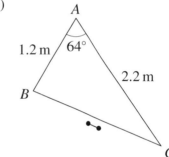

(c)

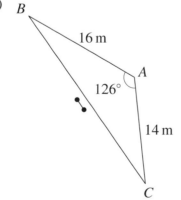

(d)

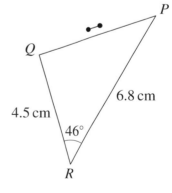

(e)

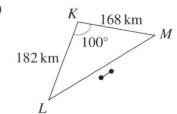

(f)

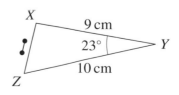

**2** Find the size of the angle marked ✪ in the diagram:

(a)
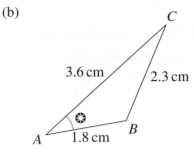

(b)
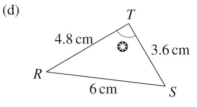

(c)
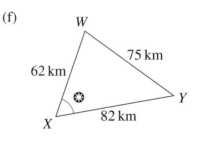

(d)

(e)
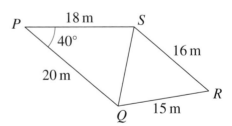

(f)
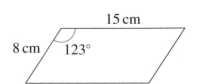

**3** Calculate the size of angle $SRQ$ in the diagram.

**4** The diagram shows a parallelogram.

Calculate the lengths of the diagonals of the parallelogram.

**5** Calculate the size of the angle marked $x°$ in the diagram.

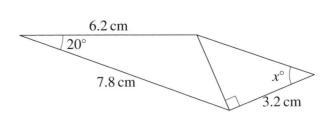

**6** With the notation in the diagram, show that $\cos \angle PQR = \frac{1}{6}$.

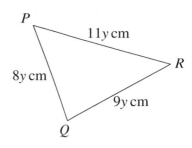

**7** With the notation in the diagram, show that $\cos \angle LKM = -\frac{1}{4}$.

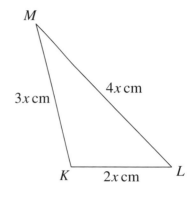

❄ **8** With the notation in the diagram, show that $y = \sqrt{4x^2 + 3}$.

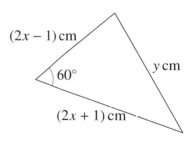

## 4.4   The area of a triangle

The following exercise will help you to practise:

❑ using the fact that the area of a triangle is $\frac{1}{2}ab \sin C$

*Where necessary, give answers to 3 significant figures.*

**Exercise 4.4**

1  Calculate the area of the triangle:

(a)

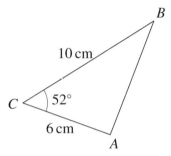

(b)

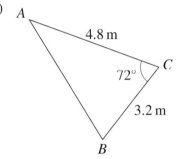

(c)

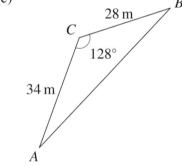

(d)

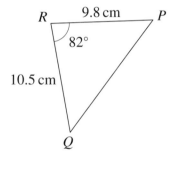

(e)

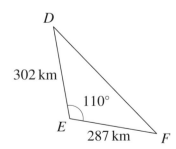

(f)

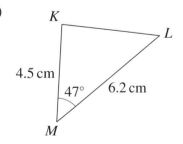

2  Triangle *PQR* is isosceles with *PQ* = *PR* = 5 cm and ∠*PRQ* = 50°.

Calculate the area of triangle *PQR*.

**3** An equilateral triangle has sides of length 12 cm.

Calculate the area of the triangle.

**4** The diagram shows a parallelogram.
Calculate the area of the parallelogram.

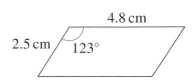

2.5 cm  123°  4.8 cm

**5** All six vertices of a regular hexagon are on the circumference of a circle of radius 16 cm.

Calculate the area of the hexagon.

**6** Calculate the area of the quadrilateral shown in the diagram.

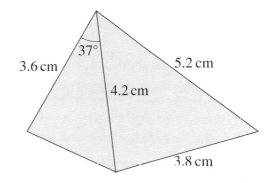

37°
3.6 cm  5.2 cm
4.2 cm
3.8 cm

**7** The diagram shows a triangle with area 1.33 cm².
Calculate the length of *PQ*.

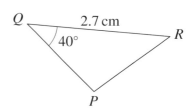

Q  2.7 cm  R
40°
P

**8** The diagram shows a triangle with area 152 m².
Calculate the length of *LM*.

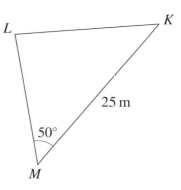

L  K
25 m
50°
M

9 The diagram shows a triangle with area $9.38\,\text{cm}^2$.
Calculate the size of the acute angle $ABC$.

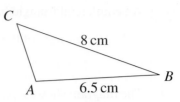

10 The diagram shows a triangle with area $17\,100\,\text{cm}^2$.

Calculate the size of the acute angle $XYZ$.

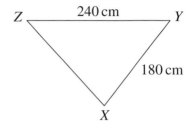

11 An isosceles triangle has equal sides of length $x$ metres.
The angle between the equal sides is $30°$ and the area of the triangle is $16\,\text{m}^2$.

Calculate the value of $x$.

12 The diagram shows a triangle with area $6\,\text{m}^2$.

Calculate the value of $x$.

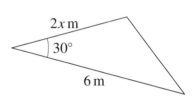

❄ 13 The diagram shows a triangle with area $8\,\text{cm}^2$.

Calculate the value of $x$.

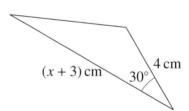

## 4.5 Miscellaneous questions

> *Where necessary, give answers to 3 significant figures.*

**Exercise 4.5**

1

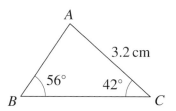

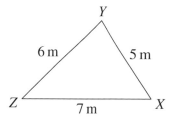

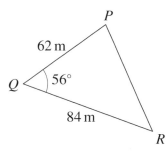

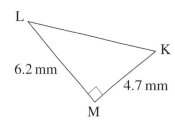

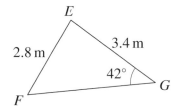

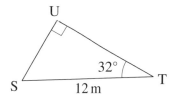

Using the information given in the diagrams above, calculate:

(a) *AB*    (b) *∠X*    (c) *PR*    (d) *∠K*    (e) *∠F*    (f) *SU*

2 Calculate the area of the triangle:

(a)

(b)

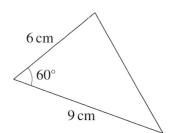

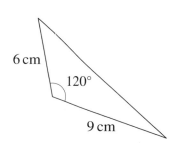

**3**

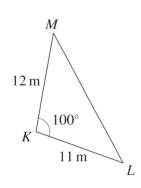

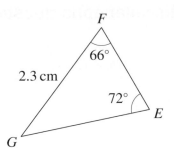

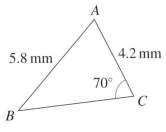

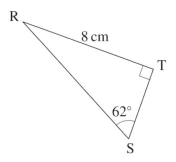

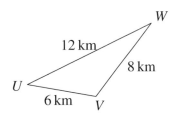

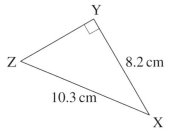

Using the information given in the diagrams above, calculate:

(a) *LM*   (b) *EF*   (c) ∠*A*   (d) *S T*   (e) ∠*V*   (f) ∠*X*

**4** Calculate the area of the isosceles triangle shown in the diagram, with *PR = QR*.

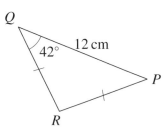

**5** Calculate the value of *x* in the diagram.

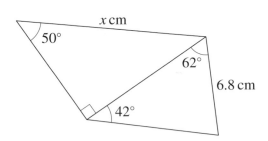

**6** Calculate the value of $x$ in the diagram.

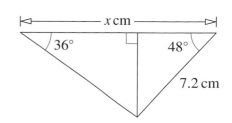

**7** Calculate the value of $x$ in the diagram.

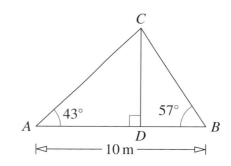

**8** The diagram shows a vertical mast $CD$ supported by two wires $AC$ and $BC$.

Calculate the height of the mast.

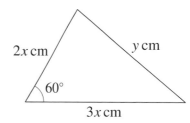

**9** In the diagram, $\sin \alpha = \frac{1}{6}$.

Prove that $q = 6p \sin \beta$.

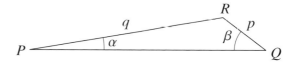

❄ **10** With the notation in the diagram, show that $y = \sqrt{7}x$.

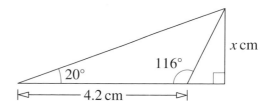

❄ **11** The diagram shows a triangle with area $19.5 \text{ m}^2$.

Calculate the value of $y$.

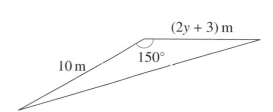

# 5 Straight lines

## 5.1 The gradient of a straight line

The following exercise will help you to practise:

❏ finding the gradient of a straight line using

$$\text{gradient} = \frac{\text{change in } y}{\text{change in } x}$$

❏ finding the gradient of a straight line through two points $(x_1, y_1)$ and $(x_2, y_2)$ using

$$\text{gradient} = \frac{y_2 - y_1}{x_2 - x_1}$$

**Exercise 5.1**

In questions 1, 2 and 3, each grid square is $1 \times 1$.

1 State the gradient of each of the straight lines shown in the diagram.

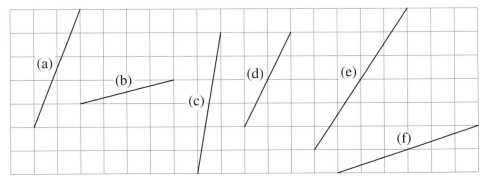

⇅ 2 State the gradient of each of the straight lines shown in the diagram.

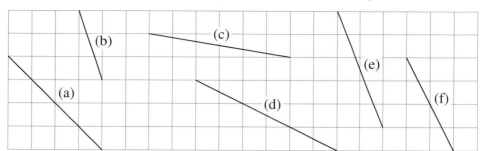

⇅ 3 State the gradient of each of the straight lines shown in the diagram.

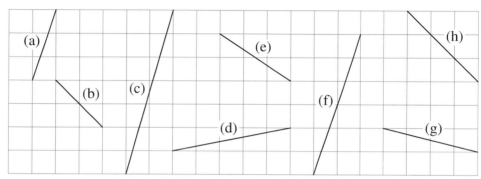

⇅ 4 On squared paper draw a straight line with gradient:

(a) $\frac{5}{6}$      (b) $-\frac{3}{4}$      (c) 3      (d) $-\frac{1}{2}$      (e) −5      (f) 2

5 Find the gradient of the straight line joining:

(a) $(2, 5)$ to $(4, 11)$      (b) $(0, 11)$ to $(-2, 1)$      (c) $(4, -2)$ to $(-2, 10)$

(d) $(-5, -3)$ to $(7, 1)$      (e) $(-5, 2)$ to $(0, -1)$      (f) $(5, 7)$ to $(4, 7)$

6 By using the coordinates of two points on the line, find the gradient of the straight line:

(a) 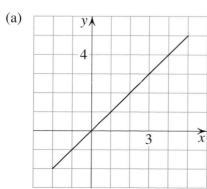      (b)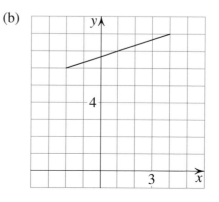

(c)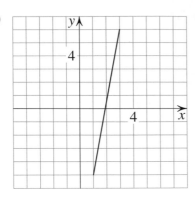

(d)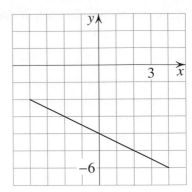

(e)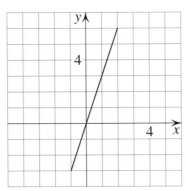

(f)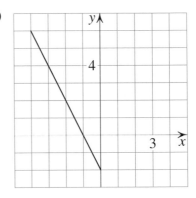

**7** By using the coordinates of two points on the line, find the gradient of the straight line:

(a)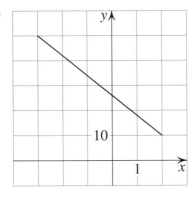

(b)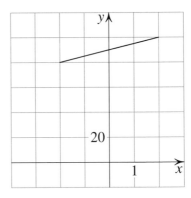

(c)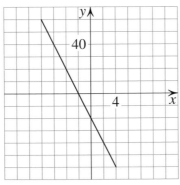

(d)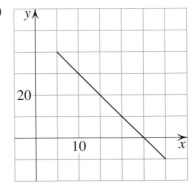

## 5.2 The equation of a straight line

The following exercise will help you to practise:

❏ relating the equation of a straight line and the coordinates of points on the line

### Exercise 5.2a

⇕ 1  Write down an equation which is satisfied by all the points:

(a)  $(1, 5)$, $(3, 7)$ and $(-2, 2)$

(b)  $(1, 4)$, $(3, 12)$ and $(-4, -16)$

(c)  $(2, -1)$, $(-3, -6)$ and $(10, 7)$

(d)  $(2, 5)$, $(-1, 8)$ and $(0, 7)$

⇕ 2  By writing down the coordinates of three points satisfying the equation, and then plotting the points, sketch the straight line with equation:

(a)  $y = x + 5$

(b)  $y = 2x - 3$

(c)  $y + x = 7$

⇕ 3  For each of the following straight lines, write down the coordinates of three points on the line and an equation which is satisfied by all three points.

(a)

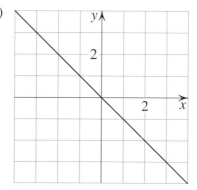

(b)

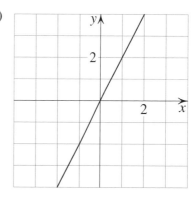

(c)

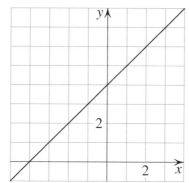

(d)

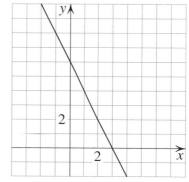

4  The point with coordinates $(5, p)$ lies on the straight line $y = 3x - 1$.
Find the value of $p$.

**5** The point with coordinates $(-4, k)$ lies on the straight line $y = -3x + 2$.
Find the value of $k$.

**6** The point with coordinates $(2, m)$ lies on the straight line $3x + 2y = 0$.
Find the value of $m$.

**7** The point with coordinates $(q, -2)$ lies on the straight line $y = -2x + 2$.
Find the value of $q$.

**8** The point with coordinates $(t, 4)$ lies on the straight line $2x - 3y = 20$.
Find the value of $t$.

**9** The point with coordinates $(m, 2m)$ lies on the straight line $y = 4x - 3$.
Find the value of $m$.

---

The following exercise will help you to practise:

❏ finding the equation of a straight line through a given point with a given
gradient, using $y = mx + c$ *or* $y - y_1 = m(x - x_1)$

❏ finding the equation of a straight line through two given points, *either* by first
finding the gradient *or* by using

$$\frac{y - y_1}{y_2 - y_1} = \frac{x - x_1}{x_2 - x_1}$$

---

## Exercise 5.2b

**1** Find the equation of the straight line:

(a)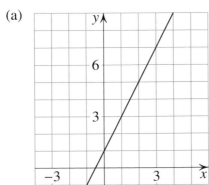

(b)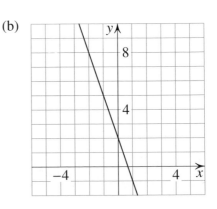

(c)

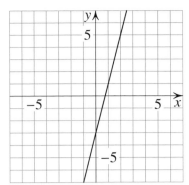

(d)

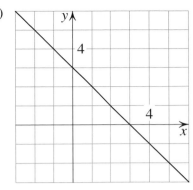

(e)

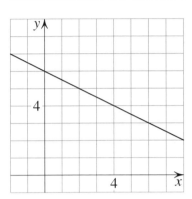

(f)

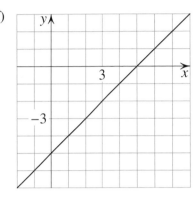

**2** Find the equation of the straight line:

(a)

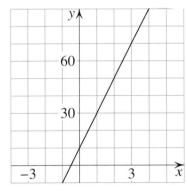

(b)

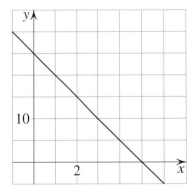

(c)

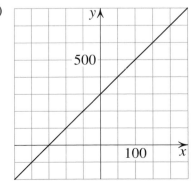

(d)

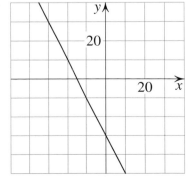

3 Find the equation of the straight line:

(a)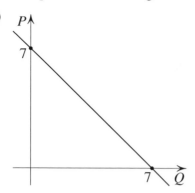

(b)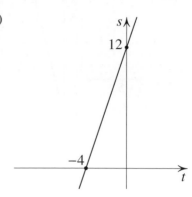

(c)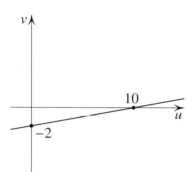

(d)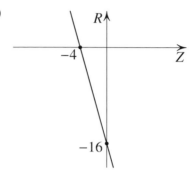

4 Sketch the straight line with equation:

(a) $y = 2x - 3$    (b) $y = 3x + 1$    (c) $y = -2x + 6$

(d) $y = x - 2$    (e) $y = x + 3$    (f) $y = -x + 7$

5 Find the equation of the straight line:

(a) through $(0, 4)$ and $(-1, 6)$    (b) through $(0, 0)$ and $(8, 4)$

(c) through $(2, 4)$ and $(0, 10)$    (d) through $(-2, -1)$ and $(0, -6)$

6 Find the equation of the straight line:

(a) through $(0, 4)$ with gradient 2    (b) through $(0, 2)$ with gradient $-1$

(c) through $(1, 1)$ with gradient 3    (d) through $(5, -3)$ with gradient $-2$

(e) through $(0, 6)$ with gradient $\frac{2}{3}$    (f) through $(4, 2)$ with gradient $-\frac{1}{2}$

7 Find the equation of the straight line:

(a) through $(2, 5)$ and $(-3, 0)$    (b) through $(4, -1)$ and $(3, -3)$

(c) through $(-4, 1)$ and $(8, 7)$    (d) through $(1, -1)$ and $(-3, 15)$

(e) through $(5, -1)$ and $(-10, 2)$    (f) through $(-3, -1)$ and $(9, 7)$

(g) through $(3, -4)$ and $(-9, 12)$

The following exercise will help you to practise:

❏ finding the points of intersection of a line with the $x$- and $y$-axes (the $x$- and $y$-intercepts)

❏ finding the gradient $m$ of a line by converting the equation to the form $y = mx + c$

❏ converting the equation of a line into a different form

### Exercise 5.2c

**1** Find the points of intersection with the $x$- and $y$-axes of the straight line with equation:

(a) $y = 2x + 4$      (b) $y = 12 - 3x$      (c) $y = 3x - 10$

(d) $x + y = 5$      (e) $3x + 5y = 30$      (f) $x - 4y = 4$

(g) $2x - 3y = 5$      (h) $x + 3y + 15 = 0$      (i) $6x - y - 9 = 0$

**2** By finding the points of intersection with the coordinate axes, sketch the straight line with equation:

(a) $x + y = 7$      (b) $x + y = 10$      (c) $x + y = 4$

(d) $x + y = -5$      (e) $x + 2y = 8$      (f) $3x - y = 12$

(g) $x + 4y = 20$      (h) $5x - y = 10$      (i) $3x + 5y = 15$

(j) $x - 3y + 6 = 0$      (k) $2x + 5y + 20 = 0$      (l) $3x - y + 12 = 0$

**3** Write down the gradient and the $y$-intercept of the straight line with equation:

(a) $y = 3x - 4$      (b) $2x + y = 7$      (c) $x + y = 10$

(d) $4y = 8x + 1$      (e) $3y = x - 6$      (f) $5x + 2y = 0$

(g) $x + 2y - 10 = 0$      (h) $x - y = 3$      (i) $5x - 4y = 7$

(j) $3x - 4y - 12 = 0$      (k) $2x = 3y$      (l) $x + 2y + 3 = 0$

**4** By converting into a form with no fractions and no negative numbers, rewrite the equation of the line:

(a) $y = \frac{2}{3}x + 5$      (b) $y = x + \frac{1}{9}$      (c) $y = 6 - \frac{2}{5}x$

(d) $y = -4 - \frac{1}{2}x$      (e) $y = \frac{4}{5}x - \frac{1}{3}$      (f) $y = \frac{1}{4}x - \frac{1}{3}$

**5** By converting into the form $ax + by + c = 0$, where $a > 0$, rewrite the equation of the line:

(a) $y = x - 4$      (b) $2y = x + 5$      (c) $4y = 6 - 3x$

(d) $y = \frac{2}{3}x - 1$      (e) $y = 2 - \frac{3}{5}x$      (f) $y = \frac{5}{6}x$

## 5.3 Parallel lines

The following exercise will help you to practise:

❑ using the fact that parallel lines have equal gradients *or* that lines with equations of the form $ax + by + c_1 = 0$ and $ax + by + c_2 = 0$ are parallel

### Exercise 5.3

1. Six points have the following coordinates.

$$A(3, -1) \quad B(-3, 2) \quad C(5, 1) \quad D(-5, -2) \quad E(1, 6) \quad F(-2, 2)$$

Are the following statements true or false?

(a) AC is parallel to BE.

(b) BC is parallel to AD.

(c) DE is parallel to EF.

2. Six lines have equations as follows.

$$\mathcal{L}: \quad y = 2x + 3 \qquad \mathcal{M}: \quad x + y = 7 \qquad \mathcal{N}: \quad y = x + 3$$
$$\mathcal{P}: \quad 2y - x + 4 = 0 \qquad \mathcal{Q}: \quad 2x - y + 10 = 0 \qquad \mathcal{R}: \quad 3x - 6y + 7 = 0$$

Are the following statements true or false?

(a) $\mathcal{L}$ is parallel to $\mathcal{Q}$.

(b) $\mathcal{M}$ is parallel to $\mathcal{N}$.

(c) $\mathcal{N}$ is parallel to $\mathcal{P}$.

(d) $\mathcal{P}$ is parallel to $\mathcal{R}$.

3. Write down the equation of the line:

(a) through the point $(0, 1)$ and parallel to the line $y = 4x + 5$

(b) through the point $(0, -2)$ and parallel to the line $2x - y = 5$

(c) through the point $(1, 2)$ and parallel to the line $x + y = 8$

(d) through the point $(-2, -3)$ and parallel to the line $3x + 2y - 1 = 0$

(e) through the point $(0, 0)$ and parallel to the line $6x - y = 7$

4. The diagram shows two straight lines $KL$ and $AB$, which are parallel.

(a) Find the equation of $KL$.

(b) Find the equation of $AB$.

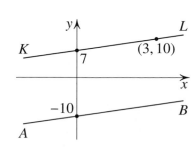

**5** The diagram shows two straight lines $CD$ and $EF$, which are parallel.

    (a) Find the equation of $CD$.

    (b) Find the equation of $EF$.

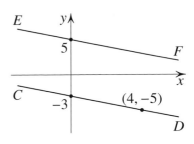

**6** The line joining the points $(7, 4)$ and $(3, k)$ is parallel to the line with equation $y = 2x + 4$.

Find the value of $k$.

**7** The line joining the points $(4, 6)$ and $(m, 15)$ is parallel to the line with equation $3x + 2y = 7$.

Find the value of $m$.

**8** Find the equation of the line through the points $(a, 4)$ and $(7, a)$ which is parallel to the line $y = 2x + 14$.

**9** The diagram shows parallelogram $PQRS$ with $P(8, 7)$, $Q(0, 2)$ and $R(0, -3)$.

    (a) Find the equation of $QP$.

    (b) Find the equation of $RS$.

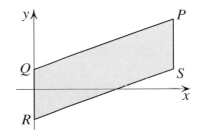

**10** In the rhombus $ABCD$ the side $AB$ has equation $y = 1 - x$ and vertex $C$ is $(1, -6)$. Write down the equation of the side $CD$.

**11** In the rectangle $KLMN$ the side $KL$ has equation $2x + 5y = 17$ and vertex $N$ is $(-1, 3)$.

Write down the equation of the side $MN$.

**12** Two of the vertices of parallelogram $ABCD$ are $A(-2, 7)$ and $C(5, -1)$.

The side $CD$ has equation $5x + y = 24$ and the side $AD$ has equation $x + 2y = 12$.

Find the equations of $AB$ and $BC$.

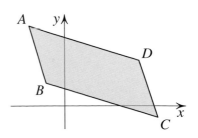

❄ **13** In the trapezium $PQRS$ the sides $PS$ and $QR$ are parallel.

Three of the vertices are $P(3, -3)$, $Q(6, 1)$ and $R(3, 2)$.

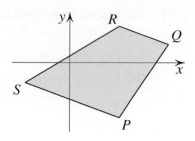

(a) Find the equation of $QR$.

(b) Find the equation of $PS$.

❄ **14** The lines $2x + py = 7$ and $qx - 5y = 4$ are parallel.
Show that $pq = -10$.

## 5.4 Perpendicular lines

The following exercise will help you to practise:

❑ using the fact that the gradients $m_1$ and $m_2$ of two perpendicular straight lines satisfy $m_1 \times m_2 = -1$

### Exercise 5.4

⇕ **1** Write down the gradient of the straight line which is perpendicular to the line with gradient:

(a) $\frac{4}{3}$    (b) $-\frac{5}{6}$    (c) $\frac{1}{5}$    (d) $-\frac{1}{4}$    (e) $-7$    (f) $6$    (g) $-1$    (h) $1$

**2** Six points have the following coordinates.

$$A\,(2,3) \quad B\,(-3,1) \quad C\,(-5,6) \quad D\,(-1,-2) \quad E\,(2,0) \quad F\,(0,3)$$

Are the following statements true of false?

(a) BD is perpendicular to DE.          (b) FE is perpendicular to DE.

(c) BA is perpendicular to EF.          (d) BA is perpendicular to BC.

**3** Six straight lines have equations as follows.

$\mathcal{L}$:   $y = 2x + 3$          $\mathcal{M}$:   $y = -\frac{1}{3}x + 2$          $\mathcal{N}$:   $y = \frac{1}{2}x + 3$
$\mathcal{P}$:   $2y + x + 4 = 0$          $\mathcal{Q}$:   $3x + y + 10 = 0$          $\mathcal{R}$:   $6x - 3y + 7 = 0$

Are the following statements true or false?

(a) $\mathcal{L}$ is perpendicular to $\mathcal{N}$.          (b) $\mathcal{M}$ is perpendicular to $\mathcal{Q}$.

(c) $\mathcal{N}$ is perpendicular to $\mathcal{P}$.          (d) $\mathcal{P}$ is perpendicular to $\mathcal{R}$.

**4** Find the gradient of a straight line perpendicular to the straight line joining $(4, -2)$ and $(-3, 5)$.

**5** Find the equation of the straight line passing through $(0, 5)$ and perpendicular to the line with equation $y = 2x - 3$.

**6** Find the equation of the straight line passing through $(0, -6)$ and perpendicular to the line with equation $x + y + 1 = 0$.

**7** Find the equation of the straight line passing through $(-2, 5)$ and perpendicular to the line with equation $3x - y - 4 = 0$.

**8** The diagram shows two straight lines $KL$ and $AB$, which are perpendicular.

   (a) Find the equation of $KL$.

   (b) Find the equation of $AB$.

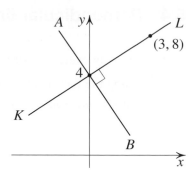

**9** The diagram shows two straight lines $CD$ and $EF$, which are perpendicular.

   (a) Find the equation of $CD$.

   (b) Find the equation of $EF$.

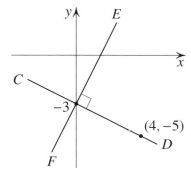

**10** The straight line joining the points $(-2, 4)$ and $(1, k)$ is perpendicular to the line with equation $y = x - 2$.

Find the value of $k$.

**11** The straight line joining the points $(-4, -3)$ and $(p, 2)$ is perpendicular to the line with equation $4x + 3y = 7$.

Find the value of $p$.

**12** The straight line joining the points $(k, 2)$ and $(-10, k)$ is perpendicular to the line through the points $(0, -1)$ and $(5, 3)$.

Find the value of $k$.

**13** The straight line with equation $2x + 4y - 7 = 0$ is perpendicular to the line with equation $4y = kx - 2$.

Calculate the value of $k$.

**14** The straight line with equation $2y = 3x + 3$ crosses the $y$-axis at point $P$.

Find the equation of the perpendicular line passing through $P$.

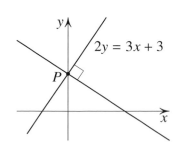

❄ **15** The straight line with equation $x + 3y - 6 = 0$ crosses the $y$-axis at point $Q$.

Find the equation of the perpendicular line passing through $Q$.

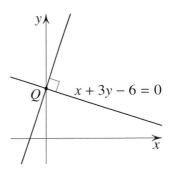

❄ **16** A straight line has equation $4x - 3y - 12 = 0$.
The line crosses the $x$-axis at $P$ and the $y$-axis at $Q$.

Find the equation of the straight line perpendicular to $PQ$ and passing through

(a) $P$      (b) $Q$

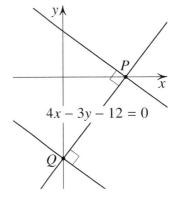

❄ **17** Two vertices of the rectangle $ABCD$ are $A\,(1, 4)$ and $C\,(7, 11)$.
The equation of $AD$ is $y = 4x$.

Find the equation of the line

(a) $CD$      (b) $BC$      (c) $AB$

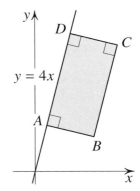

❄ **18** One vertex of the square $PQRS$ is $P\,(0, 4)$ and the diagonals intersect at the point $M\,(15, 9)$.
The equation of $PS$ is $y = 2x + 4$.

Find the equation of the line

(a) $PQ$    (b) $PR$    (c) $QS$

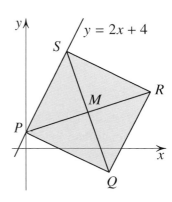

## 5.5 The intersection of two lines

The following exercise will help you to practise:

❏ finding the point of intersection of two straight lines

### Exercise 5.5

↕ 1  The diagram shows the straight lines with
equations $x = 5$ and $y = 2x + 1$.
The lines intersect at the point $B$.

Calculate the coordinates of $B$.

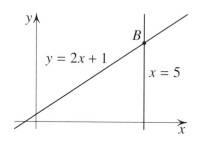

↕ 2  The diagram shows the straight lines with
equations $x = -2$ and $x + y = 7$.
The lines intersect at the point $C$.

Calculate the coordinates of $C$.

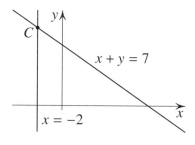

3  The diagram shows the straight lines with
equations $y = 2x - 7$ and $y = x - 2$.
The lines intersect at the point $P$.

Calculate the coordinates of $P$.

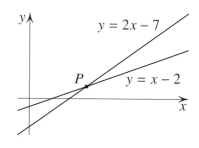

4  The diagram shows the straight lines with
equations $y = 2x - 5$ and $y = 7 - x$.
The lines intersect at the point $R$.

Calculate the coordinates of $R$.

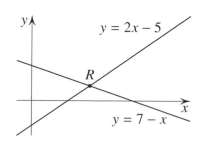

5 | The diagram shows the straight lines with equations $y = 2x$ and $y = 3x + 2$.
The lines intersect at the point $T$.

Calculate the coordinates of $T$.

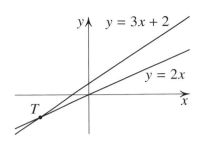

6 | The diagram shows the straight lines with equations $y = 2x + 9$ and $x + y + 6 = 0$.
The lines intersect at the point $A$.

Calculate the coordinates of $A$.

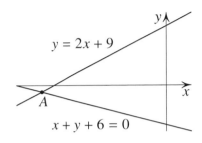

7 | The diagram shows the straight lines with equations $2x + y = 12$ and $y = x - 9$.
The lines intersect at the point $B$.

Calculate the coordinates of $B$.

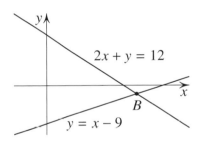

8 | The diagram shows the straight lines with equations $y = 2x + 10$ and $2x + 3y + 2 = 0$.
The lines intersect at the point $C$.

Calculate the coordinates of $C$.

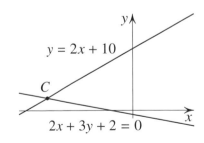

9 | The diagram shows the straight lines with equations $x + y = 4$ and $2x = y + 8$.
The lines intersect at the point $D$.

Calculate the coordinates of $D$.

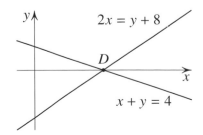

**10** The diagram shows triangle $ABC$, which has side $AB$ parallel to the $y$-axis.

   (a) Write down the equation of $AB$.

The side $BC$ is parallel to the $x$-axis.

   (b) Write down the equation of $BC$.

The line $AC$ has equation $y = 2x + 1$.

   (c) Calculate the coordinates of $A$ and $C$.

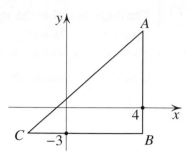

**11** The diagram shows two straight lines $AB$ and $CD$. The line $AB$ passes through $(0, 5)$ and has gradient 2. The line $CD$ passes through $(0, 15)$ and has gradient $-3$.

   (a) Write down the equation of $AB$.

   (b) Write down the equation of $CD$.

The lines $AB$ and $CD$ intersect at the point $E$.

   (c) Calculate the coordinates of $E$.

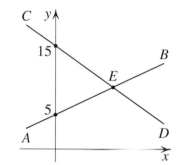

※ **12** The diagram shows triangle $PQR$.

Calculate the coordinates of the vertices $P$, $Q$ and $R$.

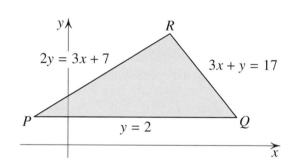
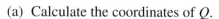

※ **13** The diagram shows parallelogram $PQRS$. The equation of $PQ$ is $y = 2x - 1$, the equation of $RQ$ is $4x + y = 35$ and $S$ is the point $(0, 5)$.

   (a) Calculate the coordinates of $Q$.

   (b) Write down the equation of $SP$.

   (c) Calculate the coordinates of $P$.

   (d) Write down the equation of $SR$.

   (e) Calculate the coordinates of $R$.

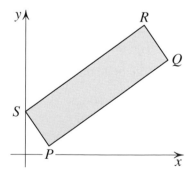

## 5.6 Miscellaneous questions

### Exercise 5.6

1. The straight line through $(2, -3)$ and $(4, p)$ has gradient $-5$.
   Calculate the value of $p$.

2. The diagram shows the curve with equation $y = 2x^2 + 3$.
   The $x$-coordinate of $P$ is $-1$ and the $x$-coordinate of $Q$
   is 2.

   Find the gradient of $PQ$.

   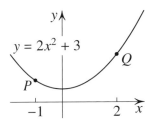

3. The line with equation $3x - 2y = 10$ passes through the point $(3, k)$.
   Find the value of $k$.

4. Find the equations of the two straight lines shown in the
   diagram.

   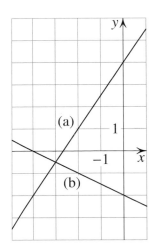

5. Find the equation of the straight line:
   (a) through the points $(2, -2)$ and $(-2, 6)$.
   (b) through the points $(6, -3)$ and $(-4, -3)$.
   (c) through the point $(-1, 8)$ and parallel to the line with equation $y = 3x - 5$.
   (d) through $(4, 2)$ and perpendicular to the line with equation $x = 6$.
   (e) through $(-4, 6)$ and parallel to the line with equation $3x + 2y = 19$.
   (f) through $(5, -4)$ and parallel to the line with equation $y = 3$.
   (g) through $(-2, 4)$ and $(-2, -3)$.

6. What is the gradient of the line perpendicular to the line with equation $4x - 6y = 3$?

7 | The straight lines with equations $y = \frac{4}{5}x - 2$ and $y = -\frac{3}{k}x + 2$ are perpendicular. Calculate the value of $k$.

8 | Calculate the point of intersection of the lines with equations $y = 2x - 5$ and $y = 6x - 1$.

9 | Two sides of a rectangle have equations $x = 4$ and $y = -6$.
One vertex of the rectangle is $(-3, 8)$.

   (a) Write down the equations of the other two sides of the rectangle.

   (b) Find the equations of the diagonals of the rectangle.

10 | The diagram shows a triangle with vertices $A (0, 7)$, $B (6, 8)$ and $C (6, -2)$.

   (a) State the equation of $BC$.

   (b) Find the equation of line $AB$.

   (c) Find the equation of line $AC$.

   (d) Calculate the length of $AC$.

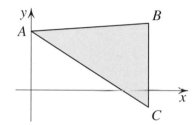

❄ 11 | In the diagram, $PQRS$ is a trapezium with $P (1, 3)$, $Q (-3, 3)$ and $R (-5, 1)$.
Angle $QRS$ is a right angle.

   (a) State the equation of $PQ$.

   (b) Find the equation of line $QR$.

   (c) Find the equation of line $RS$.

   (d) Find the coordinates of $S$.

   (e) Find the coordinates of the midpoint of $PS$.

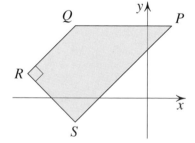

❄ 12 | Triangle $ABC$ has vertices $A (6, -5)$, $B (7, 3)$ and $C (-5, -3)$.
Line $AL$ is perpendicular to line $BC$.

   (a) Find the equation of line $AL$.

   (b) Calculate the coordinates of $L$.

   (c) Calculate the length of $AL$.

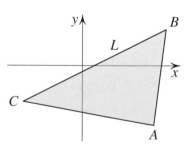

❄ 13 | The triangle $PQR$ is formed by the straight lines $PQ$ with equation $3x + 2y = 12$, $QR$ with equation $y = 6$, and $PR$ with equation $x = 4$.

Find the equation of the straight line which bisects angle $PRQ$.

# 6 Quadratic equations

## 6.1 Quadratic equations by factorising

The following exercise will help you to practise:

❏ solving a quadratic equation by factorising

❏ solving a quadratic equation not in standard form by rearranging the terms

### Exercise 6.1a

**1** Solve the equation:

(a) $x^2 + 9x + 14 = 0$      (b) $m^2 + 9m + 8 = 0$      (c) $a^2 - 10a + 21 = 0$

(d) $p^2 - 10p + 25 = 0$      (e) $x^2 + 5x - 14 = 0$      (f) $k^2 + k - 30 = 0$

(g) $t^2 - 8t - 9 = 0$      (h) $q^2 - 15q + 26 = 0$      (i) $a^2 + a - 56 = 0$

(j) $f^2 + f - 20 = 0$      (k) $x^2 - 6x - 27 = 0$      (l) $h^2 - 11h + 30 = 0$

**2** By first finding a common factor, solve the equation:

(a) $5b^2 - 5b - 60 = 0$          (b) $2s^2 + 30s + 100 = 0$

(c) $4k^2 + 32k + 48 = 0$         (d) $10t^2 + 100t - 240 = 0$

(e) $3m^2 + 54m + 216 = 0$       (f) $7w^2 - 14w - 693 = 0$

**3** Solve the equation:

(a) $x^2 + 9x = 0$      (b) $y^2 - 8y = 0$      (c) $10x - x^2 = 0$

(d) $\lambda^2 - \lambda = 0$      (e) $5t + t^2 = 0$      (f) $\alpha^2 + 0.2\alpha = 0$

**4** Solve the equation:

(a) $x^2 - 4 = 0$      (b) $16 - u^2 = 0$      (c) $a^2 - 81 = 0$

(d) $x^2 = 0$      (e) $144 - h^2 = 0$      (f) $p^2 - 49 = 0$

**5** Solve the equation:

(a) $6x^2 - 2x = 0$          (b) $21a - 14a^2 = 0$

(c) $60b^2 - 24b = 0$         (d) $4\tau^2 = 20\tau$

(e) $x(x + 1) - 10(x + 1) = 0$     (f) $(a + 3)^2 - a - 3 = 0$

**6** Solve the equation:

(a) $5x^2 - 5 = 0$            (b) $3 - 75p^2 = 0$           (c) $12a^2 - 48 = 0$

**7** Solve the equation:

(a) $9 - 4a^2 = 0$          (b) $121 - 100s^2 = 0$       (c) $64q^2 - 49 = 0$

(d) $25k^2 - 144 = 0$       (e) $81 - 100r^2 = 0$

**8** Rewrite in standard form and factorise to solve the equation:

(a) $x^2 = 7 - 6x$                     (b) $x^2 - 7x = 3x + 11$

(c) $u(u - 4) = 5$                  (d) $2h^2 + 7 = h^2 - 8h - 5$

(e) $3(2d - 1) = d^2 + 2$          (f) $k(k + 7) = 2(k - 3)$

(g) $t(2t + 1) = (t + 2)^2$        (h) $(y + 2)(2y - 1) = (y + 1)(y - 2)$

---

The following exercise will help you to practise:

❏ solving a harder quadratic equation by factorising

❏ solving a harder quadratic equation not in standard form by rearranging the terms

---

## Exercise 6.1b

**1** Solve the equation:

(a) $2x^2 - 3x + 1 = 0$      (b) $5x^2 - 6x + 1 = 0$      (c) $4e^2 + 4e + 1 = 0$

(d) $2b^2 - b - 1 = 0$        (e) $14y^2 + 5y - 1 = 0$     (f) $10z^2 + 7z + 1 = 0$

(g) $24a^2 + 2a - 1 = 0$     (h) $30h^2 + 11h + 1 = 0$     (i) $12r^2 - r - 1 = 0$

**2** Solve the equation:

(a) $1 - 10x + 21x^2 = 0$    (b) $1 - 2c - 3c^2 = 0$      (c) $1 + 4t - 12t^2 = 0$

(d) $1 - 7d - 60d^2 = 0$      (e) $1 + 5p + 6p^2 = 0$      (f) $1 - 7u + 12u^2 = 0$

**3** Solve the equation:

(a) $2x^2 - 7x + 3 = 0$              (b) $3x^2 + 5x + 2 = 0$

(c) $3q^2 + 4q - 7 = 0$            (d) $5q^2 - 34q - 7 = 0$

(e) $7y^2 - 36y + 5 = 0$          (f) $3y^2 + 2y - 5 = 0$

(g) $2z^2 - 13z + 15 = 0$        (h) $3z^2 + 19z - 14 = 0$

(i) $3t^2 - 20t - 63 = 0$         (j) $2t^2 - 3t - 9 = 0$

(k) $6a^2 + 11a - 10 = 0$       (l) $6b^2 - 13b - 28 = 0$

**4** Solve the equation:

(a) $2 - 11x + 5x^2 = 0$     (b) $11 - 9q - 2q^2 = 0$     (c) $5 + 11y + 2y^2 = 0$

(d) $2 - 11n + 12n^2 = 0$     (e) $5 - 3p - 2p^2 = 0$     (f) $7 + 26k - 8k^2 = 0$

(g) $12 + 17z - 5z^2 = 0$     (h) $9 + 30t + 25t^2 = 0$     (i) $10 + 29e + 10e^2 = 0$

(j) $8 - 10s - 3s^2 = 0$     (k) $20 - 7Q - 6Q^2 = 0$     (l) $16 + 56u + 49u^2 = 0$

**5** Rewrite in standard form and factorise to solve the equation:

(a) $15x^2 = 1 - 2x$                  (b) $5e(2e + 3) = 8e - 1$

(c) $10k(2k + 1) = (2 + k)(1 - k)$     (d) $v(5 - 2v) = 2$

(e) $(2t + 1)^2 = t + 2$            (f) $(2 - n)(n + 3) = 2(n + 1)$

❄ **6** Solve the equation:

(a) $g^2 + \frac{1}{2}g - \frac{1}{2} = 0$          (b) $a^2 - 0.4a + 0.03 = 0$

(c) $y^2 - \frac{49}{81} = 0$             (d) $q^2 - 0.25 = 0$

(e) $c^2 + 0.2c - 0.08 = 0$      (f) $t^2 - 0.72t = 0$

(g) $k^2 + \frac{1}{6}k - \frac{1}{18} = 0$        (h) $d^2 + 0.45d = 0$

(i) $x^2 - 0.9x - 2.2 = 0$       (j) $0.2d^2 + 1.06d + 0.3 = 0$

(k) $\frac{2}{3}f^2 + \frac{2}{3}f - \frac{1}{2} = 0$        (l) $\frac{6}{25}x^2 + \frac{1}{5}x - \frac{1}{3} = 0$

❄ **7** Rewrite in standard form and factorise to solve the equation:

(a) $a(a + 0.8) = 0.1(6a - 0.1)$

(b) $(n - 2)(n + 1) = -0.9(n + 1.6)$

(c) $3.5p + 4.5 = (p + 1)(p + 6)$

## 6.2 Using the quadratic formula

The following exercise will help you to practise:

❏ solving a quadratic equation of the form $ax^2 + bx + c = 0$ using the formula

$$x = \frac{-b \pm \sqrt{b^2 - 4ac}}{2a}$$

❏ solving a quadratic equation not in standard form by rearranging the terms and using the formula

Where necessary, give answers to 2 decimal places.

### Exercise 6.2

**1** Solve the equation:

(a) $x^2 + 4x + 2 = 0$             (b) $a^2 - 5a + 3 = 0$

(c) $5p^2 + p - 11 = 0$        (d) $2t^2 + 9t + 1 = 0$

(e) $19g^2 + 14g + 2 = 0$     (f) $7b^2 + 16b + 3 = 0$

(g) $1.8h^2 - 5.1h - 3.6 = 0$   (h) $4.5m^2 + m - 2.6 = 0$

**2** Solve the equation:

(a) $21w^2 = 4(w + 2)$          (b) $x(3x + 1) = 7$

(c) $0.2j^2 + 3.4j + 0.9 = 0$    (d) $\frac{1}{2}(2\tau^2 - 3) = \frac{2}{3}\tau$

**3** Solve the equation:

(a) $5x^2 - 7x - 3 = x(x + 2)$     (b) $7p - 5p^2 = 2p - 7$

(c) $G^2 + 0.75 = 0.25G^2 - 1.75G$   (d) $145c^2 = 21(c - 12)(c - 3)$

# 6.3 Special quadratic equations

The following exercise will help you to practise:

❏ solving an equation of the form $k(x - p)^2 = q$ by finding the square root of each side

### Exercise 6.3a

**1** Solve the equation:

(a) $(x + 2)^2 = 9$      (b) $(x - 4)^2 = 100$      (c) $(y + 5)^2 = 25$

(d) $4(p + 3)^2 = 81$      (e) $9(q - 1)^2 = 4$      (f) $16(r + 1)^2 = 9$

(g) $(2t + 3)^2 = 1$      (h) $(5b + 2)^2 = 9$      (i) $16(3h + 1)^2 = 25$

❄ **2** Solve the equation, leaving the answer in surd form:

(a) $(x + 3)^2 = 5$      (b) $(x - 1)^2 = 2$      (c) $(y - 7)^2 = 5$

(d) $(d + 2)^2 = 6$      (e) $(2w - 1)^2 = 3$      (f) $(2z - 5)^2 = 7$

The following exercise will help you to practise:

❏ solving an equation by making a substitution to convert it into a quadratic equation

### Exercise 6.3b

❄ **1** Solve the equation:

(a) $\cos^2 x + \cos x = 0$ for $\cos x$, by putting $c = \cos x$

(b) $4 \sin^2 x - 1 = 0$ for $\sin x$, by putting $s = \sin x$

(c) $5 \cos^2 t - 2 \cos t = 0$ for $\cos t$, by putting $c = \cos t$

(d) $6 \sin^2 t + 5 \sin t - 1 = 0$ for $\sin t$, by putting $s = \sin t$

❄ **2** Use the substitution given in the box to solve the equation:

(a) $t^4 - 10t^2 + 9 = 0$      $\boxed{x = t^2}$

(b) $k^6 + 7k^3 - 8 = 0$      $\boxed{x = k^3}$

(c) $(y + 3)^2 - 12(y + 3) - 28 = 0$      $\boxed{x = y + 3}$

(d) $A - 11\sqrt{A} + 30 = 0$      $\boxed{x = \sqrt{A}}$

(e) $a^{\frac{2}{3}} - 5a^{\frac{1}{3}} + 4 = 0$      $\boxed{x = a^{\frac{1}{3}}}$

## 6.4   Simultaneous equations where one is non-linear

The following exercise will help you to practise:

❏ solving a pair of simultaneous equations one of which is non-linear

### Exercise 6.4

1 Solve the simultaneous equations:

(a)  $y = x^2 - 6$
   $y = 2x + 2$

(b)  $y = x^2 - 2x + 7$
   $y = 6$

(c)   $x = y$
   $2x^2 - y^2 = 1$

(d)   $x + y = 0$
   $y^2 - xy = 8$

(e)  $3x + y = 4$
   $xy = 1$

(f)  $xy = 12$
   $x = y - 4$

2 Solve the simultaneous equations:

(a)  $x^2 + y^2 = 10$
   $y = x + 2$

(b)   $y = 3x + 1$
   $12x = y^2$

(c)   $a + b = 1$
   $a^2 - ab = 15$

(d)  $\alpha\beta = 4$
   $\frac{1}{2}\beta = \alpha + 1$

(e)   $3x - y = 9$
   $6x^2 - 17xy + 5y^2 = 171$

(f)   $x + 2y = -1$
   $x^2 - 2xy = 3 - 4x$

❄ 3 Solve the simultaneous equations:

(a)  $y = x + 1$
   $1 = (x + 1)^2 + (y + 1)^2$

(b)  $x^2 + y = 4$
   $3x - y = 0$

(c)  $2y^2 + 3xy - 2x^2 = 12$
   $3x + 2y = 4$

(d)   $f = 0.25g$
   $f(f - 1) = g - 4$

(e)  $3pq - 5(p + q) = 1$
   $0.8p - 0.2 = q$

(f)  $v^2 + vw = 4v - 2$
   $w = \frac{1}{2}u$

## 6.5 Miscellaneous questions

> *Where necessary, give answers to 2 decimal places.*

### Exercise 6.5

1. Solve:
   - (a) $225 - 49u^2 = 0$
   - (b) $6k^2 - 7k = 0$
   - (c) $q^2 + 16q + 64 = 0$
   - (d) $(a + 3)^2 = 25$
   - (e) $(2n - 1)^2 = 169$
   - (f) $7p^2 + 6p = 24.5$
   - (g) $4.9t^2 + 19.6t = 24.5$
   - (h) $(x - 2)^2 = 7$
   - (i) $(3e + 1)^2 = 6$
   - (j) $0.7T + 0.6T^2 = 0.5$
   - (k) $3 \tan^2 \theta - 4 \tan \theta + 1 = 0$ for $\tan \theta$
   - (l) $7e^2 - 3e - 2 = 0$
   - (m) $2.25h^2 - 1.69 = 0$
   - (n) $35z^2 - 2z - 1 = 0$
   - (o) $3.4y^2 - 0.3y - 1 = 0$
   - (p) $(3\eta - 4)(\eta + 1) = (\eta + 2)^2 + 4$
   - (q) $\dfrac{5f^2}{4} - 1 = \left(\tfrac{1}{2}f - 1\right)^2$

2. Solve the simultaneous equations:
   - (a) $x^2 + y^2 = 20$
     $x = 2y$
   - (b) $x^2 + xy = 3$
     $y = x + 1$
   - (c) $x - y - 4 = 0$
     $x^2 - 4x + y = 0$
   - (d) $(x + 1)(y + 2) = -8$
     $x + y + 1 = 0$

# 7 Curves

## 7.1 Simple quadratic curves

The following exercise will help you to practise:

❏ sketching the graph of a quadratic curve

❏ using the fact that  the $y$-intercept occurs where $x = 0$

❏ using the fact that  the turning point of $y = (x - p)^2 + q$ is at $(p, q)$

**Exercise 7.1a**

1. Sketch on the same diagram, labelling each curve clearly, the graphs of the two curves with equations:

   (a) (i) $y = x^2$      (b) (i) $y = x^2$      (c) (i) $y = -x^2$      (d) (i) $y = -3x^2$
   
       (ii) $y = 3x^2$      (ii) $y = \frac{1}{2}x^2$      (ii) $y = -2x^2$      (ii) $y = -\frac{1}{4}x^2$

2. Sketch on the same diagram, labelling the $y$-intercepts, the graphs of the two curves with equations:

   (a) (i) $y = x^2$             (b) (i) $y = -x^2$           (c) (i) $y = -x^2 - 1$
   
       (ii) $y = x^2 + 2$         (ii) $y = -x^2 + 3$        (ii) $y = x^2 + 1$

   (d) (i) $y = x^2 - 2$         (e) (i) $y = 3x^2$             (f) (i) $y = -4x^2$
   
       (ii) $y = -x^2 + 2$       (ii) $y = 3x^2 + 2$        (ii) $y = -4x^2 + 2$

3. Sketch on the same diagram, labelling the $y$-intercepts and the coordinates of the turning points, the graphs of the two curves with equations:

   (a) (i) $y = x^2$             (b) (i) $y = x^2$             (c) (i) $y = -x^2$
   
       (ii) $y = (x + 2)^2$       (ii) $y = (x - 4)^2$      (ii) $y = -(x + 3)^2$

   (d) (i) $y = -x^2$          (e) (i) $y = (x + 5)^2$      (f) (i) $y = -(x - 4)^2$
   
       (ii) $y = -(x - 2)^2$    (ii) $y = -(x - 5)^2$    (ii) $y = (x + 1)^2$

   (g) (i) $y = (x + 3)^2$
   
       (ii) $y = 2(x + 3)^2$

4  Sketch a graph, labelling the coordinates of the turning point and the intersection with the $y$-axis, of the curve with equation:

(a)  $y = (x - 1)^2 + 3$

(b)  $y = (x + 2)^2 + 5$

(c)  $y = (x + 1)^2 - 3$

(d)  $y = (x + 2)^2 - 6$

(e)  $y = 3 - (x + 1)^2$

(f)  $y = 10 - (x - 2)^2$

(g)  $y = 5 - (x - 1)^2$

(h)  $y = 4(x - 1)^2 + 2$

(i)  $y = 2(x + 3)^2 + 7$

(j)  $y = 5 - 2(x + 3)^2$

(k)  $y = 12 - 3(x + 1)^2$

(l)  $y = 3(x - 2)^2 + 4$

5  The diagram shows the curve with equation $y = (x - 3)^2 - 4$.

The point $A$ is the minimum turning point.

The curve crosses the $y$-axis at the point $B$.

The point $C$ lies on the curve and on the line through $B$ parallel to the $x$-axis.

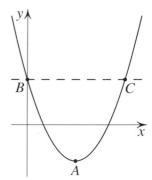

(a)  Write down the coordinates of $A$.

(b)  Find the coordinates of $B$.

(c)  Write down the coordinates of $C$.

6  The diagram shows the curve with equation $y = 12 - (x - 2)^2$.

The point $A$ is the maximum turning point.

The curve crosses the $y$-axis at the point $B$.

The point $C$ lies on the curve and on the line through $B$ parallel to the $x$-axis.

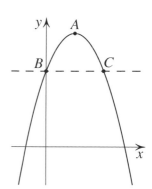

(a)  Write down the coordinates of $A$.

(b)  Find the coordinates of $B$.

(c)  Write down the coordinates of $C$.

7  The diagram shows the curve with equation $y = (x + 4)^2 + 2$.

The point $A$ is the minimum turning point.

The curve crosses the $y$-axis at the point $B$.

The point $C$ lies on the curve and on the line through $B$ parallel to the $x$-axis.

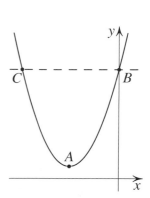

(a)  Write down the coordinates of $A$.

(b)  Find the coordinates of $B$.

(c)  Write down the coordinates of $C$.

8 | The diagram shows the curve with equation
$y = 7 - (x - 1)^2$.
The point $A$ is the maximum turning point.
The point $B(4, k)$ lies on the curve.
The point $C$ lies on the curve and on the line through $B$
parallel to the $x$-axis.

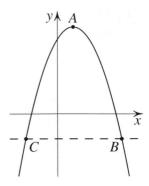

(a) Write down the coordinates of $A$.

(b) Calculate the value of $k$.

(c) Find the coordinates of $C$.

❄ 9 | The diagram shows two parabolas labelled $P$ and $Q$,
where $Q$ is a reflection of $P$ in the $y$-axis.
The curve $P$ has equation $y = 8 - (x - 3)^2$ and
maximum turning point $A$.
The curve $Q$ has maximum turning point $B$.

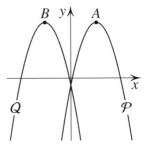

(a) Write down the coordinates of $A$.

(b) Write down the coordinates of $B$.

(c) Write down the equation of the curve $Q$.

❄ 10 | The diagram shows two parabolas labelled $P$ and $Q$.
The curve $Q$ is a reflection of $P$ in the line parallel to
the $x$-axis through the minimum turning point $A$ of $P$.
The curve $P$ has equation $y = (x - 4)^2 + 2$.

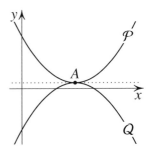

(a) Write down the coordinates of $A$.

(b) Write down the equation of the curve $Q$.

❄ 11 | The diagram shows two parabolas labelled $P$ and $Q$.
The curve $P$ crosses the $y$-axis at point $C$, and $Q$ is a
reflection of $P$ in the line parallel to the $x$-axis
through $C$.
The curve $P$ has equation $y = (x - 2)^2 - 1$.

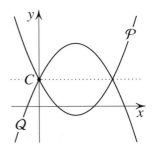

(a) Write down the coordinates of $C$.

(b) Write down the equation of the curve $Q$.

❄ **12** The diagram shows three parabolas $P$, $Q$ and $R$, whose minimum turning points lie on a straight line parallel to the $x$-axis.

The point $S$ $(-30, k)$ lies on $P$ and $T$ $(0, k)$ lies on $R$. The curves divide $ST$ into three equal parts.

The curve $P$ has equation $y = (x + 25)^2 - 17$.

(a) Calculate the value of $k$.

(b) Find the equations of the curves $Q$ and $R$.

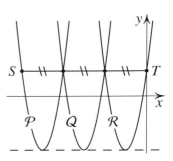

The following exercise will help you to practise:

❏ finding an equation of the form $y = kx^2$ or $y = kx^2 + q$ for a parabolic graph

## Exercise 7.1b

**1** Find an equation of the form $y = kx^2$ for the curve:

(a)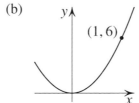

$(1, 3)$

(b)

$(1, 6)$

(c)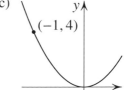

$(-1, 4)$

(d)

$(1, -5)$

(e)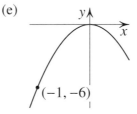

$(-1, -6)$

(f)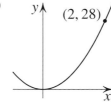

$(2, 28)$

(g)

$(-2, 32)$

(h)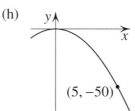

$(5, -50)$

(i)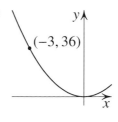

$(-3, 36)$

(j)

$(-2, -12)$

(k)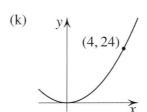

$(4, 24)$

(l)

$(6, -48)$

**2** Find an equation of the form $y = kx^2 + q$ for the curve:

(a)

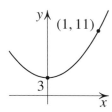

(b)

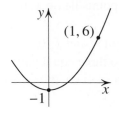

(c)

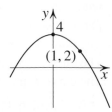

(d)

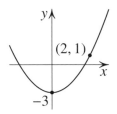

(e)

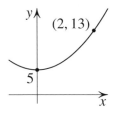

(f)

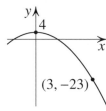

(g)

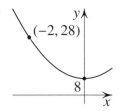

(h)

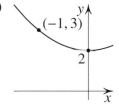

(i)

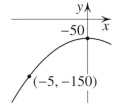

(j)

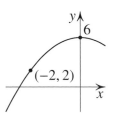

(k)

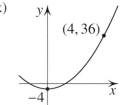

(l)

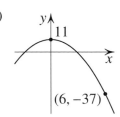

## 7.2 Quadratic curves in factorised form

The following exercise will help you to practise:

❏ using the fact that the roots occur where $y = 0$

❏ sketching the graph of a general quadratic curve

### Exercise 7.2a

**1** The diagram shows the parabola with equation
$y = (x + 2)(x - 4)$.

   (a) State the coordinates of the points $A$ and $B$.

   (b) State the coordinates of the point $C$.

   (c) Calculate the coordinates of the point $D$.

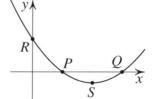

**2** The diagram shows the parabola with equation
$y = (x - 6)(x - 2)$.

   (a) State the coordinates of the points $P$ and $Q$.

   (b) State the coordinates of the point $R$.

   (c) Calculate the coordinates of the point $S$.

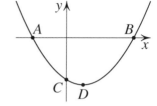

**3** The diagram shows the parabola with equation
$y = x(x + 6)$.

   (a) State the values of the roots.

   (b) Calculate the coordinates of the point $M$.

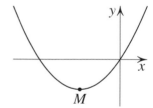

**4** The diagram shows the parabola with equation
$y = (4 - x)(8 + x)$.

   (a) State the values of the roots.

   (b) Calculate the coordinates of the point $C$.

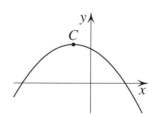

**5** The diagram shows the parabola with equation
$y = x(8 - x)$.

   (a) State the values of the roots.

   (b) Calculate the coordinates of the point $K$.

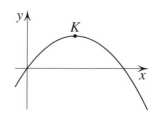

**6** The diagram shows the parabola with equation
$y = x^2 + 6x + 5$.

    (a) Find the coordinates of the points $A$ and $B$.

    (b) State the coordinates of the point $C$.

    (c) Calculate the coordinates of the point $D$.

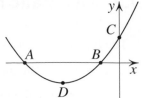

**7** The diagram shows the parabola with equation
$y = x^2 - 10x$.

Find the coordinates of the point $H$.

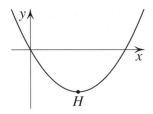

**8** The diagram shows the parabola with equation
$y = 32 - 4x - x^2$.

    (a) Find the coordinates of the points $A$ and $B$.

    (b) Calculate the coordinates of the point $C$.

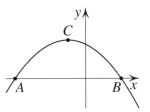

**9** Sketch a graph, showing the roots, the point of intersection with the $y$-axis and the coordinates of the turning point, of the curve with equation:

    (a) $y = x^2 + 4x + 3$     (b) $y = x^2 - 6x + 5$     (c) $y = x^2 - 3x - 4$

    (d) $y = x^2 - 16$     (e) $y = x^2 + 6x$     (f) $y = 4x - x^2$

    (g) $y = 4 - x^2$     (h) $y = 2 - x - x^2$     (i) $y = 3 + 2x - x^2$

**❋ 10** Sketch a graph, showing the roots, the intersection with the $y$-axis and the coordinates of the turning point, of the curve with equation:

    (a) $y = 2x^2 + x - 1$     (b) $y = 9 - 4x^2$     (c) $y = 2x^2 + 6x$

    (d) $y = 4x^2 - x - 3$     (e) $y = 2x^2 - 12x + 10$     (f) $y = 18 - 3x - 3x^2$

**❋ 11** A curve has equation $y = (x + 2)(x - 3)$.
The points $(4, p)$ and $(k, 14)$ lie on the curve.

    (a) Sketch the curve, showing the roots and the $y$-intercept.

    (b) Find the value of $p$.

    (c) Find the possible values of $k$.

❄ **12** A curve has equation $y = 4x^2 + 8x + 3$.
The points $(3, q)$ and $(t, 35)$ lie on the curve.

    (a) Sketch the curve, showing the $x$-intercepts and the $y$-intercept.

    (b) Find the value of $q$.

    (c) Find the possible values of $t$.

❄ **13** A curve has equation $y = 15 + 2x - x^2$.
The points $(6, m)$ and $(k, 12)$ lie on the curve.

    (a) Sketch the curve, showing the roots and the intersection with the $y$-axis.

    (b) Find the value of $m$.

    (c) Find the possible values of $k$.

---

The following exercise will help you to practise:

❑ finding an equation of the form $y = k(x - a)(x - b)$ for a parabolic graph

---

### Exercise 7.2b

**1** Find an equation of the form $y = (x - a)(x - b)$ for the curve:

(a)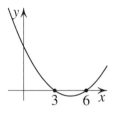

(b)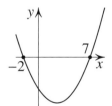

(c)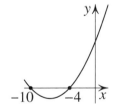

(d)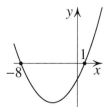

(e)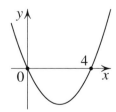

(f)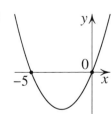

(g)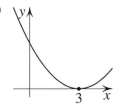

(h)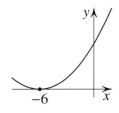

2   Find an equation of the form $y = -(x - a)(x - b)$ for the curve:

(a)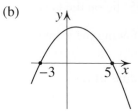

(b)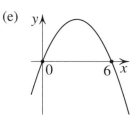

(c)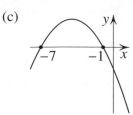

(d)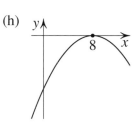

(e)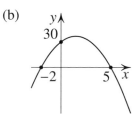

(f)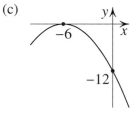

(g)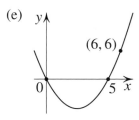

(h)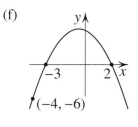

❄ 3   Find an equation of the form $y = k(x - a)(x - b)$ for the curve:

(a)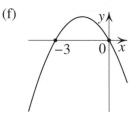

(b)

(c)

(d)

(e)

(f)

(g)

(h)

## 7.3   Cubic curves

The following exercise will help you to practise:

❑ finding the roots and the $y$-intercept of a cubic curve

❑ sketching the graph of a cubic curve

### Exercise 7.3

❄ 1   The diagram shows the cubic curve with equation $y = (x - 1)(x + 2)(x + 3)$.
The curve intersects the $x$-axis at the points $A$, $B$ and $C$, and intersects the $y$-axis at $D$.

(a) State the coordinates of $A$, $B$ and $C$.

(b) Find the coordinates of $D$.

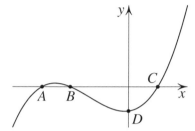

❄ 2   The diagram shows the cubic curve with equation $y = 2x + x^2 - x^3$.

(a) Fully factorise $2x + x^2 - x^3$.

(b) State the coordinates of the points where the curve intersects the $x$-axis.

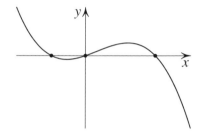

❄ 3   The diagram shows the cubic curve with equation $y = (2 - x)(3 + x^2)$.

(a) State the coordinates of the point where the curve intersects the $x$-axis.

(b) Find the coordinates of the point where the curve intersects the $y$-axis.

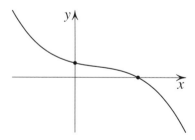

❄ 4   Sketch the graph of the cubic curve with equation:

(a) $y = (x - 5)(x - 2)(x + 1)$

(b) $y = (1 - x)(3 - x)(4 - x)$

(c) $y = 4x - x^3$

(d) $y = 3x^3 + 2x^2 - x$

(e) $y = (x - 2)(x^2 - 9)$

(f) $y = 3(x + 1)(x + 2)(x + 4)$

## 7.4   The intersection of a line and a quadratic curve

The following exercise will help you to practise:

❏ finding the points of intersection of a straight line and a quadratic curve

### Exercise 7.4

1   The diagram shows the straight line with equation $y = 8$ and the parabola with equation $y = x^2 - 8$.

The line and the parabola intersect at the points $A$ and $B$.

Calculate the coordinates of $A$ and $B$.

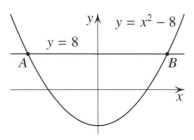

2   On the same diagram sketch the graphs of $y = 13 - x^2$ and $y = 4$.

Calculate the coordinates of the points of intersection of the line and the parabola.

3   The diagram shows the parabola with equation $y = x^2 - 4x + 3$.

The line $KL$ is parallel to the $x$-axis.

(a)  Write down the equation of $KL$.

The line and parabola intersect at $K$ and $L$.

(b)  Calculate the coordinates of $K$ and $L$.

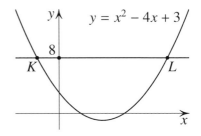

4   The diagram shows the parabola with equation $y = 3 + 2x - x^2$.

The line $AB$ is parallel to the $x$-axis.

(a)  Write down the equation of $AB$.

The line and parabola intersect at $A$ and $B$.

(b)  Calculate the coordinates of $A$ and $B$.

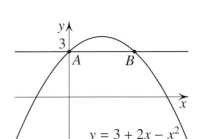

5   The diagram shows the parabola with equation $y = (x + 3)^2 - 4$.

The line through $T$ is parallel to the $x$-axis.

(a)  Write down the equation of the line through $T$.

The line and parabola intersect at $T$.

(b)  Write down the coordinates of $T$.

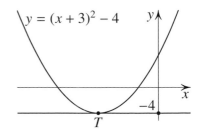

**6** The diagram shows the straight line with equation $y = 11 - x$ and the parabola with equation $y = x^2 - 3x - 4$.

The line and the parabola intersect at the points $P$ and $Q$.

Calculate the coordinates of $P$ and $Q$.

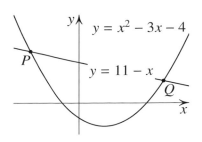

**7** Find the coordinates of the points of intersection of the curve with equation $y = 5 + 4x - x^2$ and the straight line with equation $y = x - 5$.

**8** The diagram shows the straight line with equation $y = x + 1$ and the parabola with equation $y = 2x^2$.

The line and the parabola intersect at the points $P$ and $Q$.

Calculate the coordinates of $P$ and $Q$.

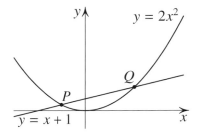

**9** The line with equation $y = 4 - 7x$ meets the curve with equation $y = 3 - 5x - x^2$ at only one point. Find the coordinates of this point.

**10** The diagram shows the straight line with equation $y = 4x$ and the parabola with equation $y = (x - 2)^2 + 11$.

The line and the parabola intersect at the points $A$ and $B$.

Calculate the coordinates of $A$ and $B$.

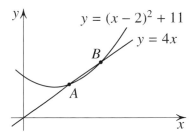

**11** The diagram shows the straight line with equation $y = 3x + 1$ and the parabola with equation $y = (x - 2)^2 - 11$.

Calculate the coordinates of the points where the line and parabola intersect.

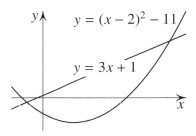

**12** On the same diagram sketch the graphs of $y = 2(x + 1)^2 - 10$ and $y = x + 1$.

Calculate the coordinates of the points where the line and parabola intersect.

☀ 13 The diagram shows a parabola and a straight line.
The parabola has an equation of the form
$y = (x - a)(x - b)$.
The line has gradient $-2$ and passes through the point
$(0, 10)$.

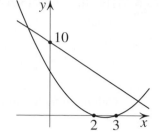

(a) Write down an equation of the parabola.

(b) Write down the equation of the line.

(c) Calculate the coordinates of the points of
intersection of the line and parabola.

☀ 14 The diagram shows a parabola and a straight line.
The parabola has an equation of the form
$y = (x - a)^2 + b$.
The line has gradient 1 and passes through the origin.

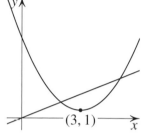

(a) Write down an equation of the parabola.

(b) Write down the equation of the line.

(c) Calculate the coordinates of the points of
intersection of the line and parabola.

☀ 15 Calculate the coordinates of the points of intersection of the straight line $y = 6x - 9$
and the parabola $y = x^2$.

What does the result tell us about the line and the curve?

## 7.5 The intersection of two quadratic curves

The following exercise will help you to practise:

❏ finding the points of intersection of two quadratic curves

### Exercise 7.5

**1** The diagram shows the curves with equations
$y = x^2$ and $y = 8 - x^2$.
The curves intersect at the points $P$ and $Q$.

Calculate the coordinates of $P$ and $Q$.

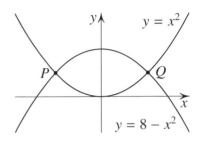

**2** On the same diagram sketch the graphs of $y = 3x^2$ and $y = 36 - x^2$.

Calculate the coordinates of the points of intersection of the two curves.

**3** The diagram shows the curves with equations
$y = x^2 - 50$ and $y = -x^2$.
The curves intersect at the points $P$ and $Q$.

Calculate the coordinates of $P$ and $Q$.

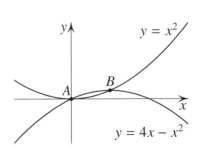

**4** The diagram shows the curves with equations
$y = x^2$ and $y = 4x - x^2$.
The curves intersect at the points $A$ and $B$.

Calculate the coordinates of $A$ and $B$.

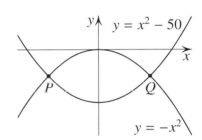

**5** The diagram shows the curves with equations
$y = 2x^2$ and $y = x^2 + 4$.
The curves intersect at the points $K$ and $L$.

Calculate the coordinates of $K$ and $L$.

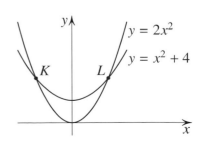

6 | The diagram shows the curves with equations
$y = x^2 - 8x$ and $y = -x^2$.
The curves intersect at the points $P$ and $Q$.

Calculate the coordinates of $P$ and $Q$.

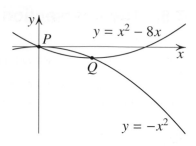

7 | On the same diagram sketch the graphs of $y = (4 - x)(2 + x)$ and $y = (x - 1)^2 + 1$.

Calculate the coordinates of the points of intersection of the two curves.

8 | The diagram shows the curves with equations
$y = (x - 4)^2 + 2$ and $y = 4 - (x - 4)^2$.
The curves intersect at the points $R$ and $S$.

Calculate the coordinates of $R$ and $S$.

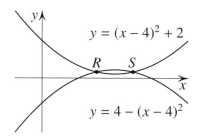

9 | The diagram shows the curves with equations
$y = 8 + 2x - x^2$ and $y = x^2 + 4$.

Calculate the coordinates of the points where the two curves intersect.

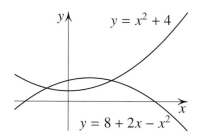

10 | Find the coordinates of the points of intersection of the curves with equations
$y = 4 - (x - 3)^2$ and $y = (x - 2)^2 - 1$.

11 | The diagram shows the curves with equations
$y = (x - 3)^2 - 6$ and $y = 3 + 4x - x^2$.

Calculate the coordinates of the points of intersection of the two curves.

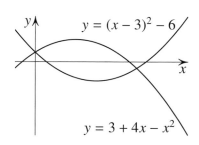

12 | Find the coordinates of the points of intersection of the curves with equations
$y = 8 + 2x - x^2$ and $y = x^2 - 8x + 16$.

## 7.6 The intersection of a line and a curve

The following exercise will help you to practise:

❏ finding the points of intersection of a line and a curve

### Exercise 7.6

**1** The diagram shows the circle with equation $x^2 + y^2 = 25$ and the straight line with equation $y = 4$.

The circle crosses the $x$-axis at points $A$ and $B$.
The circle crosses the $y$-axis at points $C$ and $D$.

(a) Find the coordinates of $A$ and $B$.

(b) Find the coordinates of $C$ and $D$.

(c) Calculate the coordinates of the points where the line with equation $y = 4$ intersects the circle.

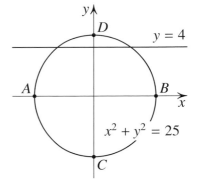

**2** The diagram shows the circle with equation $x^2 + y^2 = 169$ and the straight line with equation $x = -5$.

Calculate the coordinates of the points where the line with equation $x = -5$ intersects the circle.

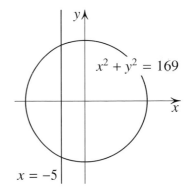

**3** The diagram shows the ellipse with equation

$$\frac{x^2}{36} + \frac{y^2}{81} = 1.$$

The ellipse crosses the $x$-axis at points $P$ and $Q$.
The ellipse crosses the $y$-axis at points $R$ and $S$.

(a) Find the coordinates of $P$ and $Q$.

(b) Find the coordinates of $R$ and $S$.

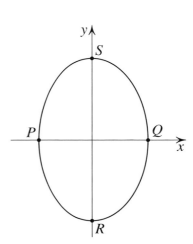

**4** The diagram shows the ellipse with equation $9x^2 + 25y^2 = 225$ and the straight line with equation $x = -4$.

Calculate the coordinates of the points of intersection of the ellipse and the line.

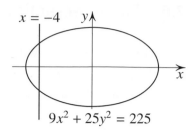

**5** The diagram shows the parabola with equation $x = y^2$ and the straight line with equation $x = 16$.

Calculate the coordinates of the points of intersection of the parabola and the line.

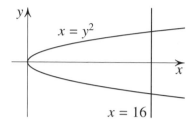

**6** The diagram shows the curve with equation

$$y = \frac{2}{x}$$

and the straight line with equation $x = \frac{1}{4}$.

Calculate the coordinates of the point of intersection of the curve and the line.

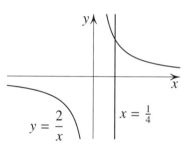

**7** The diagram shows the curve with equation

$$y = \frac{1}{x^2}$$

and the straight line with equation $y = \frac{1}{9}$.

Calculate the coordinates of the points of intersection of the curve and the line.

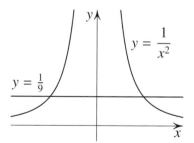

**8** The diagram shows the circle with equation $x^2 + y^2 = 225$ and the straight line with equation $y = x + 3$.

Calculate the coordinates of the points where the line and the circle intersect.

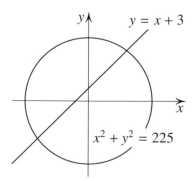

9  The diagram shows the circle with equation $x^2 + y^2 = 10$ and the straight line with equation $y + 3x = 10$.

Calculate the coordinates of the point where the line and the circle intersect.

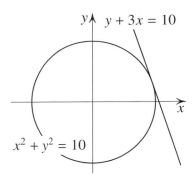

10  The diagram shows the parabola with equation $y^2 = x$ and the straight line with equation $y = x - 12$.

Calculate the coordinates of the points of intersection of the parabola and the line.

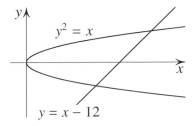

❄ 11  The diagram shows the cubic curve with equation $y = x^3 + 3x^2 - 10x + 3$ and the straight line with equation $y = 3$.

Calculate the coordinates of the points of intersection of the line and the curve.

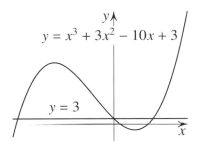

❄ 12  The diagram shows the cubic curve with equation $y = x^3 - 4x - 4$ and the straight line with equation $y = -4$.

Calculate the coordinates of the points of intersection of the line and the curve.

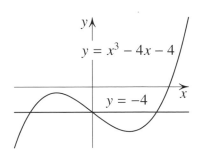

❄ 13  The diagram shows the ellipse with equation

$$\frac{x^2}{12} + \frac{y^2}{6} = 1$$

and the straight line with equation $y = x$.

Calculate the coordinates of the points of intersection of the ellipse and the line.

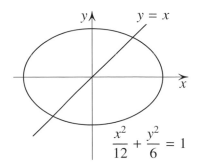

**❅ 14** The diagram shows the ellipse with equation

$$x^2 + \frac{y^2}{4} = 1$$

and the straight line with equation $x + y = 1$.

Calculate the coordinates of the points of intersection of the ellipse and the line.

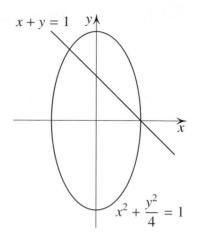

**❅ 15** The diagram shows the parabola with equation $y^2 = x$ and the straight line with equation $y = x - 12$.

Calculate the coordinates of the points of intersection of the parabola and the line.

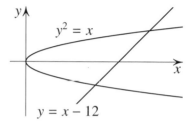

**❅ 16** The diagram shows the cubic curve with equation $y = -x^3 + 3x^2 + 12x + 2$ and the straight line with equation $y = 2x + 2$.

Calculate the coordinates of the points of intersection of the line and the curve.

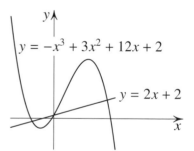

**❅ 17** The diagram shows the cubic curve with equation $y = x^3 - 3x + 5$ and the straight line with equation $y = 5 - 2x$.

Calculate the coordinates of the points of intersection of the line and the curve.

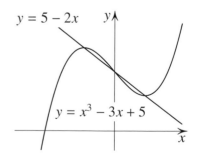

## 7.7  Miscellaneous questions

### Exercise 7.7

**1**  On one diagram, sketch graphs of the curves with the following equations. Label each curve and show the $y$-intercept.

(a)  $y = x^2 + 3$          (b)  $y = 3x^2 + 3$          (c)  $y = 3(x - 1)^2$

**2**  Sketch a graph, showing the turning point and the $y$-intercept, of the curve with equation:

(a)  $y = (x - 4)^2 + 7$          (b)  $y = 8 - (x - 2)^2$

**3**  The graph shows a curve whose equation has the form $y = (x + a)^2 + b$.
The curve crosses the $y$-axis at the point $P$.
The point $Q$ lies on the curve and on the straight line through $P$ parallel to the $x$-axis.

(a)  State the values of $a$ and $b$.

(b)  State the coordinates of $P$.

(c)  Find the coordinates of $Q$.

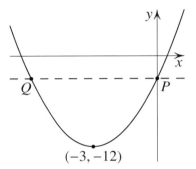

$(-3, -12)$

**4**  Find, in the form indicated, the equation of the curve:

(a)

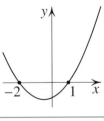

$y = (x - p)(x - q)$

(b)

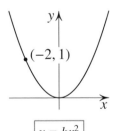

$(-2, 1)$

$y = kx^2$

(c)

$(2, 6)$

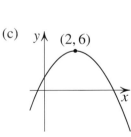

$y = p - (x - q)^2$

(d)

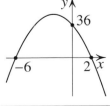

$36$

$-6$          $2$

$y = k(x - a)(x - b)$

(e)

$-3$

$(1, -32)$

$y = k(x + m)^2$

(f)

$3$

$(2, -13)$

$y = kx^2 + m$

5 | A curve has equation $y = (x - 1)(x + 5)$. Find the coordinates of the turning point.

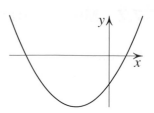

6 | A curve has equation $y = 6 - x - x^2$.
The curve crosses the $x$-axis at the points $A$ and $B$.

   (a) Find the coordinates of $A$ and $B$.

   (b) Find the coordinates of the $y$-intercept.

   (c) Find the coordinates of the turning point.

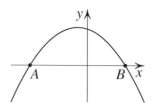

7 | The diagram shows a parabola with equation of the form $y = (x - a)^2$.
The point $Q$ is the $y$-intercept of the parabola.
A straight line with gradient $-2$ passes through $Q$.
The line and the parabola also intersect at the point $P$.

   (a) State the equation of the parabola.

   (b) Find the coordinates of $Q$.

   (c) Find the equation of the line.

   (d) Calculate the coordinates of $P$.

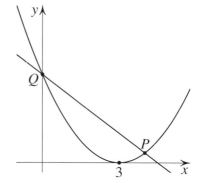

8 | The diagram shows the parabola with equation $y = (x + 6)(x - 1)$ and the straight line with equation $y = 2x + 4$.

Find the coordinates of the points of intersection of the parabola and the line.

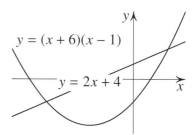

9 | On the same diagram sketch the graphs of $y = (x - 2)^2$ and $y = 2x - 1$.

Calculate the coordinates of the points of intersection of the straight line and the parabola.

10 | On the same diagram sketch the graphs of $y = x^2 + 5x$ and $y = 3x + 3$.

Calculate the coordinates of the points of intersection of the straight line and the parabola.

11 Find the points of intersection of the curves with equations $y = 2 + 4x - x^2$ and $y = 2 - x$.

12 The diagram shows two curves with equations $y = 4 - x^2$ and $y = 22 - 3x^2$.

Find the coordinates of the points of intersection of the curves.

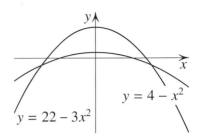

13 Find the points of intersection of the curves with equations $y = x^2 - 4x + 10$ and $y = 2 + 6x - x^2$.

14 The diagram shows the curve with equation

$$y = \frac{1}{x}$$

and the straight line with equation $x - 4y = 0$.

Find the coordinates of the points of intersection of the line and the curve.

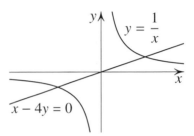

15 The diagram shows the parabola with equation $y = x^2$ and the circle with equation $x^2 + y^2 = 20$.

Find the coordinates of the points of intersection of the two curves.

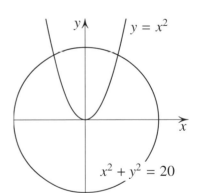

❄ 16 The diagram shows a curve with equation of the form $y^2 = kx$.
The point $(1, -2)$ lies on the curve.
A straight line with gradient 1 passes through $(1, -2)$ and meets the curve again at the point $Q$.

(a) Write down the equation of the curve.
(b) Find the coordinates of $Q$.

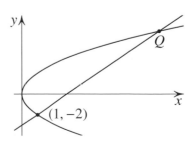

# 8 Fractions, indices and surds

## 8.1 Indices

The following exercise will help you to practise:

❑ evaluating an expression with indices

❑ using $a^0 = 1$, $a^{-p} \equiv \dfrac{1}{a^p}$ and $a^{\frac{m}{n}} \equiv \left(\sqrt[n]{a}\right)^m \equiv \sqrt[n]{a^m}$

❑ using $\left(\dfrac{a}{b}\right)^p = \dfrac{a^p}{b^p}$

This is a non-calculator exercise.

### Exercise 8.1a

**1** Evaluate:

(a) $4^3$      (b) $2^5$      (c) $3^5$      (d) $7^0$

(e) $1.1^3$      (f) $\left(\frac{1}{2}\right)^7$      (g) $\left(-\frac{1}{3}\right)^4$      (h) $\left(\frac{1}{6}\right)^3$

**2** Evaluate:

(a) $2^{-3}$      (b) $4^{-2}$      (c) $5^{-1}$      (d) $\left(-\frac{1}{2}\right)^{-5}$

(e) $0.1^{-1}$      (f) $\left(\frac{1}{9}\right)^0$      (g) $\left(\frac{1}{3}\right)^{-2}$      (h) $0.2^{-4}$

**3** Evaluate:

(a) $\left(-\frac{2}{5}\right)^3$      (b) $\left(\frac{3}{4}\right)^{-1}$      (c) $0.6^3$      (d) $0.04^{-2}$

**4** Evaluate:

(a) $16^{\frac{1}{4}}$      (b) $(-125)^{\frac{1}{3}}$      (c) $400^{\frac{1}{2}}$      (d) $0.64^{0.5}$

(e) $64^{\frac{2}{3}}$      (f) $81^{\frac{3}{4}}$      (g) $625^{\frac{3}{4}}$      (h) $32^{\frac{3}{5}}$

**5** Evaluate:

(a) $4^{-\frac{1}{2}}$ (b) $27^{-\frac{1}{3}}$ (c) $100\,000^{-\frac{1}{5}}$ (d) $625^{-\frac{1}{4}}$

(e) $16^{-\frac{3}{4}}$ (f) $125^{-\frac{2}{3}}$ (g) $32^{-\frac{2}{5}}$ (h) $8000^{-\frac{2}{3}}$

**6** Evaluate:

(a) $\left(\dfrac{8}{27}\right)^{\frac{2}{3}}$ (b) $\left(\dfrac{64}{49}\right)^{\frac{1}{2}}$ (c) $0.216^{\frac{1}{3}}$ (d) $0.49^{\frac{3}{2}}$

(e) $\left(\dfrac{36}{25}\right)^{-\frac{3}{2}}$ (f) $0.0025^{-\frac{1}{2}}$ (g) $0.000008^{-\frac{2}{3}}$ (h) $1.69^{-0.5}$

**7** When $p = 5$, $q = 12$, $r = 7$ and $s = 4$, evaluate:

(a) $\left(p^2 + q^2\right)^{\frac{1}{2}}$ (b) $(3p - r)^{\frac{2}{3}}$ (c) $(9r + 1)^{-\frac{1}{3}}$ (d) $(q - r)^{-2}$

(e) $(p - s)^{-5}$ (f) $(pr - 2s)^{\frac{5}{3}}$ (g) $4p^0 + s^{\frac{3}{2}}$

---

The following exercise will help you to practise:

❏ using $a^p \times a^q \equiv a^{p+q}$ , $\dfrac{a^p}{a^q} \equiv a^{p-q}$ and $(a^p)^q \equiv a^{pq}$

---

### Exercise 8.1b

**1** Write as a single power:

(a) $5^2 \times 5^5$ (b) $7^4 \times 7^{-2}$ (c) $9^5 \times 9^{-5}$

(d) $1.4^{-3} \times 1.4^{-4}$ (e) $0.4^{-5} \times 0.4 \times 0.4^2$ (f) $\left(\frac{2}{5}\right)^3 \times \left(\frac{2}{5}\right)^{-1} \times \left(\frac{2}{5}\right)^{-2}$

**2** Write as a single power:

(a) $\dfrac{6^5}{6^4}$ (b) $\dfrac{1.5^7}{1.5^{-5}}$ (c) $5^{10} \div 5^7$

(d) $217^5 \div 217^{-2}$ (e) $0.9^{-2} \div 0.9$ (f) $\dfrac{4}{4^{-7}}$

**3** Write as a single power:

(a) $\dfrac{14^3 \times 14^8}{14}$ (b) $\dfrac{0.3^{-11} \times 0.3^{12}}{0.3^{-13}}$ (c) $\dfrac{\left(\frac{1}{2}\right)^{10} \times \left(\frac{1}{2}\right)^0 \times \left(\frac{1}{2}\right)^{-2}}{\frac{1}{2}}$

**4** Write as a single power:

(a) $\left(2^2\right)^3$

(b) $\left(5^{-2}\right)^{-1}$

(c) $\left(3^{-2}\right)^3$

(d) $\left(0.1^2\right)^2$

(e) $\left(\left(\frac{2}{3}\right)^4\right)^2$

(f) $\left(6^0\right)^2$

(g) $\left(\left(\frac{3}{2}\right)^{-3}\right)^{-1}$

(h) $\left(0.2^{-1}\right)^2$

The following exercise will help you to practise:

❏ simplifying an expression with indices

## Exercise 8.1c

**1** Simplify:

(a) $v^2 \times v^7$

(b) $7y^2 \times y^4$

(c) $3m^3 \times 4m^5$

(d) $5t^3 \times 2t^5 \times t^2$

(e) $\rho \times \rho^2 \times \frac{1}{2}\rho^3$

(f) $\omega^{-2} \times 3\omega^7 \times \omega^{-1}$

(g) $8\zeta^2 \times 3\zeta^{-2}$

(h) $0.5j \times 4j^{-\frac{2}{5}}$

(i) $30u^{\frac{1}{2}} \times 5u^{\frac{1}{3}}$

**2** Simplify:

(a) $\dfrac{x^7}{2x^2}$

(b) $\dfrac{28\alpha^{10}}{7\alpha^6}$

(c) $\dfrac{4.5p^9}{1.5p^{10}}$

(d) $\dfrac{3a^8b}{a^5b^2}$

(e) $45p^3q^7 \div \left(20pq^3\right)$

(f) $27xy^3 \div \left(9x^2y\right)$

**3** Simplify:

(a) $\dfrac{a^3 \times a^6}{a^4}$

(b) $\dfrac{h \times h^4}{7h^5}$

(c) $\dfrac{15\gamma^4 \times \gamma}{5\gamma^7}$

(d) $\dfrac{2r^2 \times r^2}{16r^5}$

(e) $\dfrac{5t^3 \times 12t^2}{0.6t}$

(f) $\dfrac{0.3e^3 \times 12e^2}{0.8e^9}$

**4** Simplify:

(a) $\dfrac{3c^3 \times 4d^2}{2c^4 \times 6d}$

(b) $\dfrac{2p \times d^3}{6p^4 \times 5d}$

(c) $\dfrac{0.2a^2 \times 0.1b^7}{0.4a^3 \times 0.5b^2}$

**5** Simplify:

(a) $\dfrac{a^{\frac{1}{2}} \times a^{\frac{5}{2}}}{a^2}$

(b) $\dfrac{b^{\frac{5}{2}} \times b^{-\frac{1}{2}}}{b}$

(c) $\dfrac{6x^{\frac{3}{2}}}{2x^{\frac{1}{2}}}$

(d) $\dfrac{\alpha^{\frac{1}{4}} \times \alpha^{\frac{7}{4}}}{\alpha^2}$

(e) $\dfrac{p^{\frac{5}{2}} \times p^{\frac{3}{2}}}{p^{-1}}$

(f) $\dfrac{4\sigma^{\frac{3}{4}} \times \sigma^{\frac{5}{4}}}{12\sigma}$

6　Simplify:

(a) $\left(n^6\right)^5$　　　　(b) $\left(c^{-1}\right)^{-4}$　　　　(c) $\left(z^2\right)^{-\frac{1}{2}}$　　　　(d) $\left(b^{12}\right)^{-\frac{5}{6}}$

(e) $\left(\tau^{\frac{3}{2}}\right)^4$　　　　(f) $\left(d^4\right)^{-1}$　　　　(g) $\left(f^3\right)^0$　　　　(h) $\left(w^{-2}\right)^{\frac{1}{2}}$

7　Simplify:

(a) $\left(h^2 j^6\right)^2$　　　　(b) $\left(u^{\frac{2}{3}} v^4\right)^3$　　　　(c) $\left(\dfrac{x^2}{y^5}\right)^5$　　　　(d) $\left(\dfrac{5\alpha^3}{2\beta}\right)^3$

8　Simplify:

(a) $\left(\dfrac{a}{b^3}\right)^{-2}$　　　　(b) $\left(\dfrac{p^3}{q^2}\right)^{-3}$　　　　(c) $\left(\tfrac{1}{3}f^2 g^7\right)^{-1}$　　　　(d) $\left(\dfrac{2r^{\frac{1}{2}}t^3}{3s^4}\right)^{-4}$

9　Simplify:

(a) $\left(\dfrac{t^2}{s^4}\right)^{\frac{1}{2}}$　　　　(b) $\left(\dfrac{y^6}{z^9}\right)^{\frac{2}{3}}$　　　　(c) $\left(\dfrac{h^{10}}{k^{25}}\right)^{\frac{3}{5}}$

(d) $\left(\dfrac{p^6}{q^{12}}\right)^{\frac{5}{6}}$　　　　(e) $\left(\dfrac{4a^2 b^{10}}{49c^4}\right)^{-\frac{1}{2}}$　　　　(f) $\left(\dfrac{10\,000\mu^8}{81v^{12}}\right)^{-\frac{3}{4}}$

❋ 10　Simplify:

(a) $\left(3n^2\right)^{-1} \times 2n^4$　　　　　　　　(b) $\left(5r^3\right)^{-1} \times 10r^4$

(c) $\dfrac{\left(4f^2 g\right)^3 \times \left(0.2f^{-1}g^4\right)^2}{0.8fg^{-3}}$　　　　(d) $\dfrac{(2ab)^2 \times \left(0.1a^2 b^{-5}\right)^{-1}}{4a^3 b^7}$

---

The following exercise will help you to practise:
❑ rewriting an expression in index form

## Exercise 8.1d

❋ 1　Express in index form:

(a) $\dfrac{1}{x^2}$　　(b) $\dfrac{2}{x}$　　(c) $\dfrac{1}{3x^2}$　　(d) $\dfrac{2}{5x}$　　(e) $\sqrt{x}$　　(f) $x\sqrt{x}$

(g) $5x\sqrt{x}$　　(h) $\dfrac{x^2}{\sqrt{x}}$　　(i) $\dfrac{\sqrt{x}}{2x}$　　(j) $4\sqrt[3]{x}$　　(k) $\dfrac{2x}{\sqrt[3]{x^2}}$　　(l) $\dfrac{5\sqrt[3]{x}}{3x}$

❉ 2 Express as a sum of separate terms in index form:

(a) $d^2 \left(d^4 - 2\right)$

(b) $4r^3 \left(r - r^2 + 5r^4\right)$

(c) $3z^4 \left(z + 7z^3 - 2z^6\right)$

(d) $a^2 \left(2a^{-\frac{1}{2}} + a\right)$

(e) $b^{\frac{1}{2}}(2b^{-\frac{1}{2}} + b^{\frac{1}{2}})$

(f) $x\left(5x^{\frac{1}{2}} - x^{\frac{5}{2}}\right)$

(g) $u\left(u^{-\frac{1}{2}} + 3u\right)$

(h) $e^2 \left(e^{-\frac{3}{2}} + e^{-2}\right)$

(i) $\rho^{-1} \left(\rho^{-\frac{1}{2}} + 3\rho^{\frac{3}{2}}\right)$

❉ 3 Express as a sum of separate terms in index form:

(a) $\dfrac{x^3 - 4x^2 + 5x}{x}$

(b) $\dfrac{3c^3 - c^2 + c}{c^2}$

(c) $\dfrac{2z + 3}{z^4}$

(d) $\dfrac{t - 5t^2 + t^4}{t^3}$

(e) $\dfrac{(2p - 5)^2}{p}$

(f) $\dfrac{\left(m^2 - 2\right)^2}{m^2}$

(g) $\dfrac{y + 2}{y^{\frac{1}{2}}}$

(h) $\dfrac{\sigma^2 + 3\sigma}{\sigma^{\frac{3}{2}}}$

(i) $\dfrac{2t^{\frac{1}{2}} + t^3}{t^{\frac{1}{2}}}$

❉ 4 Express as a sum of separate terms in index form:

(a) $\dfrac{2d^3 - d}{2d}$

(b) $\dfrac{5r - r^4}{5r}$

(c) $\dfrac{h^3 + 4h^2}{2h}$

(d) $\dfrac{3x^7 - x^5 + 5x^3}{3x^2}$

(e) $\dfrac{c^3 - c - 7}{3c^3}$

(f) $\dfrac{5v^4 - 6v^2 + 1}{2v^3}$

(g) $\dfrac{(\alpha + 4)^2}{2\alpha^2}$

(h) $\dfrac{(2z - 3)^2}{5z}$

(i) $\dfrac{\left(p^2 - 2\right)^2}{3p}$

## 8.2  Equations with powers

The following exercise will help you to practise:

❏ solving an equation of the form $(px + q)^n = r$ by finding the $n$th root of each side

❏ solving a pair of simultaneous equations involving powers above 2

❏ solving an equation with unknown powers

### Exercise 8.2

❊ 1 | Solve the equation:

(a) $(x + 2)^3 = -27$

(b) $(x - 5)^4 = 256$

(c) $(6 - y)^5 = 1$

(d) $(4f + 1)^4 = 625$

(e) $(2t - 7)^3 = -1$

(f) $(5v + 2)^3 = -27$

(g) $2(a + 3)^5 = 6250$

(h) $3(4p - 1)^2 = 363$

(i) $\frac{1}{5}(1 - 2m)^4 = 125$

❊ 2 | Solve the simultaneous equations:

(a) $ar^3 = 500$
$ar^5 = 125$

(b) $ar^2 = 9$
$ar^5 = \frac{1}{3}$

(c) $ar^4 = 1000$
$ar^5 = 10\,000$

(d) $ar^6 = 896$
$ar^3 = 112$

(e) $ar = 8$
$ar^4 = \frac{1}{125}$

(f) $ar = 1$
$ar^7 = 729$

(g) $xy^5 = 1$
$xy = 16$

(h) $\alpha\beta = 14$
$\alpha\beta^6 = 448$

❊ 3 | Solve the equation:

(a) $3^e = 81$

(b) $2^r = 128$

(c) $9^x = 3$

(d) $6^f = \dfrac{1}{36}$

(e) $7^t = 1$

(f) $4 \times 3^a = 108$

(g) $20 \times 5^z = 4$

(h) $125 = 25^p$

(i) $8 = 32^q$

## 8.3 Algebraic fractions

The following exercise will help you to practise:

❑ simplifying an algebraic fraction by cancelling

❑ recognising that $(a - b)$ and $(b - a)$ are related: $(b - a) = -(a - b)$

### Exercise 8.3a

**1** Simplify:

(a) $\dfrac{4x^5}{8x^7}$

(b) $20p \div \left(5p^9\right)$

(c) $\dfrac{32a^8}{8a^5}$

(d) $\dfrac{15t^3}{40t^{10}}$

(e) $\dfrac{6b^3}{4b^4}$

(f) $\dfrac{30u^{10}}{20u^5}$

(g) $9e^7 \div \left(3e^2\right)$

(h) $\dfrac{42a^7}{84a^8}$

**2** Simplify:

(a) $\dfrac{2(a + b)^2}{3(a + b)}$

(b) $\dfrac{12(x - 3)^4}{4(x - 3)^5}$

(c) $\dfrac{25(x + 4t)^3}{15(x + 4t)^7}$

(d) $(8h + j)^9 \div \left(4(8h + j)^{10}\right)$

❄ **3** Simplify:

(a) $\dfrac{t - s}{s - t}$

(b) $\dfrac{2(m - n)}{5(n - m)}$

(c) $(p - 2q) \div (2q - p)$

(d) $\dfrac{7(x - 3y)}{3y - x}$

(e) $\dfrac{3u - v}{2(v - 3u)}$

(f) $\dfrac{4(a - 6b)}{5(6b - a)}$

The following exercise will help you to practise:

❑ simplifying an algebraic fraction by factorising and cancelling

### Exercise 8.3b

**1** Simplify:

(a) $\dfrac{12x - 21}{15}$

(b) $\dfrac{6 + 2a + 4b^2}{10}$

(c) $\dfrac{4t + 8s}{16}$

(d) $\dfrac{12}{9b - 6c + 15}$

(e) $\dfrac{18}{14 - 6y^2}$

(f) $\dfrac{20e + 14f}{6}$

2 Simplify:

(a) $\dfrac{4w}{8w + 12x}$

(b) $\dfrac{2y - y^2}{4yz}$

(c) $\dfrac{\pi r^2}{r + \pi r + r^2}$

(d) $\dfrac{3k^2 l^2}{kl^2 + l^2 - l^4}$

(e) $\dfrac{5pq + p}{3p}$

(f) $\dfrac{4r^2 - r}{7r}$

3 Simplify:

(a) $\dfrac{x^3 + x^5}{x^2}$

(b) $\dfrac{a^7 - a^4}{a}$

(c) $\dfrac{6y^3 + 2y^5 + y^7}{y^3}$

(d) $\dfrac{(x + 5)^6 + (x + 5)^5}{(x + 5)^5}$

(e) $\dfrac{15k^3}{25k^3 + 10k^7}$

(f) $\dfrac{4u}{8u^2 - 2u^6}$

4 Simplify:

(a) $\dfrac{3x + 6}{6x - 9}$

(b) $\dfrac{2a + 4b + 6c}{8a - 10b}$

(c) $\dfrac{9 - 6k}{12k + 3}$

(d) $\dfrac{a^2 + a}{6a + ab}$

(e) $\dfrac{x^2 + x^3}{x^2 + x^4 + x^6}$

(f) $\dfrac{3a^2 + 6a^3b + 9a}{12a^3 - 21a}$

5 Simplify:

(a) $\dfrac{x^2 + xy}{x + y}$

(b) $\dfrac{v + u}{v^3 + v^2u}$

(c) $\dfrac{6c + 6d}{12c + 12d}$

(d) $\dfrac{3a - 6b}{5a - 10b}$

(e) $\dfrac{2s^2 - st}{2s - t}$

(f) $\dfrac{2a - 8}{a - 4}$

(g) $\dfrac{\gamma^2 + \gamma}{\gamma + 1}$

(h) $\dfrac{a + 3}{a^2 + 3a}$

(i) $\dfrac{\alpha^2 + 2\alpha\beta}{2\alpha + 4\beta}$

❄ 6 Simplify:

(a) $\dfrac{2a - 2b}{b - a}$

(b) $\dfrac{3p - 3q}{4q - 4p}$

(c) $\dfrac{4x - 16x^2}{12x - 3}$

(d) $\dfrac{5s - 20t}{8t - 2s}$

(e) $\dfrac{a^2 - a}{7 - 7a}$

7 Simplify:

(a) $\dfrac{x^2 + 3x - 4}{2x + 8}$

(b) $\dfrac{2z + 4}{z^2 - 4}$

(c) $\dfrac{x^2 + x - 2}{4x - 4}$

(d) $\dfrac{g^2 - 1}{5g + 5}$

(e) $\dfrac{5a - 10}{a^2 + 3a - 10}$

(f) $\dfrac{h^2 - 6h + 8}{6h - 12}$

(g) $\dfrac{6p + 3}{2p^2 + 9p + 4}$ 

(h) $\dfrac{4x^2 + 4x + 1}{8x + 4}$ 

(i) $\dfrac{b^2 + 3b}{4b + 12}$

8  Simplify:

(a) $\dfrac{x^2 + 3x - 4}{x^2 + 6x + 8}$ 

(b) $\dfrac{a^2 + a - 6}{a^2 - 3a + 2}$ 

(c) $\dfrac{e^2 - 2e + 1}{e^2 + e - 2}$

(d) $\dfrac{\beta^2 - 3\beta - 10}{\beta^2 + 3\beta + 2}$ 

(e) $\dfrac{n^2 + 8n + 16}{n^2 + 9n + 20}$ 

(f) $\dfrac{m^2 - 4}{m^2 - 9m + 14}$

9  Simplify:

(a) $\dfrac{4 + 4y + y^2}{y^2 + 5y + 6}$ 

(b) $\dfrac{25 - x^2}{13x + x^2 + 40}$ 

(c) $\dfrac{k^2 + 18 + 11k}{81 - k^2}$

(d) $\dfrac{9 - c^2}{24 + c^2 + 11c}$ 

(e) $\dfrac{35 + 2h - h^2}{7 + 6h - h^2}$ 

(f) $\dfrac{11 + 12z + z^2}{z^2 - 8z - 9}$

The following exercise will help you to practise:

❑ multiplying and dividing algebraic fractions

## Exercise 8.3c

1  Simplify:

(a) $\dfrac{5t^2}{4b} \times \dfrac{3t}{b^3}$ 

(b) $3k \times \dfrac{2k^5}{7m}$ 

(c) $\dfrac{v}{w} \times \dfrac{2v}{3w^2} \times v^3$

(d) $\dfrac{7p^4}{15q} \times \dfrac{3p}{q}$ 

(e) $\dfrac{20a}{21b^2} \times \dfrac{14a^4}{15b^3}$ 

(f) $\dfrac{12}{5x} \times 3y^2 \times \dfrac{10y}{9x^3}$

(g) $27k^3 \times \dfrac{2}{9m} \times \dfrac{5k}{3m^7}$ 

(h) $\dfrac{70a^2bc}{13d^2} \times \dfrac{65b^2c}{14d}$ 

(i) $\dfrac{4f}{5g} \times \dfrac{10f^3}{3g^3} \times \dfrac{3}{8g^5}$

2  Simplify:

(a) $\dfrac{p^2}{q} \div (3p)$ 

(b) $\dfrac{5t^2}{4b} \div \dfrac{3t}{b^3}$ 

(c) $\dfrac{4r^2}{s} \div \dfrac{r}{3s}$

(d) $\dfrac{2c}{5d^3} \div \dfrac{2c}{d}$ 

(e) $14k \div \dfrac{2k^5}{7m}$ 

(f) $\dfrac{10d^2}{7e^3} \div \dfrac{2d^5}{e}$

(g) $\dfrac{3k^2n}{m^4} \div \dfrac{6k^5n^2}{m^2}$ 

(h) $\left(\dfrac{15}{4v^2} \div \dfrac{wz}{6v}\right) \div 5w^3v$ 

(i) $\dfrac{30a}{7b^3c^2} \div \left(5a \div \dfrac{7b^3c^2}{6}\right)$

**3** Simplify:

(a) $\dfrac{6\beta + 15}{4} \div \dfrac{21}{2\beta + 5}$

(b) $\dfrac{12z}{5z + 15} \times \dfrac{25z}{4z + 8}$

(c) $\dfrac{3x - 6}{20} \div \dfrac{9}{5x + 10}$

(d) $7p \div \dfrac{14p - 35}{p^2}$

(e) $\dfrac{3a - 6b}{c^2} \div \dfrac{a - 2b}{c}$

(f) $\dfrac{x^2 - xy}{y} \times \dfrac{xy}{x^2 - y^2}$

**4** Simplify:

(a) $\dfrac{5r}{\frac{2}{3}}$

(b) $\dfrac{6y}{\frac{1}{3}}$

(c) $\dfrac{25t^7}{\frac{1}{2}}$

(d) $\frac{3}{4} \div \left(3s^3\right)$

(e) $12x^4 \div \frac{4}{3}$

(f) $\dfrac{\frac{5}{12}}{10p^2}$

**5** Simplify:

(a) $\dfrac{6a^2}{\frac{1}{2}a}$

(b) $\dfrac{14h^6}{\frac{2}{3}h^2}$

(c) $\dfrac{\frac{2}{5}k}{5k^4}$

(d) $\frac{3}{4}p \div \left(5p^4\right)$

(e) $20a^9 \div \left(\frac{4}{5}a^4\right)$

(f) $\dfrac{\frac{5}{9}x^2}{3x^7}$

**6** Simplify:

(a) $\dfrac{\frac{1}{2}y^2}{\frac{1}{4}y}$

(b) $\dfrac{\dfrac{a^2}{18}}{\dfrac{a^3}{6}}$

(c) $\dfrac{p}{10} \div \left(\dfrac{p^4}{40}\right)$

(d) $\dfrac{\dfrac{5}{w}}{\dfrac{15}{w^2}}$

(e) $\frac{3}{7}t^3 \div \left(\frac{1}{14}t\right)$

(f) $\dfrac{\dfrac{3}{5j}}{\dfrac{6}{5j^2}}$

**7** Expand and simplify:

(a) $\left(2 + \dfrac{1}{x}\right)^2$

(b) $\left(p - \dfrac{1}{p}\right)^2$

(c) $\left(k^2 + \dfrac{1}{k}\right)^2$

(d) $\left(x + \dfrac{5}{x}\right)\left(x - \dfrac{5}{x}\right)$

(e) $\left(2t + \dfrac{1}{t}\right)\left(t - \dfrac{2}{t}\right)$

(f) $(2a + 3)\left(\dfrac{5}{a} + 1\right)$

> The following exercise will help you to practise:
>
> ❑ simplifying an algebraic fraction by multiplying the numerator and denominator by the same expression

## Exercise 8.3d

**1** Simplify:

(a) $\dfrac{2 + \dfrac{3}{t}}{\dfrac{1}{t} - 4}$
(b) $\dfrac{1 + \dfrac{1}{x}}{3 - \dfrac{1}{x}}$
(c) $\dfrac{2 - \dfrac{3}{r}}{4 + \dfrac{1}{r}}$
(d) $\dfrac{\dfrac{1}{a}}{a - \dfrac{5}{a}}$

**2** Simplify:

(a) $\dfrac{\dfrac{1}{\tan x} + 1}{1 - \dfrac{1}{\tan x}}$
(b) $\dfrac{5 - \dfrac{2}{n^2}}{\dfrac{3}{n^2}}$
(c) $\dfrac{\dfrac{3}{2y^2} - 4}{5 - \dfrac{7}{2y^2}}$
(d) $\dfrac{2 + \dfrac{3}{a^2 + 1}}{\dfrac{1}{a^2 + 1} + 4}$

**3** Simplify:

(a) $\dfrac{7}{\dfrac{1}{x} + 2}$
(b) $\dfrac{4 - \dfrac{1}{2z}}{3}$
(c) $\dfrac{4}{\dfrac{1}{3y} - 2}$
(d) $\dfrac{\dfrac{1}{7t} - 2}{5}$

**4** Simplify:

(a) $\dfrac{2 + g^2}{3 - \dfrac{1}{g}}$
(b) $\dfrac{7 + \sin x}{5 - \dfrac{\sin x}{\cos x}}$
(c) $\dfrac{8 + a}{\dfrac{a}{b}}$
(d) $\dfrac{\sin C - 4}{\dfrac{\cos C}{\sin C}}$

❄ **5** Simplify:

(a) $\dfrac{\dfrac{1}{e^2} - 2}{\dfrac{1}{e} + 4}$
(b) $\dfrac{\dfrac{v + 1}{v} + 1}{\dfrac{2}{v^2} + 5}$
(c) $\dfrac{\dfrac{5}{b^3} - 3}{\dfrac{6}{b} + 7}$
(d) $\dfrac{\dfrac{2a + 3}{a} - 1}{1 + \dfrac{1}{a^2}}$

✳ **6** Simplify:

(a) $\dfrac{1 + \dfrac{2}{s}}{\dfrac{7}{t} + 1}$  (b) $\dfrac{4m + \dfrac{1}{n}}{n + \dfrac{1}{m}}$  (c) $\dfrac{\sin t + \dfrac{1}{\cos t}}{\cos t + \dfrac{1}{\sin t}}$  (d) $\dfrac{2 + \dfrac{1}{f^2}}{2 + \dfrac{1}{g}}$

✳ **7** Simplify:

(a) $\dfrac{\dfrac{4}{t} + \dfrac{1}{3}}{\dfrac{2}{3} - \dfrac{1}{t}}$  (b) $\dfrac{\dfrac{5}{a} + \dfrac{3}{4}}{\dfrac{1}{4} - \dfrac{2}{a}}$  (c) $\dfrac{\dfrac{2}{5} - \dfrac{1}{\omega}}{\dfrac{3}{\omega} + \dfrac{4}{5}}$

✳ **8** Simplify:

(a) $\dfrac{\dfrac{2}{p} - \dfrac{3}{p+1}}{\dfrac{5}{p+1} + \dfrac{4}{p}}$  (b) $\dfrac{\dfrac{3}{a-1} + \dfrac{2}{a}}{\dfrac{3}{a} - \dfrac{2}{a-1}}$  (c) $\dfrac{\dfrac{1}{\sin\theta} - \dfrac{3}{\cos\theta}}{\dfrac{2}{\cos\theta} + \dfrac{5}{\sin\theta}}$

---

The following exercise will help you to practise:

❏ adding and subtracting expressions with algebraic fractions

---

### Exercise 8.3e

⤱ **1** Express as a single fraction:

(a) $\dfrac{5}{x} - \dfrac{1}{x}$  (b) $\dfrac{2}{b} + \dfrac{1}{b}$  (c) $\dfrac{1}{w+5} - \dfrac{2}{w+5}$

(d) $\dfrac{4}{2p-1} - \dfrac{3}{2p-1}$  (e) $\dfrac{5}{3y} - \dfrac{4}{3y} + \dfrac{7}{3y}$  (f) $\dfrac{1}{t+7} - \dfrac{7}{t+7} + \dfrac{5}{t+7}$

**2** Express as a single fraction:

(a) $\dfrac{k}{9} + k$  (b) $\dfrac{5s}{4} - s$  (c) $r - \dfrac{4r}{5}$  (d) $\dfrac{2a}{3} - a + \dfrac{5a}{3}$

**3** Express as a single fraction:

(a) $\dfrac{2}{x} - 1$  (b) $\dfrac{2}{m} + n$  (c) $p - \dfrac{2}{q}$

(d) $\dfrac{a}{2b} - 3$  (e) $3\beta - \dfrac{2}{\beta}$  (f) $\dfrac{a}{b} + 4b$

4 Express as a single fraction:

(a) $\dfrac{3x+1}{2} + \dfrac{5x-4}{3}$

(b) $\dfrac{4a}{5} + \dfrac{3a+1}{2}$

(c) $\dfrac{p-7}{2} - \dfrac{2p+1}{4}$

(d) $\dfrac{3b+1}{7} - \dfrac{b}{6}$

(e) $\dfrac{s}{2} + \dfrac{s+1}{3} - \dfrac{2s+3}{5}$

(f) $\dfrac{2d+3}{4} - \dfrac{d-5}{5} + \dfrac{6-d}{3}$

5 Express as a single fraction:

(a) $\dfrac{1}{x} + \dfrac{2}{y}$

(b) $\dfrac{5}{3p} - \dfrac{2}{7q}$

(c) $\dfrac{4}{3s} + \dfrac{1}{t}$

(d) $\dfrac{7}{xy} - \dfrac{2}{z}$

6 Express as a single fraction:

(a) $\dfrac{2}{n} - \dfrac{3}{n^2}$

(b) $\dfrac{1}{x} + \dfrac{3}{x^2}$

(c) $\dfrac{5}{m^3} - \dfrac{2}{m}$

(d) $\dfrac{2}{v^8} + \dfrac{9}{v^5}$

(e) $\dfrac{1}{p} + \dfrac{2}{p^2} - \dfrac{5}{p^3}$

(f) $\dfrac{3}{r^5} - \dfrac{4}{r^4} + \dfrac{1}{r^2} - \dfrac{9}{r}$

7 Express as a single fraction:

(a) $3 + \dfrac{2}{b-2}$

(b) $\dfrac{d+1}{2d+1} - 7$

(c) $\dfrac{5p-1}{2p+1} + 3$

(d) $\dfrac{\alpha^2+2}{\alpha^2-1} - 1$

(e) $2 - \dfrac{\cos x}{\sin x}$

(f) $\dfrac{1}{\tan \theta} + 1$

(g) $1 + \dfrac{2}{\cos A}$

(h) $\cos t - \dfrac{1}{\sin t}$

❄ 8 Express as a single fraction:

(a) $\dfrac{5}{x+3} - \dfrac{1}{x}$

(b) $\dfrac{5}{s-7} + \dfrac{1}{s}$

(c) $\dfrac{2}{w+3} + \dfrac{3}{w+1}$

(d) $\dfrac{4}{t+7} + \dfrac{5}{t}$

(e) $\dfrac{3}{\alpha-2} + \dfrac{2}{\alpha+5}$

(f) $\dfrac{4}{v-4} - \dfrac{3}{v+1}$

❄ 9 Express as a single fraction:

(a) $\dfrac{x+1}{x-9} + \dfrac{3}{x}$

(b) $\dfrac{5n+1}{n+4} + \dfrac{7n}{n-3}$

(c) $\dfrac{2}{t-1} - \dfrac{5t}{t+7}$

(d) $\dfrac{e+5}{e-6} + \dfrac{e}{e+1}$

(e) $\dfrac{d}{d+3} - \dfrac{1}{d-4}$

(f) $\dfrac{\rho+1}{\rho-3} + \dfrac{\rho-4}{\rho+1}$

❄ 10 Express as a single fraction:

(a) $\dfrac{1}{x-7} - \dfrac{1}{(x-7)^2}$

(b) $\dfrac{1}{m+2} + \dfrac{4}{m^2-4}$

(c) $\dfrac{4p-9}{p^2-5p+6} - \dfrac{1}{p-2}$

# 8.4 Equations with algebraic fractions

The following exercise will help you to practise:

❏ solving an equation with algebraic fractions that leads to a linear equation

## Exercise 8.4a

**1** Solve the equation:

(a) $\dfrac{1}{a} = 3$

(b) $\dfrac{5}{p} = 2$

(c) $\dfrac{7}{e} = \dfrac{1}{2}$

(d) $\dfrac{2}{r} + 3 = 4$

(e) $\dfrac{1}{u} + 7 = \dfrac{7}{u}$

(f) $\dfrac{5}{x} = \dfrac{1}{x} - \dfrac{2}{3}$

(g) $\dfrac{1}{z} - \dfrac{2}{3} = \dfrac{4}{z}$

(h) $\dfrac{2}{p} + 1 = \dfrac{3}{p} + \dfrac{1}{2}$

(i) $\dfrac{5}{v} - \dfrac{1}{2} = \dfrac{1}{4} + \dfrac{2}{v}$

**2** Solve the equation:

(a) $\dfrac{6}{2 - c} = \dfrac{5}{3}$

(b) $\dfrac{3}{1 + x} = \dfrac{4}{7}$

(c) $\dfrac{2}{0.1 + y} = 5$

(d) $\dfrac{2 + a}{3a - 4} = 2$

(e) $\dfrac{1 + p}{2 - p} = 7$

(f) $\dfrac{u - 2}{3u - 4} = 0.4$

(g) $\dfrac{5}{t - 4} = \dfrac{2}{t - 2}$

(h) $\dfrac{4}{13 - \alpha} = \dfrac{3}{2\alpha - 15}$

(i) $\dfrac{z}{z + 2} = \dfrac{z - 2}{z - 3}$

**3** Solve the equation:

(a) $\dfrac{9}{z} = 13 + \dfrac{1}{3z}$

(b) $\dfrac{3}{2t} + 5 = 7 + \dfrac{4}{3t}$

(c) $\dfrac{5}{2m} + 3 = \dfrac{2}{m}$

(d) $\dfrac{7}{2k} + \dfrac{1}{4} = \dfrac{2}{k}$

(e) $\dfrac{5}{2p} - \dfrac{2}{3p} = \dfrac{11}{12}$

(f) $\dfrac{1}{4q} - \dfrac{2}{5q} + \dfrac{3}{10} = 0$

The following exercise will help you to practise:

❏ solving an equation with algebraic fractions that leads to a quadratic equation

## Exercise 8.4b

❋ **1** Remove the denominators and rewrite as a quadratic equation to solve:

(a) $\dfrac{t + 5}{t} = t - 3$

(b) $p + \dfrac{3}{p + 4} = 0$

(c) $\dfrac{2}{v + 4} + \dfrac{3}{v} = 1$

(d) $\dfrac{1}{q+3} + \dfrac{2}{q+8} = \dfrac{1}{6}$    (e) $\dfrac{6}{r+2} - \dfrac{1}{r-4} = \dfrac{1}{3}$    (f) $\dfrac{5}{x+3} - \dfrac{1}{x} = \dfrac{1}{2}$

❄ 2   Remove the denominators and rewrite as a quadratic equation to solve:

(a) $2h + 1 = \dfrac{3}{h}$

(b) $\dfrac{1+s}{3-5s} = 3s$

(c) $\dfrac{w-4}{7} = \dfrac{2}{3w-1}$

(d) $\dfrac{3}{v} = 2 - \dfrac{2}{v-1}$

(e) $\dfrac{17a-5}{5a-2} = a + 3$

(f) $\dfrac{3}{y+2} - \dfrac{2}{2y-3} = \dfrac{1}{7}$

---

The following exercise will help you to practise:

❏ solving a pair of simultaneous equations with algebraic fractions

---

## Exercise 8.4c

1   Solve the simultaneous equations:

(a) $\dfrac{3}{m} + 7n = 20$

    $\dfrac{3}{m} - n = 4$

(b) $\dfrac{2}{h} - 5g = -19$

    $g = \dfrac{6}{h} + 1$

(c) $p - \dfrac{2}{q} = 7$

    $p = \dfrac{1}{q} + 6$

❄ 2   Solve the simultaneous equations:

(a) $xy = 20$

    $\dfrac{x}{y} = 5$

(b) $xy^2 = 54$

    $\dfrac{x^3}{y^2} = 24$

(c) $x(y+1) = -36$

    $\dfrac{y+1}{x} = -4$

❄ 3   Solve the simultaneous equations:

(a)   $ar = -12$

    $\dfrac{a}{1-r} = 1$

(b)   $ar = 2$

    $\dfrac{a}{1-r} = 9$

(c)   $\dfrac{a}{1-r} = \dfrac{8}{3}$

    $ar = -2$

(d)   $ar = 10$

    $\dfrac{a}{1-r} = -5$

(e)   $\dfrac{a}{1-r} = 1$

    $ar = \tfrac{1}{4}$

# 8.5 Surds

The following exercise will help you to practise:

❏ simplifying an expression involving surds

❏ using $\sqrt{ab} \equiv \sqrt{a} \times \sqrt{b}$ and $\sqrt{\dfrac{a}{b}} \equiv \dfrac{\sqrt{a}}{\sqrt{b}}$ (provided $a, b > 0$)

❏ simplifying a fraction with surds into a form with a rational denominator, by multiplying the numerator and denominator by the same value *or* by using

$$\dfrac{a}{\sqrt{a}} = \sqrt{a}$$

This is a non-calculator exercise.

## Exercise 8.5

**1** Simplify:

(a) $\sqrt{8}$      (b) $\sqrt{24}$      (c) $\sqrt{28}$      (d) $\sqrt{50}$      (e) $\sqrt{98}$

(f) $\sqrt{75}$      (g) $\sqrt{200}$      (h) $\sqrt{90}$      (i) $\sqrt{48}$      (j) $\sqrt{125}$

**2** Simplify:

(a) $\sqrt{2} \times \sqrt{6}$      (b) $\sqrt{2} \times 2\sqrt{3}$      (c) $3 \times 2\sqrt{3}$

(d) $\sqrt{2} \times 4\sqrt{2}$      (e) $\sqrt{3} \times \sqrt{6}$      (f) $\sqrt{12} \times \sqrt{6}$

(g) $3\sqrt{2} \times \sqrt{18}$      (h) $2\sqrt{3} \times \sqrt{27}$      (i) $3\sqrt{75} \times 2\sqrt{6}$

(j) $2\sqrt{20} \times \sqrt{125}$      (k) $\sqrt{24} \times 3\sqrt{12}$      (l) $\sqrt{28} \times \sqrt{63}$

(m) $2\sqrt{2} \times 2\sqrt{3} \times \sqrt{12}$      (n) $\sqrt{12} \times 2\sqrt{6} \times \sqrt{18}$      (o) $\sqrt{14} \times 2\sqrt{7} \times \sqrt{8}$

**3** Simplify:

(a) $4\sqrt{5} + 3\sqrt{2} - \sqrt{5}$      (b) $6\sqrt{3} + 3\sqrt{2} + 2\sqrt{2}$

(c) $2\sqrt{2} + 3\sqrt{2} - \sqrt{5}$      (d) $5\sqrt{7} + 2\sqrt{3} + 6\sqrt{3} - 2\sqrt{7}$

(e) $2\sqrt{3} + 12\sqrt{3} + 6\sqrt{3} - 4\sqrt{2}$      (f) $\sqrt{7} + 2\sqrt{5} + 8\sqrt{5} - 2\sqrt{7}$

**4** Simplify:

(a) $\sqrt{12} + \sqrt{27}$      (b) $\sqrt{125} + \sqrt{20}$      (c) $\sqrt{32} - \sqrt{8}$

(d) $\sqrt{20} + \sqrt{45}$      (e) $\sqrt{63} - \sqrt{7}$      (f) $\sqrt{50} + \sqrt{32}$

(g) $\sqrt{48} - \sqrt{3}$      (h) $\sqrt{8} + \sqrt{18}$      (i) $\sqrt{5} + \sqrt{20}$

**5** Simplify:

(a) $\sqrt{12} - \sqrt{18} + \sqrt{8}$      (b) $\sqrt{27} - \sqrt{3} + \sqrt{8}$      (c) $\sqrt{45} + 2\sqrt{3} + \sqrt{5}$

(d) $5\sqrt{3} - \sqrt{18} + 2\sqrt{8}$      (e) $\sqrt{32} - \sqrt{28} + \sqrt{8}$      (f) $3\sqrt{2} - \sqrt{48} + \sqrt{8}$

**6** Simplify:

(a) $\sqrt{\dfrac{1}{128}}$      (b) $\sqrt{\dfrac{8}{49}}$      (c) $\sqrt{\dfrac{18}{125}}$      (d) $\sqrt{\dfrac{147}{50}}$      (e) $\sqrt{\dfrac{200}{121}}$

**7** Expand the brackets and simplify:

(a) $\sqrt{2}\left(\sqrt{2} - 1\right)$      (b) $\sqrt{5}\left(3 - \sqrt{5}\right)$

(c) $\sqrt{3}\left(4\sqrt{3} - 5\right)$      (d) $\sqrt{7}\left(\sqrt{14} - 3\sqrt{7}\right)$

**8** Simplify:

(a) $\left(\sqrt{2} - 1\right)\left(\sqrt{2} + 1\right)$      (b) $\left(3 - \sqrt{5}\right)\left(3 + \sqrt{5}\right)$

(c) $\left(4 - \sqrt{3}\right)\left(4 + \sqrt{3}\right)$      (d) $\left(\sqrt{3} - 2\right)\left(\sqrt{3} + 2\right)$

(e) $\left(\sqrt{5} + \sqrt{3}\right)\left(\sqrt{5} - \sqrt{3}\right)$      (f) $\left(\sqrt{7} - \sqrt{2}\right)\left(\sqrt{7} + \sqrt{2}\right)$

**9** Expand the brackets and simplify:

(a) $\left(\sqrt{2} - 1\right)\left(\sqrt{2} + 3\right)$      (b) $\left(\sqrt{5} - 2\right)\left(3\sqrt{5} + 4\right)$

(c) $\left(5\sqrt{2} + 3\right)\left(\sqrt{2} - 1\right)$      (d) $\left(6 - \sqrt{5}\right)\left(2 + \sqrt{5}\right)$

**10** Simplify:

(a) $\dfrac{8\sqrt{6}}{\sqrt{3}}$      (b) $\dfrac{5\sqrt{10}}{\sqrt{2}}$      (c) $\dfrac{2\sqrt{21}}{4\sqrt{3}}$      (d) $\dfrac{4\sqrt{15}}{3\sqrt{5}}$

(e) $\dfrac{\sqrt{7} \times 3\sqrt{2}}{3\sqrt{14}}$      (f) $\dfrac{\sqrt{2} \times 5\sqrt{6}}{2\sqrt{3}}$      (g) $\dfrac{4\sqrt{55} \times 3\sqrt{2}}{5\sqrt{5} \times 2\sqrt{11}}$      (h) $\dfrac{\sqrt{3} \times 12\sqrt{10}}{4\sqrt{6} \times \sqrt{2}}$

**11** Simplify into a form with a rational denominator:

(a) $\dfrac{2}{\sqrt{2}}$      (b) $\dfrac{10}{\sqrt{5}}$      (c) $\dfrac{6}{\sqrt{3}}$

(d) $\dfrac{21}{\sqrt{7}}$      (e) $\dfrac{12}{\sqrt{3}}$      (f) $\dfrac{18}{\sqrt{2}}$

(g) $\dfrac{2 + \sqrt{2}}{\sqrt{2}}$      (h) $\dfrac{3\sqrt{5} + 5}{\sqrt{5}}$      (i) $\dfrac{5\sqrt{3} + \sqrt{6}}{\sqrt{3}}$

(j) $\dfrac{\sqrt{7} + 14}{\sqrt{7}}$      (k) $\dfrac{5\sqrt{2} + 2\sqrt{3}}{\sqrt{6}}$      (l) $\dfrac{\sqrt{2} + 4}{5\sqrt{2}}$

## 8.6 Miscellaneous questions

This is a non-calculator exercise.

### Exercise 8.6

**1** Evaluate:

(a) $0.02^{-3}$

(b) $\left(\frac{5}{6}\right)^{-2}$

(c) $\left(\frac{256}{81}\right)^{-\frac{3}{4}}$

(d) $0.125^{-\frac{1}{3}}$

**2** Simplify:

(a) $0.2^{-3} \times 0.2^7$

(b) $2\alpha^5 \times 3\alpha^{-1}$

(c) $\dfrac{6j \times j^6}{2j^2}$

(d) $\dfrac{d^{\frac{3}{2}} \times d^{\frac{5}{2}}}{d}$

(e) $\dfrac{(0.2t)^4}{(0.1t^2)^3}$

(f) $\dfrac{0.2x^5 \times \left(6x^2\right)^3}{(0.3x)^2}$

❄ **3** Express as a sum of separate terms in index form:

(a) $\dfrac{1}{2x} + \dfrac{2}{x^2} + 3x^2\sqrt{x}$

(b) $2t^{\frac{1}{2}}\left(t + t^2 + 4t^5\right)$

(c) $\dfrac{x^3 - 4x}{x^{\frac{1}{2}}}$

**4** Solve the equation:

(a) $5^y = \dfrac{1}{625}$

(b) $5 \times 2^y = 320$

(c) $(5t + 1)^3 = 64$

**5** Simplify:

(a) $\dfrac{\frac{3}{4}c^3}{4c}$

(b) $\dfrac{5}{z^2} \div \dfrac{2}{z}$

(c) $\dfrac{7(x + 4)^2}{(x + 4)^{-2}}$

(d) $\dfrac{\alpha^2\beta^4}{\alpha + \alpha\beta + \alpha^2\beta}$

(e) $\dfrac{14n^2 - 2m}{3m - 21n^2}$

(f) $\dfrac{t + 4}{t^2 + 6t + 8}$

(g) $\dfrac{s^2 + 5s - 6}{s^2 - 1}$

(h) $\dfrac{2w^2 - w - 1}{4w^2 + 4w + 1}$

(i) $\dfrac{\frac{1}{3}(r - 1) + 2}{1 - \frac{1}{2}(r - 1)}$

**6** Simplify:

(a) $\dfrac{\frac{3}{b} + 1}{6}$

(b) $\dfrac{5}{5 - \frac{3}{2e^2}}$

(c) $\dfrac{\sin\theta}{1 + \frac{\cos\theta}{\sin\theta}}$

(d) $\dfrac{\frac{1}{y + 2} + 1}{1 - \frac{4}{y + 2}}$

**7** Express as a single fraction:

(a) $\dfrac{4}{p} + \dfrac{8}{p} - \dfrac{2}{p}$

(b) $\dfrac{\pi}{4x} - \dfrac{\pi}{6x^2}$

(c) $\dfrac{4e - 3}{e + 2} + 2$

(d) $3 \sin \psi + \dfrac{2}{\cos \psi}$

(e) $\dfrac{5}{x} + \dfrac{2}{y} - 3$

(f) $\dfrac{5}{s^2} - \dfrac{q - r}{s}$

(g) $\dfrac{4}{2q + 1} + \dfrac{1}{q - 5}$

(h) $\dfrac{2\alpha - 3}{\alpha + 1} - \dfrac{\alpha}{\alpha + 2}$

(i) $\dfrac{2}{a - b} + \dfrac{5}{b - a}$

**8** Solve the equation:

(a) $\dfrac{2}{f} = 5$

(b) $\dfrac{7}{2g} = 4$

(c) $\dfrac{5}{a} + \dfrac{1}{3} = \dfrac{1}{4} - \dfrac{2}{a}$

(d) $\dfrac{4}{0.2 + 3x} = 10$

(e) $\dfrac{3r + 7}{2r - 5} = \dfrac{2}{3}$

(f) $\dfrac{5}{2s + 1} = \dfrac{3}{1 - s}$

**❄ 9** Solve the equation:

(a) $\dfrac{3}{v + 3} - \dfrac{1}{v + 2} = \dfrac{5}{12}$

(b) $\dfrac{n + 1}{4} - \dfrac{3}{n - 6} = \dfrac{3}{2}$

(c) $\dfrac{1}{x} + \dfrac{x + 1}{9} = \dfrac{11}{9}$

(d) $\dfrac{2}{d - 2} = \dfrac{3d}{4d + 12}$

**10** Solve the simultaneous equations:

(a) $x^2 = y^2$

$x = y + 1$

(b) $ar^2 = 1000$

$ar^5 = -125$

(c) $5a + \dfrac{3}{b} = -1$

$2a + \dfrac{1}{b} = -1$

(d) $\dfrac{1}{s} + 3t = \dfrac{7}{2}$

$\dfrac{3}{s} - 2t = \dfrac{26}{3}$

(e) $ar = 14$

$ar^6 = 448$

(f) $cd = 0.8$

$cd^3 = 0.032$

**❄ 11** Solve the simultaneous equations:

(a) $\dfrac{x}{1 - y} = 2$

$xy = -4$

(b) $x + y = 8$

$2y + \dfrac{1}{x - 3} = 9$

**12** Simplify:

(a) $\sqrt{128}$

(b) $\sqrt{45}$

(c) $2\sqrt{3} \times 5\sqrt{2}$

(d) $5\sqrt{75} \times 2\sqrt{8}$

(e) $\dfrac{6}{\sqrt{3}}$

(f) $\dfrac{5}{\sqrt{5}}$

(g) $\dfrac{27}{\sqrt{3}}$

(h) $\sqrt{\dfrac{72}{20}}$

13. Simplify:
    (a) $2\sqrt{3} - \sqrt{7} + 4\sqrt{3}$
    (b) $\sqrt{11} - \sqrt{10} - 4\sqrt{11} + 5\sqrt{10}$
    (c) $\sqrt{75} + \sqrt{27}$
    (d) $\sqrt{200} + \sqrt{8}$

14. Simplify:
    (a) $\sqrt{5}\left(1 + 7\sqrt{5}\right)$
    (b) $\sqrt{2}\left(\sqrt{2} + 3\sqrt{3}\right)$
    (c) $2\sqrt{3}\left(\sqrt{3} + 5\sqrt{6}\right)$
    (d) $\left(\sqrt{5} - 1\right)\left(\sqrt{5} + 1\right)$
    (e) $\left(\sqrt{7} - 1\right)^2$
    (f) $\left(5\sqrt{2} + \sqrt{3}\right)\left(\sqrt{2} - \sqrt{3}\right)$

15. Evaluate the area and the length of the perimeter of the rectangle:

    (a)
    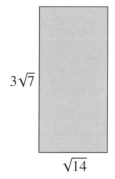
    $3\sqrt{7}$
    $\sqrt{14}$

    (b)
    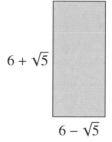
    $6 + \sqrt{5}$
    $6 - \sqrt{5}$

    (c)
    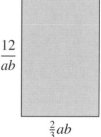
    $\dfrac{12}{ab}$
    $\frac{2}{3}ab$

16. Solve the simultaneous equations $\quad x + \sqrt{2}y = 3\sqrt{2}$
    $$\sqrt{2}x + y = 4.$$

17. The diagram shows a kite $OABC$, where $A$ is on the $x$-axis and $C$ is the point $(1, 1)$.
    (a) Calculate the length $OC$.
    (b) Write down the coordinates of $A$.
    The length of the perimeter of the kite is 4.
    (c) Calculate the area of the kite.

    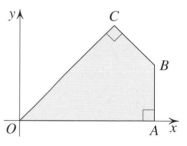

# 9 More algebra

## 9.1 Constructing equations

The following exercise will help you to practise:
- ❏ constructing an expression from given information
- ❏ using one expression in the construction of a second

### Exercise 9.1a

**1** A rectangle has width $x$ cm and the length is 6 cm longer than the width.

Write down an expression for the area of the rectangle in terms of $x$.

**2** The perimeter of a rectangle is 56 cm.
The length of the rectangle is $l$ cm.

  (a) Write down an expression for the width of the rectangle in terms of $l$.
  (b) Find an expression for the area of the rectangle in terms of $l$.

**3** The sum of two numbers is 34.
One of the numbers is $n$.

Write down an expression for the other number in terms of $n$.

**4** The area of a rectangle is three times that of a square of side $s$.

Write down an expression, in terms of $s$, for the total area of the two shapes.

**5** A 200 cm length of wire is used to form a skeletal cuboid with a square base of side $s$.

  (a) Write down an expression for the height of the cuboid in terms of $s$.
  (b) Write down an expression, in terms of $s$, for the volume of the cuboid.

**6** A number $p$ is 3 more than the number $n$.

    (a) Write down an expression for $p$ in terms of $n$.

The product of $n$, $p$ and a third number is 89.

    (b) Write down, in terms of $n$, an expression for the third number.

**7** The diagram shows a solid cuboid with width $b$.
The length of the cuboid is twice the width.

    (a) Write down an expression for the length of the
        cuboid in terms of $b$.

    (b) Write down an expression, in terms of $b$, for the
        area of the top face of the cuboid.

The volume of the cuboid is 10.

    (c) Find an expression, in terms of $b$, for the height of
        the cuboid.

    (d) Find an expression for the surface area of the
        cuboid in terms of $b$.

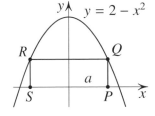

**8** A piece of wire of length 60 cm is cut into two parts.
One part is bent to form a square of side $w$ cm and the other part is bent to form a
rectangle of width $w$ cm.

Find an expression for the length of the rectangle in terms of $w$.

**9** The diagram shows the curve with equation $y = 2 - x^2$
and the rectangle $PQRS$, where $P$, $S$ are on the $x$-axis
and $Q$, $R$ are on the curve.
The point $P$ has coordinates $(a, 0)$.

    (a) Find an expression, in terms of $a$, for the height of
        the rectangle $PQRS$.

    (b) Find an expression, in terms of $a$, for the area of
        the rectangle $PQRS$.

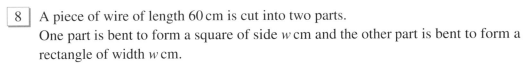

**10** The diagram shows the point $P(x, 4 - x)$ on the line with
equation $x + y = 4$.

Find an expression for the length of the line segment
$OP$ in terms of $x$.

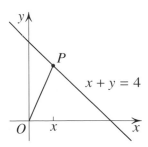

❄ **11** A rectangular sheet of paper measuring 30 cm × 24 cm has four squares cut from the corners, as shown.

Each square has sides of length $x$ cm.

The resulting shape is then folded to form an open box in the shape of a cuboid.

Write down expressions, in terms of $x$, for:

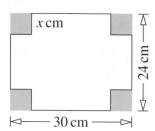

(a) the height of the box;

(b) the length of the box;

(c) the width of the box;

(d) the volume of the box;

(e) the surface area of the box.

❄ **12** The diagram shows a closed box whose base length is three times its width $w$ cm.

Write down an expression, in terms of $w$, for:

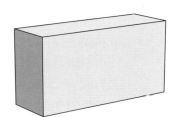

(a) the length of the box;

(b) the area of the top face of the box.

The box has a surface area of 34 cm².

Find an expression, in terms of $w$, for:

(c) the height of the box;

(d) the volume of the box.

❄ **13** A car travelling at $v$ km h⁻¹ uses petrol at the rate of $7 + 0.02v^3$ litres per hour. The car travels 100 km at a steady speed of $v$ km h⁻¹.

(a) Write down an expression for the time taken for the journey, in terms of $v$.

(b) Write down an expression, in terms of $v$, for the amount of petrol used on the journey.

---

The following exercise will help you to practise:

❏ forming and solving an equation

❏ solving a word problem

---

## Exercise 9.1b

**1** Find the values of $x$, $y$ and $p$ so that each rectangle has the given area.

(a)

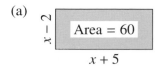

$x - 2$ · Area = 60 · $x + 5$

(b)

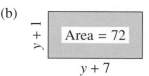

$y + 1$ · Area = 72 · $y + 7$

(c)

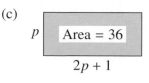

$p$ · Area = 36 · $2p + 1$

**2** When $t = 2$ is substituted into the expression $t^3 - 4t^2 + 6t - a$ the answer is $-3$.

Find the value of $a$.

**3** The perimeter of the shape shown on the right has length 79 cm.

All the indicated lengths are measured in centimetres.

Form and solve an equation to calculate the value of $y$.

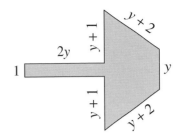

**4** A pen costs £2.50 more than a pencil.
Together the pen and pencil cost £3.90.

By letting the cost of a pencil be $x$ pence, form and solve an equation to find the cost of a pencil.

**5** The solid cuboid shown alongside has a volume of 324 cm³.

Calculate the value of $a$.

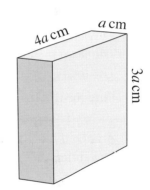

**6** A metal rod 5 m long is cut three times so that each piece cut off is 10 cm longer than the one before.

Form and solve an equation to find the lengths of the four pieces of rod.

❄ **7** A car tank was $\frac{1}{4}$ full.
After 26 litres of petrol were added the tank was then 90% full.

Form and solve an equation to calculate how much more petrol needed to be added to fill the tank completely.

❄ **8** The area of the symmetrical shape shown alongside is 48.

Find the length of the perimeter of the shape.

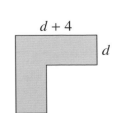

❄ 9  The sum of two positive integers is 8.
The sum of the squares of the two integers is 34.

Form and solve a quadratic equation to find the integers.

❄ 10  The triangle shown in the diagram is right-angled.
Find the value of $h$.

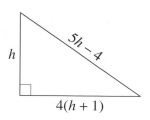

❄ 11  Adding an integer to twice its square gives a total of 21.
Find the integer.

❄ 12  Adding an integer to its reciprocal gives $\frac{5}{2}$.
Find the integer.

❄ 13  The length of a rectangular lawn is 7 metres more than the width.
The lawn is surrounded by a gravel path, 2 metres wide.
The total area of the lawn and path is $144 \, \text{m}^2$.

Find the dimensions of the lawn.

❄ 14  A cuboid has dimensions $w$ cm, $(w + 4)$ cm and $(w + 5)$ cm.
The surface area of the cuboid is $472 \, \text{cm}^2$.

Calculate the volume of the cuboid.

❄ 15  The diagram shows a rectangular-based pyramid.
The base has dimensions $2l$ m and $4l$ m, and all the slant lengths are $3l$ m.

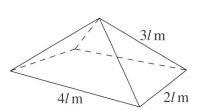

(a)  Find an expression in terms of $l$ for the perpendicular height of the pyramid.

The volume of the pyramid is $144 \, \text{m}^3$.

(b)  Calculate the value of $l$.

❄ 16  A closed metal cube has sides of length $l$ cm.
The cube is hollow, with a shell 1 cm thick, and the volume of metal used to form the cube is $296 \, \text{cm}^3$.

Calculate the value of $l$.

## 9.2 Changing the subject

The following exercise will help you to practise:

❑ changing the subject of a formula

### Exercise 9.2

**1** Make $x$ the subject of the formula:

(a) $x + a = 3b$      (b) $x - 4t = 7t$      (c) $2x = c$      (d) $-4x = t$

(e) $\dfrac{x}{a} = s$      (f) $\dfrac{x}{r} = 2r$      (g) $x(h - 2) = h$      (h) $5x + k = c$

(i) $6 + ax = b$      (j) $2 - x = m$      (k) $\pi - 5x = 3\pi$      (l) $c - x = 6g$

**2** Make $x$ the subject of the formula:

(a) $\dfrac{x}{8k} = n$      (b) $\dfrac{x}{gh} = h$      (c) $\dfrac{3}{x} = h$      (d) $\dfrac{g}{x} = 9$

(e) $\dfrac{a}{x} = c^2$      (f) $\dfrac{\pi}{x} = 4$      (g) $\dfrac{1}{x} + \dfrac{1}{y} = 0$      (h) $\dfrac{1}{x} + \dfrac{2}{\pi} = 0$

(i) $\dfrac{\pi}{x} + \dfrac{1}{2} = 3$      (j) $\dfrac{4x}{a} = b$      (k) $p = \dfrac{1}{2x}$      (l) $q = \dfrac{1}{5px}$

**3** Make $x$ the subject of the formula:

(a) $\sqrt{x} = y$      (b) $2 + \sqrt{x} = p$      (c) $\sqrt{x} - b = c$

(d) $\sqrt{sx} = t$      (e) $\dfrac{\sqrt{x}}{g} = h$      (f) $\dfrac{1}{\sqrt{x}} = q$

(g) $\sqrt{x - f} = j$      (h) $\sqrt{\dfrac{x}{u} + 1} = v$      (i) $\dfrac{\sqrt{x}}{b} = c + d$

**4** Make $x$ the subject of the formula:

(a) $x^2 = m$      (b) $\pi x^2 = s$      (c) $\dfrac{a}{x^3} = b$

(d) $x^3 - k = 7k$      (e) $6 - x^2 = gh$      (f) $\dfrac{f + 5}{x^4} = b$

(g) $\dfrac{x}{g} + h = 4$      (h) $(x + j)^2 = k$      (i) $\dfrac{x - c}{d} = b^3$

(j) $(p + 2q)x^2 = 4$      (k) $\dfrac{f}{x} - g = 2f$      (l) $(x - e)^3 = d$

(m) $\sqrt{\dfrac{x}{n - m}} = n$      (n) $\sqrt{\dfrac{t}{x + 1}} = s$      (o) $\left(\dfrac{x}{v} + u\right)^2 = w$

**5** Make $x$ the subject of the formula:

(a) $y^2 = ax$

(b) $k = \dfrac{x}{m+n}$

(c) $2 + p = \dfrac{7}{x}$

(d) $y = p - qx$

(e) $y = \sqrt{x-4}$

(f) $r = \dfrac{px}{q}$

(g) $h = \left(\dfrac{x}{d}\right)^2$

(h) $a^2 = \sqrt{x} + 1$

(i) $y = \dfrac{1}{x+2}$

(j) $p = a + \dfrac{x}{b}$

(k) $m = (3-x)^2$

(l) $k = 8 - \dfrac{x}{3}$

**6** Make $x$ the subject of the formula:

(a) $x - kx = k$

(b) $xu - x = u^2$

(c) $x + cx - c = d$

(d) $ax + b = x$

(e) $x - p = rx$

(f) $px - p = x$

(g) $ax + b = cx + d$

(h) $hx - g = x + g$

(i) $cx - d = dx + c$

(j) $ax - bx = c - dx$

(k) $2x - px = qx + 3$

(l) $u^2x - g = v^2x + a$

(m) $\dfrac{bx - a}{3} = 2x$

(n) $\dfrac{ax + b}{cx + d} = 2$

(o) $\dfrac{px + q}{3} = \dfrac{qx - p}{4}$

**7** Change the subject of the formula to the term given in the box:

(a) $C = 2\pi r$  $\boxed{r}$

(b) $v = u + at$  $\boxed{u}$

(c) $a = b + \cos\theta$  $\boxed{\cos\theta}$

(d) $V = lbh$  $\boxed{l}$

(e) $V = \dfrac{d}{t}$  $\boxed{t}$

(f) $V = iR$  $\boxed{i}$

(g) $A = \pi r^2$  $\boxed{r}\,(>0)$

(h) $P = 2(l + b)$  $\boxed{b}$

(i) $A = \frac{1}{2}bh$  $\boxed{h}$

(j) $P = I^2R$  $\boxed{I}\,(>0)$

(k) $v = u + at$  $\boxed{t}$

(l) $V = \pi r^2 h$  $\boxed{r}\,(>0)$

(m) $v^2 - u^2 = 2as$  $\boxed{u}\,(>0)$

(n) $S = 5x^2 + 6xh$  $\boxed{h}$

(o) $s = \dfrac{k}{d^2}$  $\boxed{d}\,(>0)$

(p) $F = \dfrac{GMm}{r^2}$  $\boxed{m}$

(q) $E = \frac{1}{2}mv^2$  $\boxed{v}\,(>0)$

(r) $\dfrac{a}{\sin 40°} = \dfrac{b}{\sin B}$  $\boxed{\sin B}$

(s) $d = \dfrac{k - m}{t}$  $\boxed{m}$

(t) $A = \pi\left(R^2 - r^2\right)$  $\boxed{R}\,(>0)$

(u) $D = 2\pi\rho + 3\rho + 6\alpha$  $\boxed{\rho}$

(v) $T = 2\pi\sqrt{\dfrac{l}{g}}$  $\boxed{l}$

(w) $P = \dfrac{n^2 + a}{n + a}$  $\boxed{a}$

(x) $\dfrac{l}{r} = 1 + e\cos\theta$  $\boxed{e}$

## 9.3 Completing the square

The following exercise will help you to practise:

❏ completing the square

❏ solving a quadratic equation by completing the square

### Exercise 9.3

1. Write in the form $(x + p)^2 + q$:

   (a) $x^2 + 6x$   (b) $x^2 - 12x$   (c) $x^2 + 10x$

   (d) $x^2 - 4x$   (e) $x^2 - x$   (f) $x^2 + 11x$

   (g) $x^2 - 8x + 5$   (h) $x^2 - 2x - 6$   (i) $x^2 + 16x + 70$

   (j) $x^2 - 14x + 50$   (k) $x^2 - 10x + 12$   (l) $x^2 + 4x - 3$

   (m) $x^2 + 3x + 1$   (n) $x^2 - 7x + 4$   (o) $x^2 + 5x - 1$

❄ 2. Write in the form $q - (x + p)^2$:

   (a) $4x - x^2$   (b) $6x - x^2$   (c) $-12x - x^2$

   (d) $1 + 8x - x^2$   (e) $20 - 2x - x^2$   (f) $6 - x - x^2$

❄ 3. Write in the form $k(x + p)^2 + q$:

   (a) $2x^2 + 12x$   (b) $5x^2 + 20x$   (c) $7x^2 - 56x$

   (d) $4x^2 - 24x - 5$   (e) $5x^2 + 10x + 6$   (f) $3x^2 + 60x + 400$

   (g) $2x^2 + 10x + 3$   (h) $7x^2 - 21x + 4$   (i) $3x^2 + x - 3$

❄ 4. Write in the form $q - k(x + p)^2$:

   (a) $8x - 2x^2$   (b) $30x - 3x^2$   (c) $10 - 16x - 2x^2$

   (d) $-3 + 8x - 4x^2$   (e) $42x - 7x^2$   (f) $1 - x - x^2$

❄ 5. Write in the form $k(x + p)^2 + q$:

   (a) $2x^2 - 12x + 1$   (b) $8x^2 + 16x - 3$   (c) $4 - 40x - 5x^2$

   (d) $2x^2 + 1.6x + 1$   (e) $0.1x^2 + 0.6x + 2$   (f) $12x - x^2$

❄ 6. Leaving the answer in the form $r \pm s\sqrt{t}$, solve the equation:

   (a) $x^2 + 4x + 1 = 0$   (b) $y^2 - 6y + 2 = 0$   (c) $\phi^2 + \phi - 1 = 0$

   (d) $2t^2 + 4t - 5 = 0$   (e) $5 + 12s - 3s^2 = 0$   (f) $1 - 10\omega - 5\omega^2 = 0$

❄ **7** Leaving the answer in the form $r \pm s\sqrt{t}$, solve the equation:

(a) $x^2 - x - 3 = 3x - 4$

(b) $y(y + 8) = 5$

(c) $(11 + z)(1 - z) = 30$

(d) $(t + 3)(t - 2) = (3t + 1)(t - 4)$

(e) $\dfrac{3u + 1}{u + 2} = \dfrac{4}{u + 5}$

(f) $\dfrac{1}{v} + \dfrac{1}{v + 2} = 3$

## 9.4 Functions

The following exercise will help you to practise:

❏ using functional notation

### Exercise 9.4a

1  The function $f$ is defined by $f(x) = 5x + 7$.

   (a) Find the value of:

   i) $f(3)$ ii) $f(-2)$ iii) $f(0)$ iv) $f(0.1)$

   (b) What value of $x$ satisfies $f(x) = 27$?

2  The function $f$ is defined by $f(x) = \frac{3}{4}x - 1$.

   (a) Find the value of:

   i) $f(2)$ ii) $f(-5)$ iii) $f(2.4)$ iv) $f(-0.5)$

   (b) What value of $m$ satisfies $f(m) = -10$?

3  The function $f$ is defined by $f(x) = 2x^2 - 1$.

   (a) Find the value of:

   i) $f(5)$ ii) $f(-3)$ iii) $f(0)$ iv) $f(1.1)$

   (b) What values of $x$ satisfy $f(x) = 17$?

4  The function $k$ is defined by $k(x) = 4^x$.

   (a) Find the value of:

   i) $k(3)$ ii) $k(0)$ iii) $k(-1)$ iv) $k\left(\frac{1}{2}\right)$

   (b) What value of $x$ satisfies $k(x) = 16$?

   (c) What value of $x$ satisfies $k(x) = \frac{1}{16}$?

5  The function $f$ is defined by $f(x) = x^2 - 2$.

   (a) Find the value of:

   i) $f(5)$ ii) $f(-3)$

   (b) Calculate the values of $m$ satisfying $f(m) = 14$.

   (c) Find an expression for:

   i) $f(a)$ ii) $f(t)$ iii) $f(r)$

6 The function $h$ is defined by $h(x) = x^2 + 2x$.

    (a) Given that $h(t) = -1$, find the value of $t$.

    (b) Given that $h(p) = 15$, find the possible values of $p$.

    (c) Find an expression for:

        i) $h(a)$         ii) $h(m)$

7 The function $k$ is defined by $k(x) = 3x - 2$.
Find an expression for:

    (a) $k(m)$         (b) $k(2t)$         (c) $k\left(a - \frac{1}{3}\right)$

8 The function $g$ is defined by $g(x) = 2x^2 + 7$.
Find and simplify an expression for:

    (a) $g(a)$         (b) $g(3t)$         (c) $g(m + 3)$

9 A function $f$ is defined by $f(x) = x(x + 3)$.
Find an expression for:

    (a) $f(t)$         (b) $f(2a)$         (c) $f(3m - 1)$

10 A function $h$ is defined by $h(t) = t(4 - t)$.
Find and simplify an expression for:

    (a) $h(x)$         (b) $h(x^2)$         (c) $h(x^3)$

11 A function $g$ is defined by $g(x) = 3x - 1$.

    (a) Find and simplify an expression for:

        i) $g(a + 1)$         ii) $g(2 - a)$

    (b) Find the value of $a$ such that $g(a + 1) = g(2 - a) + 3$.

12 A function $h$ is defined by $h(x) = \sqrt{2x + 3}$.

    (a) Find and simplify an expression for:

        i) $h(a + 3)$         ii) $h(2b)$

    (b) Find the value of $a$ such that $h(a + 3) = 5$.

    (c) Find the value of $b$ such that $h(2b) = 1$.

❋ 13 A function $g$ is defined by $g(t) = 2t^2 - 3$.

    (a) Find the values of $a$ such that $g(a + 1) = 5$.

    (b) Find the values of $p$ such that $g(3p) = 15$.

✳ 14 The function $h$ is defined by $h(x) = x(x - 3)$.
Find the values of $p$ such that $h(p - 2) = 0$.

✳ 15 A function $f$ is defined by $f(t) = 2t^2 - t$.
  (a) Find the possible values of $m$ such that $f(2m) = 10$.
  (b) Find the possible values of $a$ such that $f(a - 3) = 3$.

The following exercise will help you to practise:
  ❏ finding the values of unknown coefficients in a function

## Exercise 9.4b

1 The function $f$ is defined by $f(x) = ax + b$.
Given that $f(2) = 7$ and $f(3) = 15$, find the values of $a$ and $b$.

2 The function $g$ is defined by $g(x) = mx^2 + n$.
Given that $g(-2) = 14$ and $g(4) = 50$, find the values of $m$ and $n$.

3 The function $h$ is defined by $h(t) = At^2 - B$.
Given that $h(4) = 8$ and $h(6) = 18$, find the values of $A$ and $B$.

4 The function $F$ is defined by $F(x) = px^2 + qx + r$.
Given that $F(0) = 7$, $F(9) = 52$ and $F(-3) = 4$, find the values of $p$, $q$ and $r$.

5 The function $s$ is defined by $s(t) = t^3 + at^2 + bt + 6$.
Given that $s(3) = -6$ and $s(-3) = -18$, find the values of $a$ and $b$.

✳ 6 The function $Q$ is defined by $Q(x) = (x + \alpha)(x + \beta)$.
Given that $Q(0) = -6$ and $Q(1) = -4$, find the values of $\alpha$ and $\beta$.

✳ 7 The function $\rho$ is defined by $\rho(x) = x^3 + ax^2 + bx + c$.
Given that $\rho(1) = 12$, $\rho(-1) = -2$ and $\rho(-2) = 0$, find the values of $a$, $b$ and $c$.

## 9.5 Miscellaneous questions

### Exercise 9.5

1   The sum of two numbers is 14.
One of the numbers is $n$.

Write down an expression for the product of the two numbers.

2   The diagram shows the circle with equation
$x^2 + y^2 = 20$ and the straight line with equation
$x = a$.
The line and circle intersect at the points $P$ and $Q$,
and $O$ is the origin.

Find an expression for the area of the triangle $OPQ$
in terms of $a$.

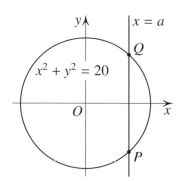

3   A square has sides of length 4 cm.
An equilateral triangle with sides of length $2s$ cm is cut out from inside the square.

Find an expression for the remaining area.

❋ 4   A solid cylinder has total surface area $20\pi$ cm$^2$.
The cylinder has radius $r$ cm and height 3 cm.

Calculate the value of $r$.

5   The volume, in cm$^3$, of the solid cuboid shown on the
right is numerically equal to the surface area, in cm$^2$.

Calculate the value of $b$.

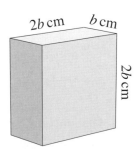

❋ 6   The diagram shows a triangle with area 7 cm$^2$.

Calculate the value of $t$.

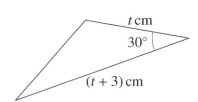

**7** Change the subject of the formula to the term given in the box:

(a) $S = 8r^2 + 5rh$    $\boxed{h}$       (b) $t(u + 2v) = 3u$    $\boxed{u}$

(c) $\dfrac{v + u}{v - u} = 2$    $\boxed{v}$       (d) $(p - a)(p - b) = ab$    $\boxed{p}\,(\neq 0)$

(e) $k - 2 = \dfrac{m}{k + 2}$    $\boxed{k}\,(> 0)$       (f) $\dfrac{1}{\sqrt{\gamma}} + \alpha = \beta^2$    $\boxed{\gamma}$

(g) $\dfrac{x^2}{a^2} + \dfrac{y^2}{b^2} = 1$    $\boxed{x}$       (h) $\dfrac{r}{h} = \sin(\theta - \alpha)$    $\boxed{\theta}$ (acute)

**8** Make $\sin A$ the subject of the formula $\dfrac{a}{\sin A} = \dfrac{b}{\sin B}$.

**9** Make $\cos A$ the subject of the formula $a^2 = b^2 + c^2 - 2bc \cos A$.

**10** Write in the form $k(x + p)^2 + q$:

(a) $x^2 + 6x + 1$       (b) $1 + 8x - x^2$       (c) $3x^2 + 12x - 2$

(d) $5x^2 + 2x$       (e) $2 - 3x - 2x^2$       (f) $7x^2 + 21x + 16$

**11** Leaving the answer in the form $r \pm s\sqrt{t}$, solve the equation:

(a) $x^2 + 6x + 2 = 0$       (b) $y^2 + 7 = 2y(y - 5)$       (c) $\dfrac{1}{t} + 1 = \dfrac{t}{3t + 1}$

**12** The function $f$ is defined by $f(x) = 4x + 5$.

(a) Find the value of $f(7)$.

(b) What value of $a$ satisfies $f(1 + a) = 21$?

**13** The function $\tau$ is defined by $\tau(t) = t^2 + t + 1$.

Find the values of $s$ so that $\tau(2s) = \tau(3s)$.

**14** The function $p$ is defined by $p(x) = ax^2 + bx - 4$.

Given that $p(-2) = 30$ and $p(4) = 48$, find the values of $a$ and $b$.

❄ **15** The function $f$ is defined by $f(x) = x^2 - 7x - 18$.

(a) Factorise $f(p)$.

(b) Evaluate $f\left(9 + \sqrt{3}\right)$.

❄ **16** The function $\sigma$ is defined by $\sigma(p) = p(p + 1)$.

(a) Solve the equation $\sigma(a + 4) = 6$.

(b) Solve the equation $\sigma(b^2) = 20$.

# Answers

**1.** (a) $7t$

(b) $s^2$

(c) $5g^2$

(d) $m^3$

(e) $5t^2$

(f) $15\beta^2$

(g) $12a^2$

(h) $8q^3$

**2.** (a) $xy$

(b) $\alpha\beta$

(c) $6rs$

(d) $12tz$

(e) $8mn$

(f) $30pq$

(g) $24t^2$

(h) $8\pi\omega$

**3.** (a) $12pq$

(b) $6tz$

(c) $\alpha^2\beta$

(d) $12h^2k^2$

(e) $12\pi\omega^2$

(f) $30p^2q$

(g) $3v^2w^2$

(h) $2c^2d^2$

**4.** (a) $p^3q$

(b) $12hk^3$

(c) $f^3g^3$

(d) $\pi x^3 y$

(e) $6p^3q^3$

(f) $6\alpha^3\beta^2$

(g) $10a^2b^2$

(h) $6\theta t^3$

**5.** (a) $4x^2$

(b) $9y^2$

(c) $25\omega^2$

(d) $p^3q^3$

(e) $r^2s^2$

(f) $4c^2d^2$

(g) $9\alpha^2\beta^4$

(h) $9a^4b^4$

**6.** (a) $16\omega^2$

(b) $54rt$

(c) $0.25m^2$

(d) $12t^3$

(e) $0.2m^2n$

(f) $0.02\alpha^2$

(g) $9\pi r^2 st$

(h) $24d^2e^2$

(i) $8.4\pi p^3 q$

**7.** (a) $2xy$

(b) $6t$

(c) $18\mu$

(d) $4xy$

(e) $\frac{1}{2}x^3 y$

(f) $\frac{1}{4}\beta^3$

(g) $4p^2q^2$

(h) $9y^3z$

(i) $\frac{1}{100}s^4$

(j) $4k^2$

(k) $\frac{1}{8}d^3$

(l) $\frac{1}{3}t^4$

**1.** (a) $15x$

(b) $-\pi$

(c) $-2e$

(d) $\alpha$

(e) $0$

(f) $-4\beta$

**2.** (a) $3x + 3$

(b) $6p - 9$

(c) $11c + 1$

(d) $-3\pi + 3$

(e) $mn - m + 3$

(f) $-2$

(g) $2 + 4xy$

(h) $8 - 2\beta\gamma$

(i) $2pq - 7$

**3.** (a) $2x + 5y$

(b) $-6a + 6b$

(c) $7pq - r$

(d) $2g + 4h$

(e) $8\pi - t$

(f) $6\alpha + \beta$

(g) $10s + 3st + 2t$

(h) $3c - 2d$

(i) $8m - 5mn$

**4.** (a) $5x^2 + 3x$

(b) $7 - 6x^2$

(c) $5y^2 + 4y + 3$

(d) $6t - 5t^2$

(e) $-\beta - 1$

(f) $2s^3 - s^2$

**5.** (a) $7y - 6$

(b) $4q + 9r$

(c) $2m^2 + 7m$

(d) $3 - 7n^2$

(e) $-2x^3 - 3x^2$

(f) $8\lambda - 3e$

**6.** (a) $f^2 - 4f + 3$

(b) $5t^2 - 9t + 7$

(c) $-2s^3 + 2s^2 + 6s + 10$

(d) $10x^2 - x - 1$

(e) $t^2 - 3t - 3$

(f) $6y^2 - 3y - 4$

7. (a) $7.9y$

(b) $0$

(c) $0.6uv - 0.7$

(d) $10.2\alpha - 0.1\beta$

(e) $10.4 - 2.2\sigma^2$

(f) $6.6 - 0.4z + 0.4z^2$

(g) $-0.3e^2 + 4.4e^3$

(h) $3.9 + 0.5m^2$

8. (a) $\frac{5}{6}q$

(b) $\frac{1}{12}\pi$

(c) $\frac{1}{3}a + \frac{2}{3}$

(d) $\frac{5}{12}\theta$

(e) $\frac{5}{12}\pi - \frac{1}{6}t$

(f) $\frac{3}{14}r - \frac{11}{100}s$

(g) $\frac{3}{10}\omega^3 - \frac{1}{6}\omega$

(h) $\frac{5}{6} - \frac{8}{45}x - \frac{8}{15}x^2$

---

**Exercise 1.2a**  *page 4*

1. (a) $2x - 2y$

(b) $6\lambda + 15$

(c) $30y - 24$

(d) $6a + 9b - 12c$

(e) $2\pi - 4x + 2x^2$

(f) $5t^3 - 10t^2 + 20t - 25$

2. (a) $-2x - 2y$

(b) $-5a + 5b$

(c) $-2\alpha + 3\beta$

(d) $-4a + 12b - 16c$

(e) $-\pi x^2 + 4\pi x$

(f) $-5 + 10t + 5t^2$

3. (a) $7x - y$

(b) $-a + 19b$

(c) $5t - 8$

(d) $26 + 10\pi$

(e) $11m^2 - 16m + 2$

(f) $2n^3 - 3n^2 + 6n - 11$

4. (a) $10\omega + 17$

(b) $-2y - 6$

(c) $16u + 6v + w$

(d) $11z + 5t + 2q$

(e) $13 - 2w - 4t$

(f) $10 - 5x - y$

5. (a) $x^2 - 2x$

(b) $2e^2 - 5e$

(c) $12h^2 - 6h$

(d) $-6\omega^2 - 9\omega$

(e) $-2x + 4x^2 - 2x^3$

(f) $5p^4 - 10p^3 + 20p^2 - 25p$

6. (a) $-2 - 2x$

(b) $-2 + 4\mu$

(c) $6 + 8z$

(d) $-p^2 + p$

(e) $-2h^2 - 9h$

(f) $-2\beta^3 - 7\beta^2$

7. (a) $2p^2 - 7p$

(b) $t + 3t^3$

(c) $ab + a^3 - b^2$

(d) $3x^2 + 3xy$

(e) $12m - 3mn + m^2$

(f) $2z^2 - z$

8. (a) $8x^2 - 12x$

(b) $a^2 - 7a - 1$

(c) $6n + 12mn - 5m^2$

(d) $4\alpha^2 - 4\alpha + 7$

(e) $2\beta^3 - 3\beta^2 - 3\beta$

(f) $k^4 - k^3 + 2k^2 + 4k - 5$

9. (a) $3.2y - 8$

(b) $-4 - 0.8x$

(c) $23.8y + 13.4z$

(d) $4a^4 - 8a^3 + 160a^2 - 20a$

(e) $-t^2 + 1.1t$

(f) $-1.3k^3 + 12.9k^2$

10. (a) $3s + 2t$

(b) $\frac{1}{6}a^2 - \frac{1}{12}a$

(c) $4 - 3c + 2c^2$

(d) $4q^3 - 8q^2 + 14q - 10$

(e) $\frac{1}{7} - \frac{2}{7}e$

(f) $-\frac{1}{4}z - \frac{1}{8}t$

11. (a) $\sigma - 2$

(b) $-\frac{1}{2}t^3 - \frac{1}{2}t^2 - \frac{3}{2}t + \frac{3}{2}$

(c) $-\frac{7}{3}z + \frac{5}{6}z^2$

(d) $-\frac{1}{3}m^2 - \frac{1}{3}m^3$

---

**Exercise 1.2b**  *page 5*

1. (a) $x^2 + 4x + 3$

(b) $12m^2 + 31m + 7$

(c) $18t^2 + 31t + 6$

(d) $n^2 + 5n + 6$

(e) $2z^2 + 9z + 4$

(f) $15s^2 + 28s + 12$

2. (a) $x^2 - 5x + 4$

(b) $15e^2 - 16e + 4$

(c) $5b^2 - 8b + 3$

(d) $z^2 - 3z + 2$

(e) $6t^2 - 11t + 3$

(f) $10n^2 - 29n + 10$

3. (a) $x^2 - x - 6$

(b) $p^2 - 16$

(c) $42 + q - q^2$

(d) $9 - 25n^2$

(e) $z^2 + z - 2$

(f) $6h^2 - h - 12$

4. (a) $5x^2 - 14x - 3$

(b) $12m^2 - 11m - 5$

(c) $4k^2 - 1$

(d) $8p^2 - 10p - 3$

(e) $12m^2 + 8m - 15$

(f) $-10\beta^2 + 29\beta - 21$

(g) $4 - 81n^2$

(h) $2p^2 - 5p + 3$

(i) $-2y^2 - 3y + 5$

5. (a) $x^2 + 6x + 9$

(b) $y^2 - 8y + 16$

(c) $4a^2 + 4a + 1$

(d) $9x^2 - 12x + 4$

(e) $25m^2 + 40m + 16$

(f) $4t^2 - 28t + 49$

(g) $9 - 6t + t^2$

(h) $100 - 60m + 9m^2$

**6.** (a) $xy + 2x + 3y + 6$

(b) $st + 2t - 4s - 8$

(c) $yz - 3z - y + 3$

(d) $20 - 5w + 4r - rw$

(e) $8pq + 6q - 12p - 9$

(f) $2 - c - 2d + cd$

**7.** (a) $x^2 - 2xy - 3y^2$

(b) $25\lambda^2 - 20\lambda + 4$

(c) $12p^2 + 5pq - 2q^2$

(d) $\alpha^2 - 3\alpha - 4$

(e) $2t^2 - 13t + 20$

(f) $9c^2 - 12cd + 4d^2$

(g) $20 + 7\omega - 3\omega^2$

(h) $2n^2 + 12n + 18$

(i) $4s^2 - 36$

**8.** (a) $2n^2 + 2n + 5$

(b) $4y^2 - 6y + 7$

(c) $-m^2 + m + 6$

(d) $-\lambda - 7$

(e) $2\alpha^3$

(f) $-s^2 - 24s + 6$

**9.** (a) $x^3 + 3x^2 + 3x + 1$

(b) $2p^3 - 9p^2 + 8p + 5$

(c) $3y^3 + 8y^2 - 1$

(d) $t^3 - t^2 + 3t + 5$

**10.** (a) $a^2 + 3a - b^2 - b + 2$

(b) $p^2 + 2pr - q^2 + r^2$

(c) $5x + x^2 + y + 6 - y^2$

(d) $r^2 - 4rs + 6rt +$
$4s^2 - 12st + 9t^2$

**11.** (a) $n^3 + 9n^2 + 27n + 27$

(b) $\gamma^3 - 6\gamma^2 + 12\gamma - 8$

(c) $64 - 48q + 12q^2 - q^3$

(d) $8s^3 - 12s^2 + 6s - 1$

(e) $27e^3 + 54e^2 + 36e + 8$

(f) $p^3 - 6p^2q +$
$12pq^2 - 8q^3$

---

## Exercise 1.3          page 7

**1.** (a) $3(x + y)$

(b) $5(z - t)$

(c) $3(\theta + 3)$

(d) $6(4 - k)$

(e) $\pi(1 + t)$

(f) $5(3y - 2)$

(g) $5(3t + 2r - 5s)$

(h) $10(5m - 3z + 4x)$

(i) $6(4x + 5y - 7z)$

**2.** (a) $x(x + 5)$

(b) $n(n - 2)$

(c) $t(\pi - t)$

(d) $p(p + 7)$

(e) $p(q + 2)$

(f) $r(4 + s)$

(g) $q(t + r + s - 6)$

(h) $v(z + w - v)$

(i) $x(s - r + 3x - x^2)$

**3.** (a) $2x(x - 3)$

(b) $4y(y - 1)$

(c) $3m(2 - m)$

(d) $6\alpha(2 - \alpha)$

(e) $3n(2n + 5)$

(f) $3q(5q - 6)$

(g) $4\omega(2\omega + 3)$

(h) $2\beta(3 - 2\beta + 10\beta^2)$

(i) $5s(5s^2 + 3 - 2s)$

**4.** (a) $q(p^2 + 1)$

(b) $s(3rs + 1)$

(c) $5r^2(\pi - 2)$

(d) $3rt(t^2 + 2r - 1)$

(e) $\beta(3\alpha - 2\beta^2)$

(f) $cd(5 + 6cd)$

(g) $s^2(2s + 1)$

(h) $ab(5b + ab + a)$

(i) $ar(1 + r + r^2)$

**5.** (a) $(x + 3)(2 + z)$

(b) $(m - 1)(m + n)$

(c) $(t + 1)(r - 4)$

(d) $(r + 2s)(q + 1)$

(e) $(2x + 1)(1 + 3x^2)$

(f) $(k - 2)(5k - 1)$

**6.** (a) $(x - 2)(5 - z)$

(b) $(m - 1)(k - n)$

(c) $(2q - 3)(r - p)$

(d) $(m - 3)(2 + m)$

(e) $(t - 1)(p + 3)$

(f) $(x - 4)(2x - 11)$

(g) $(q - 1)(p + q - 1)$

(h) $(7m - 1)(7km - k - r)$

**7.** (a) $(x + 4)(3x + 12 + z)$

(b) $(b - 1)(a + b^2 - b)$

(c) $(7p - 1)(7pt - t + r)$

(d) $x(x + 3)(x - 1)$

(e) $(y + 1)^2(x - zy - z)$

(f) $r(t + 1)^2(t + 1 - 4)$

**8.** (a) $\cos x(\sin x + 1)$

(b) $\tan A(3 \cos A - 1)$

(c) $2 \cos \alpha(3 - 5 \sin \alpha)$

(d) $5 \tan t(\tan t + 1)$

(e) $\cos C(\cos C - 3)$

(f) $\tan \theta(\cos \theta + \sin \theta)$

---

## Exercise 1.4a          page 9

**1.** (a) $(x - y)(x + y)$

(b) $(\rho - 3)(\rho + 3)$

(c) $(t - 5)(t + 5)$

(d) $(q - 4)(q + 4)$

(e) $(b - \frac{1}{2})(b + \frac{1}{2})$

(f) $(7 - x)(7 + x)$

(g) $(\frac{2}{3} - \alpha)(\frac{2}{3} + \alpha)$

(h) $(c - 6)(c + 6)$

**2.** (a) $(2x - 3)(2x + 3)$

(b) $(5m - 7)(5m + 7)$

(c) $(1 - 3t)(1 + 3t)$

(d) $(3 - 4\beta)(3 + 4\beta)$

(e) $(p - 2q)(p + 2q)$

(f) $(7k - 5m)(7k + 5m)$

(g) $(3z - 2x)(3z + 2x)$

(h) $(10 - 9t)(10 + 9t)$

(i) $(\frac{1}{5}b - a)(\frac{1}{5}b + a)$

(j) $(\frac{1}{2}c - \frac{1}{5}d)(\frac{1}{2}c + \frac{1}{5}d)$

(k) $(\frac{1}{7}y - 1)(\frac{1}{7}y + 1)$

(l) $(\frac{1}{3}r - \frac{1}{4}t)(\frac{1}{3}r + \frac{1}{4}t)$

3. (a) $2(x - 2)(x + 2)$

(b) $3(t - 5)(t + 5)$

(c) $3(2 - m)(2 + m)$

(d) $5(3y - 1)(3y + 1)$

(e) $\pi(q - p)(q + p)$

(f) $c(d - e)(d + e)$

(g) $z(x - 4)(x + 4)$

(h) $b(2a - 3)(2a + 3)$

(i) $k(5m - 2t)(5m + 2t)$

(j) $\pi(\frac{1}{3}y - z)(\frac{1}{3}y + z)$

(k) $4y(y - 3)(y + 3)$

(l) $\frac{1}{3}s(t - s)(t + s)$

4. (a) $(z - 1)(z + 1)(z^2 + 1)$

(b) $t(2t - 1)(2t + 1)$

(c) $(1 - p)(1 + p)(1 + p^2)$

(d) $ar^2(1 - r)(1 + r)$

---

**Exercise 1.4b** *page 9*

1. (a) $(x + 5)(x + 1)$

(b) $(y + 1)(y + 3)$

(c) $(m + 7)(m + 1)$

(d) $(t + 2)(t + 3)$

(e) $(b + 4)(b + 2)$

(f) $(e + 6)(e + 2)$

2. (a) $(p - 2)(p - 1)$

(b) $(x - 1)(x - 1)$

(c) $(q - 4)(q - 3)$

(d) $(z - 2)(z - 8)$

(e) $(y - 8)(y - 3)$

(f) $(n - 15)(n - 1)$

3. (a) $(x + 2)(x - 1)$

(b) $(t - 1)(t + 5)$

---

(c) $(c + 1)(c - 3)$

(d) $(p - 3)(p + 2)$

(e) $(z + 4)(z - 1)$

(f) $(r - 2)(r + 6)$

(g) $(a + 2)(a - 8)$

(h) $(e + 3)(e - 8)$

(i) $(h - 12)(h + 1)$

4. (a) $(2x + 5)(x + 1)$

(b) $(5y + 3)(y + 1)$

(c) $(3m + 7)(m + 1)$

(d) $(5n - 1)(n - 1)$

(e) $(5q - 2)(q - 1)$

(f) $(2z + 3)(z - 2)$

(g) $(7a + 2)(2a + 3)$

(h) $(3e - 4)(4e - 3)$

(i) $(8w - 3)(w + 2)$

5. (a) $(1 + x)(1 + 2x)$

(b) $(1 + m)(1 + 5m)$

(c) $(1 + c)(4 + c)$

(d) $(2 + z)(5 + z)$

(e) $(3 + a)(4 + a)$

(f) $(3 + x)(2 + x)$

(g) $(5 - b)(1 - b)$

(h) $(2 + 3s)(3 + 2s)$

(i) $(1 - 9\beta)(2 - \beta)$

6. (a) $(1 - x)(1 + 2x)$

(b) $(1 - 3y)(1 + y)$

(c) $(1 + 3t)(1 - 2t)$

(d) $(4 - t)(2 + t)$

(e) $(6 - m)(1 + m)$

(f) $(8 + w)(3 - w)$

(g) $(3 - 2y)(1 + y)$

(h) $(4 + n)(3 - 5n)$

(i) $(4 - p)(2 + 3p)$

7. (a) $(x - 2)(6 + x)$

(b) $(3t - 4)(t - 1)$

(c) $(2m - 1)(m + 3)$

(d) $(3\omega + 2)(5\omega + 1)$

(e) $(1 - z)(2 + z)$

(f) $(3 - g)(5 - g)$

---

(g) $(2c - 1)(c - 1)$

(h) $(3 - 2s)(3 + 4s)$

(i) $(6r + 5)(r - 1)$

8. (a) $2(x + 1)(x + 3)$

(b) $5(e - 1)(e + 3)$

(c) $3(m - 5)(m - 2)$

(d) $4(\alpha - 1)(\alpha + 7)$

(e) $x(y + 3)(y - 2)$

(f) $0.3p(q - 6)(q + 1)$

9. (a) $(2p + q)(p - 2q)$

(b) $(5t - r)(t + 5r)$

(c) $(x + 3y)(3x - y)$

(d) $(2a + 5b)(a - 2b)$

(e) $(5w - 2x)(w + 2x)$

(f) $(k + 5m)(3k - m)$

10. (a) $(\tan \beta + 3)(\tan \beta - 1)$

(b) $(\sin B + 2)(\sin B - 3)$

(c) $(\tan \theta - 5)(\tan \theta - 2)$

(d) $(2\tan \lambda - 1)(\tan \lambda + 1)$

(e) $(3\sin P - 2)(2\sin P + 1)$

(f) $(10\sin \phi - 3)(\sin \phi + 1)$

(g) $(5\cos X - 2)(\cos X - 1)$

(h) $(5\tan C + 2)(\tan C + 6)$

---

**Exercise 1.5** *page 12*

1. (a) 1

(b) 12

(c) −4

(d) −3

(e) 2

(f) −2

(g) 2

(h) 0

2. (a) 12

(b) −15

(c) −20

(d) 45

(e) 60

(f) −13

(g) −11

(h) 8

**3.** (a) −8
  (b) 18
  (c) 27
  (d) 16
  (e) 36
  (f) 18
  (g) 48
  (h) 48

**4.** (a) −3
  (b) −8
  (c) −6
  (d) $\frac{1}{5}$
  (e) −1
  (f) −10
  (g) −9
  (h) $-\frac{1}{2}$

**5.** (a) 2
  (b) 2
  (c) 4
  (d) −4
  (e) −6
  (f) 3
  (g) $\frac{1}{3}$
  (h) 0

**6.** (a) −4.7
  (b) −18
  (c) 12
  (d) −0.875
  (e) 0.32
  (f) 3
  (g) −7.5
  (h) 36

**7.** (a) $\frac{1}{12}$
  (b) $\frac{7}{20}$
  (c) $\frac{3}{25}$
  (d) $\frac{2}{9}$
  (e) $\frac{1}{2}$
  (f) $\frac{3}{4}$
  (g) $\frac{36}{35}$
  (h) $\frac{1}{12}$

**8.** (a) 5
  (b) 155.925
  (c) 170.52
  (d) 3.2
  (e) 24.75
  (f) 158.57
  (g) 11.43 (2dp)
  (h) 5.3
  (i) 18.90 (2dp)

---

### Exercise 1.6    *page 14*

**1.** (a) $3q^2$
  (b) $m^3 n^2$
  (c) $1.5a^3 b^2$
  (d) $-5s$
  (e) 0
  (f) $-g^2 - 1$
  (g) $19t - 76$
  (h) $2 + 48\pi$
  (i) $5q^2 + 8q - 1$

**2.** (a) $2c^2 + c - 21$
  (b) $12 - 7w - 10w^2$
  (c) $16x^2 - 24x + 9$
  (d) $km + k - 2m - 2$
  (e) $14t^2 - 36t + 25$
  (f) $f^3 + 9f^2 + 27f + 27$
  (g) $\frac{1}{4}x^2 + 2x + 4$
  (h) $\frac{5}{6}n^2 - \frac{1}{2}n$

**3.** (a) $10x$ cm, $6x^2$ cm$^2$
  (b) $(8y + 6x)$ cm,
      $24xy$ cm$^2$
  (c) $(10a - 10)$ m,
      $(6a^2 - 15a)$ m$^2$

**4.** (a) $18x$ m, $17x^2$ m$^2$
  (b) $(18\ell + 4)$ cm,
      $(20\ell^2 - 10\ell + 4)$ cm$^2$

**5.** $4\pi h$ cm, $2(2 + \pi)h^2$ cm$^2$

**6.** $2(a + \pi b)$ m,
    $(2ab + \pi b^2)$ m$^2$

**7.** (a) $3(p + 1)^2$

  (b) $\pi(r - 1)(r + 1)$
  (c) $5(2m - 1)(m + 1)$
  (d) $2(\mu - 5)(\mu + 5)$
  (e) $2(3t + 1)(t - 1)$
  (f) $0.3b(2b + 1)$
  (g) $(3 + a)^2$
  (h) $(2y + 1)(y - 3)$
  (i) $(t - \frac{1}{3}s)(t + \frac{1}{3}s)$
  (j) $3(2 - k)(2 + k)$
  (k) $(q - 1)(p + 5)$
  (l) $(t + 1)(t^2 - t + 3)$

**8.** (a) $(2x - 1)(2x + 1)$
  (b) $4(x^2 + 1)$
  (c) $4x(x + 1)$
  (d) $4(x - 1)(x + 1)$
  (e) $3(y^2 + 1)$
  (f) $3(y - 1)(y + 1)$
  (g) $3y(y - 1)$
  (h) $3y^2(1 - y)$

**9.** (a) $\tan \phi (3 + 4 \tan \phi)$
  (b) $\sin x(3 \sin^2 x +$
      $5 \sin x - 7)$
  (c) $(\cos t - 2)(\cos t - 1)$
  (d) $(3 \sin \alpha - 5)(\sin \alpha + 1)$

**10.** (a) −30
  (b) −23
  (c) 25
  (d) 21
  (e) 4
  (f) 10
  (g) −3
  (h) $\frac{1}{2}$

---

### Exercise 2.1    *page 16*

**1.** (a) $a = 9$
  (b) $b = \frac{2}{5}$
  (c) $d = \frac{7}{3}$
  (d) $f = -3.1$
  (e) $m = 1$
  (f) $t = -4$

(g) $e = \frac{13}{2}$

(h) $f = -\frac{5}{2}$

2. (a) $q = -\frac{1}{6}$

(b) $r = \frac{4}{3}$

(c) $\mu = 0.1$

(d) $T = \frac{5}{6}$

(e) $v = 5$

(f) $w = -8$

(g) $\theta = -\frac{2}{3}$

(h) $u = \frac{7}{2}$

3. (a) $g = -4$

(b) $P = \frac{1}{6}$

(c) $y = \frac{5}{8}$

(d) $\alpha = \frac{1}{2}$

(e) $n = 6$

(f) $X = \frac{4}{3}$

(g) $k = 12$

(h) $\rho = \frac{1}{4}$

4. (a) $n = 2$

(b) $r = -6$

(c) $t = 13$

(d) $u = 4$

(e) $\lambda = \frac{3}{2}$

(f) $W = 1$

(g) $\beta = \frac{2}{3}$

(h) $e = \frac{1}{11}$

5. (a) $n = \frac{3}{2}$

(b) $a = -\frac{3}{2}$

(c) $b = -1$

(d) $p = -5$

(e) $k = 1.9$

(f) $x = 8$

(g) $y = -3$

(h) $z = -3.5$

(i) $t = 10$

(j) $w = -3$

6. (a) $\sin x = 1$

(b) $\tan x = 2.5$

(c) $\cos x = 0.376$

(d) $\tan x = 0.51$

(e) $\sin x = 0.577$

(f) $\cos x = 0.102$

## Exercise 2.2 *page 18*

1. (a) $a = 6$

(b) $x = 8$

(c) $p = -10$

(d) $t = \frac{28}{3}$

(e) $z = -\frac{6}{7}$

(f) $t = 5$

(g) $a = 4$

(h) $k = 20$

(i) $f = 2$

2. (a) $r = -\frac{4}{3}$

(b) $p = \frac{8}{9}$

(c) $F = -\frac{3}{4}$

(d) $g = 24$

(e) $d = \frac{2}{3}$

3. (a) $\alpha = -\frac{2}{3}$

(b) $j = \frac{2}{5}$

(c) $e = -18$

(d) $v = 6$

(e) $b = -3$

(f) $t = 2.4$

4. (a) $s = -\frac{4}{3}$

(b) $t = -6$

(c) $a = -\frac{9}{5}$

(d) $p = -4.6$

(e) $r = -0.1$

(f) $f = 40$

5. (a) $p = 9$

(b) $q = -6$

(c) $x = 6$

(d) $y = 9$

## Exercise 2.3 *page 19*

1. (a) 0, 1

(b) 0, 1, 2, …, 10

(c) 0, 1, 2, …, 7

(d) 6, 7, 8, 9, 10

(e) 1, 2, 3, 4, 5

(f) 6, 7, 8, 9, 10

(g) 0, 1, 2, 3, 4

(h) 0, 1, 2, 3, 4

(i) 0

(j) no values

(k) 3, 4, 5, 6

(l) 0, 1, 7, 8, 9, 10

2. (a) 7, 8, 9, 10

(b) 0, 1, 2, 3

(c) 0, 1, 2, 3, 4, 5, 6

(d) 6, 7, 8, 9, 10

(e) 10

(f) 3, 4, 5, …, 10

3. (a) $c < 3$

(b) $x > -6$

(c) $d < 7$

(d) $f \leq -10$

(e) $t > -\frac{5}{4}$

(f) $e > 0.6$

(g) $g \geq -\frac{36}{5}$

4. (a) $-5 < x < 4$

(b) $-2 \leq c \leq 8$

(c) $-10 < t < 5$

## Exercise 2.4 *page 20*

1. (a) $x = 3, y = 1$

(b) $a = 4, b = 1$

(c) $p = 5, q = -2$

(d) $y = \frac{3}{2}, z = 0$

(e) $g = -2, h = -3$

(f) $x = 3, y = -1$

2. (a) $x = 4, y = -1$

(b) $a = 0, b = 5$

(c) $p = \frac{1}{2}, q = \frac{1}{4}$

(d) $\theta = 0.2, \phi = 0.4$

(e) $x = 12, y = -4$

(f) $a = -\frac{1}{2}, b = \frac{1}{6}$

**3.** (a) $m = 5, n = -1$

(b) $a = 3, d = -1$

(c) $f = -\frac{1}{2}, g = \frac{5}{2}$

(d) $x = 10, y = 2$

(e) $r = 12, s = -4$

(f) $h = -3, k = 8$

**4.** (a) $\alpha = 2, \beta = 1$

(b) $a = \frac{5}{2}, d = -\frac{1}{2}$

(c) $s = 0.1, t = 0.2$

(d) $h = 0.3, w = -0.25$

(e) $p = -4, q = -2$

(f) $c = -3, d = 0$

**5.** (a) $x = 20, y = -10$

(b) $p = 0.2, q = 1.4$

(c) $k = 4, l = 6$

(d) $\eta = 1.5, \lambda = 4$

(e) $a = 25, b = 50$

(f) $w = 20, z = 10$

**6.** (a) $x = 1, y = 5$

(b) $x = 2, y = -3$

(c) $a = 3, b = -3$

(d) $c = 4, d = \frac{7}{3}$

(e) $m = 8, n = 3$

(f) $s = 5, t = 12$

**7.** (a) $u = 5, j = -3$

(b) $e = -1, f = -5$

(c) $\sigma = 7, \tau = 10$

(d) $k = 9, m = 4$

(e) $r = 8, t = 20$

(f) $A = -2, B = 8$

**8.** (a) $x = -7, y = 4$

(b) $u = 3, v = 2$

(c) $a = 7, b = -2$

(d) $p = -3, q = -4$

(e) $m = 4, n = 10$

(f) $d = 3, e = 0.2$

**9.** (a) $x = 6, y = -2$

(b) $x = 4, y = 1$

(c) $s = -2, t = 3$

(d) $a = -10, b = 4$

(e) $e = 0, f = 3$

(f) $u = 4, v = -1$

(g) $p = 5, q = 0$

(h) $a = 3, b = -3$

(i) $\theta = 4\pi, \phi = \pi$

(j) $\alpha = -\frac{2\pi}{3}, \beta = -\frac{4\pi}{3}$

---

**Exercise 2.5**  *page 22*

**1.** (a) $-9$

(b) $45$

(c) $10$

(d) $7$

(e) $-3$

**2.** (a) $a < -\frac{1}{2}$

(b) $f \geq 20$

**3.** $-1, 0, 1$

**4.** (a) $a = 5, b = 1$

(b) $a = 1.5, T = 725$

(c) $u = 8, v = -1$

(d) $h = -1, k = -3$

(e) $x = 1, y = 5$

(f) $p = \frac{11}{6}, q = \frac{25}{6}$

(g) $s = \frac{5}{3}, t = \frac{37}{3}$

(h) $a = 0.1, b = 0.4$

(i) $g = 0.7, h = 4$

(j) $P = 0.6, Q = 1$

**5.** (a) $x = 27$

(b) $m = 0.2, T = 3.2$

(c) $\lambda = 1.5, \mu = -1$

(d) $u = 4, v = 2.8$

(e) $\mu = 0.17$

(f) $y = 5.07$

(g) $P = 519, R = 750$

---

**Exercise 3.1**  *page 23*

**1.** (a) $Q, T, V$

(b) $Q, S$

(c) $P, S, W$

(d) $R, T$

**2.** $P, R, S$

**3.** $K, L, M$

**4.** $A, C, D$

**5.** $A$

**6.** $K, L, N$

**7.** $C, D$

**8.** $P(3, 18), Q(-2, 8)$

**9.** $A(4, 1), B(-2, -2)$

**10.** $K(3, 4), L(3, -4)$

**11.** (a) $31$

(b) $-2$

**12.** $1$

**13.** $\pm 6$

**14.** $\pm 2$

**15.** $\pm 3$

---

**Exercise 3.2**  *page 26*

**1.** (a) $(8, 6)$

(b) $(7, 2)$

(c) $(-2, 1)$

(d) $(1, 3)$

(e) $(-4, -4)$

(f) $\left(-\frac{13}{2}, 0\right)$

**2.** $(4, 6)$

**3.** $(-9, 7)$

**4.** $(-14, -2)$

**5.** $(4, 1)$

**6.** $(12, -5)$

**7.** $(4a, 2b)$

**8.** $(2p, p)$

---

**Exercise 3.3**  *page 27*

**1.** (a) $5$

(b) 10

(c) 7

(d) 5

(e) 9

(f) 7

2. (a) 5

(b) 13

(c) 13

(d) $\sqrt{50} = 5\sqrt{2}$

(e) $\sqrt{18} = 3\sqrt{2}$

(f) 5

4. 5 or −3

5. (0, 1) or (−6, 1)

6. $10x + 12y = 61$

7. $\pm\sqrt{5}$

8. $3x^2 + 3y^2 + 16x + 24y + 52 = 0$

---

**Exercise 3.4**      *page 28*

1. (b)

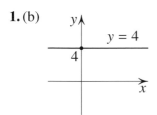

2. (b)

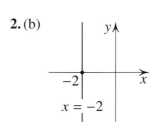

3. (a)

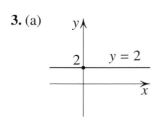

(b)

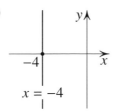

$x = -4$

(c)

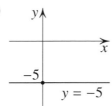

$y = -5$

(d)

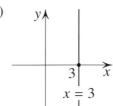

$x = 3$

4. (a) $y = 5$

(b) $x = -3$

(c) $y = -3$

(d) $x = 10$

(e) $y = 8$

(f) $x = -7$

5. $y = 3$, $x = 4$, $y = -3$, $x = -6$

6. $x = -2$, $y = 1$

7. (a) $(3, -1)$

(b) $y = 3$, $x = 3$

8. $y = -3$, $x = 2$

9. (a) $y = 3$

(b) $y = 4$

(c) $x = 2$

(d) $y = 1$

(e) $y = 4$

10. $y = 4$

11. (a) $(-2, 5)$

(b) $(-4, 5)$, $(-2, 2)$

12. (a) $x = 9$, $y = 1$;
$x = 10$, $y = 3$

(b) $x = 13$, $y = 1$;
$x = 20$, $y = 3$

---

**Exercise 3.5**      *page 30*

1. 14

2. 10

3. 20

4. 32.5

5. 30

6. 68

7. 5

8. 96

9. 56

10. (a) $(-7, -5)$

(b) 70

11. (a) $(9, 2)$, $(-1, 2)$

(b) 50

12. 48

13. 6.5

---

**Exercise 3.6**      *page 32*

1. (a) $(-1, 12)$

(b) 5

2. (a) $(4, -1)$

(b) $\sqrt{8} = 2\sqrt{2}$

3. $(0, 2)$

4. *A* inside, *B* on the circle, *C* outside, *D* outside, *E* inside

5. $(2, 2)$, $(-2, 2)$, $(2, -2)$, $(-2, -2)$

6. $(7, 7)$, 7

7. $(6, 6)$, $(6, -6)$, $(-6, -2)$, $(-2, 2)$

8. $(40, 30)$, $(85, 15)$, $(55, 35)$

9. (a) 2, 2, 1
   (b) (2, 4), (14, 4), (8, 9)

10. (a) 10
    (b) 3

11. 1

14. $\sqrt{8} = 2\sqrt{2}$

15. $\sqrt{5}$

## Exercise 3.7     page 35

1. (a) 6
   (b) −1

2. (−2, 14), (−3, 29)

3. −4

4. (5, 1)

5. 10

6. (a) $\sqrt{85}$
   (b) $\left(-\frac{1}{2}, 2\right)$

7. (a) 10
   (b) $y = -2$
   (c) $x = 2$

8. (a) −6
   (b) −16
   (c) $x = -3, y = -7$

9. 31.5

10. 2

11. (4, 11), 2

12. (a) (−4, −1)
    (b) $x = -2, y = 3$
    (c) (−3, 1), $\sqrt{5}$

13. 5

14. (5, −22), 26

## Exercise 4.1a     page 37

1. (a) $\angle R = 51.3°$
   (b) $\angle C = 65.4°$
   (c) $\angle N = 40.8°$
   (d) $\angle Z = 46.2°$

(e) $\angle G = 50.9°$
(f) $\angle W = 55.6°$

2. (a) $BC = 7.71$ m
   (b) $JL = 4230$ m
   (c) $XZ = 5.70$ cm
   (d) $TU = 1.09$ cm
   (e) $PR = 34.6$ m
   (f) $MO = 10.0$ cm

3. (a) $RT = 3.40$ cm
   (b) $VW = 12.1$ cm
   (c) $AB = 4.44$ mm
   (d) $TV = 11.8$ m
   (e) $IK = 10.4$ cm
   (f) $EF = 1.45$ cm

4. (a) 31.5
   (b) 1.70
   (c) 2.80
   (d) 25.8
   (e) 30.5
   (f) 5.85

5. 18.4°

6. 1.42 cm

7. (a) 25.5 cm
   (b) 49.1°
   (c) 12.7 cm
   (d) 12.6 cm

8. $2d(\sin x° + \cos x°)$ cm

9. (a) $y \tan \alpha°$
   (b) $D \sin \beta°$
   (c) $\dfrac{k}{\cos \theta°}$
   (d) $\dfrac{T}{\tan \gamma°}$
   (e) $5 \sin \phi°$
   (f) $\dfrac{10}{\cos \psi°}$

10. (a) $X = F \cos 35°$,
         $Y = F \sin 35°$
    (b) $X = F \sin 56°$,
         $Y = F \cos 56°$

(c) $X = F \sin 67°$,
     $Y = F \cos 67°$
(d) $X = F \cos 19°$,
     $Y = F \sin 19°$

## Exercise 4.1b     page 42

1. 49.2°

2. 6.49 cm

3. 89 cm

4. 10.6 cm

5. $\left(\dfrac{\ell}{\sin \frac{1}{2}\theta°} + \ell\right)$ mm

## Exercise 4.2     page 43

1. (a) $BC = 3.88$ cm
   (b) $AB = 17.2$ mm
   (c) $AC = 627$ cm
   (d) $KL = 3.86$ m
   (e) $XZ = 27.6$ m
   (f) $DE = 6.20$ cm

2. (a) $\angle A = 84.2°$
   (b) $\angle C = 54.5°$
   (c) $\angle C = 49.2°$
   (d) $\angle M = 64.2°$
   (e) $\angle Y = 37.4°$
   (f) $\angle G = 72.8°$

4. 13.1

## Exercise 4.3     page 45

1. (a) $BC = 3.36$ cm
   (b) $BC = 1.99$ m
   (c) $BC = 26.7$ m
   (d) $PQ = 4.90$ cm
   (e) $LM = 268$ km
   (f) $XZ = 3.91$ cm

2. (a) $\angle A = 58.4°$
   (b) $\angle A = 32.7°$
   (c) $\angle A = 119°$
   (d) $\angle T = 90°$

(e) $\angle E = 136°$

(f) $\angle X = 60.9°$

**3.** $50°$

**4.** $20.5\,\text{cm}, 12.6\,\text{cm}$

**5.** $42.2°$

---

**Exercise 4.4**     *page 48*

**1.** (a) $23.6\,\text{cm}^2$

(b) $7.30\,\text{m}^2$

(c) $375\,\text{m}^2$

(d) $50.9\,\text{cm}^2$

(e) $40\,700\,\text{km}^2$

(f) $10.2\,\text{cm}^2$

**2.** $12.3\,\text{cm}^2$

**3.** $62.4\,\text{cm}^2$

**4.** $10.1\,\text{cm}^2$

**5.** $665\,\text{cm}^2$

**6.** $12.4\,\text{m}^2$

**7.** $1.53\,\text{cm}$

**8.** $15.9\,\text{m}$

**9.** $21.1°$

**10.** $52.3°$

**11.** $8$

**12.** $2$

**13.** $5$

---

**Exercise 4.5**     *page 51*

**1.** (a) $2.58\,\text{cm}$

(b) $57.1°$

(c) $71.2\,\text{m}$

(d) $52.8°$

(e) $54.3°$

(f) $6.36\,\text{cm}$

**2.** (a) $23.4\,\text{cm}^2$

(b) $23.4\,\text{cm}^2$

**3.** (a) $17.6\,\text{m}$

(b) $1.62\,\text{cm}$

(c) $67.1°$

(d) $4.25\,\text{cm}$

(e) $117°$

(f) $37.2°$

**4.** $32.4\,\text{cm}^2$

**5.** $12.9$

**6.** $12.2$

**7.** $1.86$

**8.** $5.81\,\text{m}$

**11.** $2.40$

---

**Exercise 5.1**     *page 54*

**1.** (a) $\frac{5}{2}$

(b) $\frac{1}{4}$

(c) $6$

(d) $2$

(e) $\frac{3}{2}$

(f) $\frac{1}{3}$

**2.** (a) $-1$

(b) $-3$

(c) $-\frac{1}{6}$

(d) $-\frac{1}{2}$

(e) $-\frac{5}{2}$

(f) $-2$

**3.** (a) $3$

(b) $-1$

(c) $\frac{7}{2}$

(d) $\frac{1}{5}$

(e) $-\frac{2}{3}$

(f) $3$

(g) $-\frac{1}{4}$

(h) $-1$

**4.** (a)

(b)

(c)

(d)

(e)

(f)

**5.** (a) $3$

(b) $5$

(c) $-2$

(d) $\frac{1}{3}$

(e) $-\frac{3}{5}$

(f) $0$

**6.** (a) $1$

(b) $\frac{1}{3}$

(c) $\frac{11}{2}$

(d) $-\frac{1}{2}$

(e) $3$

(f) $-2$

**7.** (a) $-8$

(b) $5$

(c) $-10$

(d) $-2$

Answers

**Exercise 5.2a**    *page 57*

1. (a) $y = x + 4$
   (b) $y = 4x$
   (c) $y = x - 3$
   (d) $x + y = 7$

2. (a)
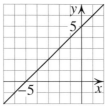

   (b)
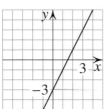

   (c)
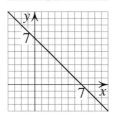

3. (a) $y = x + 4$
   (b) $y = 2x$
   (c) $y = -x$
   (d) $y = 6 - 2x$

4. 14

5. 14

6. $-3$

7. 2

8. 16

9. $\frac{3}{2}$

**Exercise 5.2b**    *page 58*

1. (a) $y = 2x + 1$
   (b) $y = -3x + 2$
   (c) $y = 4x - 3$
   (d) $y = -x + 3$

(e) $y = -\frac{1}{2}x + 6$
(f) $y = x - 5$

2. (a) $y = 20x + 10$
   (b) $y = -5x + 25$
   (c) $y = 2x + 300$
   (d) $y = -2x - 30$

3. (a) $P = -Q + 7$
   (b) $s = 3t + 12$
   (c) $v = \frac{1}{5}u - 2$
   (d) $R = -4Z - 16$

4. (a)
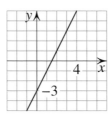

   (b)
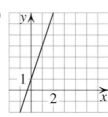

   (c)
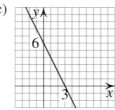

   (d)
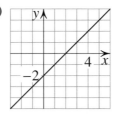

   (e)
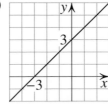

(f)
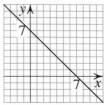

5. (a) $y = -2x + 4$
   (b) $2y = x$
   (c) $y = 10 - 3x$
   (d) $2y + 5x + 12 = 0$

6. (a) $y = 2x + 4$
   (b) $y = -x + 2$
   (c) $y = 3x - 2$
   (d) $y = -2x + 7$
   (e) $3y = 2x + 18$
   (f) $x + 2y = 8$

7. (a) $y = x + 3$
   (b) $y = 2x - 9$
   (c) $2y = x + 6$
   (d) $y = -4x + 3$
   (e) $x + 5y = 0$
   (f) $3y = 2x + 3$
   (g) $4x + 3y = 0$

**Exercise 5.2c**    *page 61*

1. (a) $(-2, 0)$ and $(0, 4)$
   (b) $(4, 0)$ and $(0, 12)$
   (c) $\left(\frac{10}{3}, 0\right)$ and $(0, -10)$
   (d) $(5, 0)$ and $(0, 5)$
   (e) $(10, 0)$ and $(0, 6)$
   (f) $(4, 0)$ and $(0, -1)$
   (g) $\left(\frac{5}{2}, 0\right)$ and $\left(0, -\frac{5}{3}\right)$
   (h) $(-15, 0)$ and $(0, -5)$
   (i) $\left(\frac{3}{2}, 0\right)$ and $(0, -9)$

2. (a)
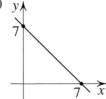

(b)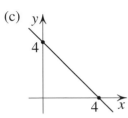

(c)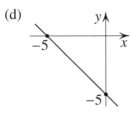

(d)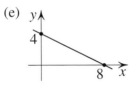

(e)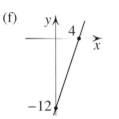

(f)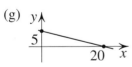

(g)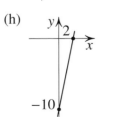

(h)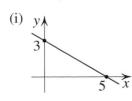

(i)

(j)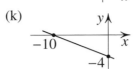

(k)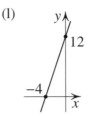

(l)

3. (a) 3, −4

(b) −2, 7

(c) −1, 10

(d) 2, $\frac{1}{4}$

(e) $\frac{1}{3}$, −2

(f) $-\frac{5}{2}$, 0

(g) $-\frac{1}{2}$, 5

(h) 1, −3

(i) $\frac{5}{4}$, $-\frac{7}{4}$

(j) $\frac{3}{4}$, −3

(k) $\frac{2}{3}$, 0

(l) $-\frac{1}{2}$, $-\frac{3}{2}$

4. (a) $3y = 2x + 15$

(b) $9y = 9x + 1$

(c) $2x + 5y = 30$

(d) $x + 2y + 8 = 0$

(e) $15y + 5 = 12x$

(f) $4 + 12y = 3x$

5. (a) $x - y - 4 = 0$

(b) $x - 2y + 5 = 0$

(c) $3x + 4y - 6 = 0$

(d) $2x - 3y - 3 = 0$

(e) $3x + 5y - 10 = 0$

(f) $5x - 6y = 0$

---

**Exercise 5.3**    *page 62*

1. (a)  True

(b)  False

(c)  True

2. (a)  True

(b)  False

(c)  False

(d)  True

3. (a) $y = 4x + 1$

(b) $y = 2x - 2$

(c) $x + y = 3$

(d) $3x + 2y + 12 = 0$

(e) $y = 6x$

4. (a) $y = x + 7$

(b) $y = x - 10$

5. (a) $x + 2y + 6 = 0$

(b) $x + 2y = 10$

6. −4

7. −2

8. $y = 2x - 8$

9. (a) $8y = 5x + 16$

(b) $8y = 5x - 24$

10. $x + y + 5 = 0$

11. $2x + 5y = 13$

12. $5x + y + 3 = 0$,
    $x + 2y = 3$

13. (a) $x + 3y = 9$

(b) $x + 3y + 6 = 0$

---

**Exercise 5.4**    *page 65*

1. (a) $-\frac{3}{4}$

(b) $\frac{6}{5}$

(c) −5

(d) 4

(e) $\frac{1}{7}$

(f) $-\frac{1}{6}$

(g) 1

(h) −1

2. (a)  True

(b)  True

(c) False

(d) True

**3.** (a) False

(b) False

(c) False

(d) True

**4.** 1

**5.** $x + 2y = 10$

**6.** $y = x - 6$

**7.** $x + 3y = 13$

**8.** (a) $3y = 4x + 12$

(b) $3x + 4y = 16$

**9.** (a) $x + 2y + 6 = 0$

(b) $y = 2x - 3$

**10.** 1

**11.** $\frac{8}{3}$

**12.** $-58$

**13.** 8

**14.** $4x + 6y = 9$

**15.** $y = 3x + 2$

**16.** (a) $3x + 4y = 9$

(b) $3x + 4y + 16 = 0$

**17.** (a) $x + 4y = 51$

(b) $y = 4x - 17$

(c) $x + 4y = 17$

**18.** (a) $x + 2y = 8$

(b) $3y = x + 12$

(c) $3x + y = 54$

---

## Exercise 5.5 *page 68*

**1.** $(5, 11)$

**2.** $(-2, 9)$

**3.** $(5, 3)$

**4.** $(4, 3)$

**5.** $(-2, -4)$

**6.** $(-5, -1)$

**7.** $(7, -2)$

**8.** $(-4, 2)$

**9.** $(4, 0)$

**10.** (a) $x = 4$

(b) $y = -3$

(c) $(4, 9), (-2, -3)$

**11.** (a) $y = 2x + 5$

(b) $y = -3x + 15$

(c) $(2, 9)$

**12.** $(-1, 2), (5, 2), (3, 8)$

**13.** (a) $(6, 11)$

(b) $4x + y = 5$

(c) $(1, 1)$

(d) $y = 2x + 5$

(e) $(5, 15)$

---

## Exercise 5.6 *page 71*

**1.** $p = -13$

**2.** 2

**3.** $k = -\frac{1}{2}$

**4.** (a) $2y = 3x + 8$

(b) $2y + x + 4 = 0$

**5.** (a) $2x + y = 2$

(b) $y = -3$

(c) $y = 3x + 11$

(d) $y = 2$

(e) $3x + 2y = 0$

(f) $y = -4$

(g) $x = -2$

**6.** $-\frac{3}{2}$

**7.** $k = \frac{12}{5}$

**8.** $(-1, -7)$

**9.** (a) $x = -3, y = 8$

(b) $y = -2x + 2; y = 2x$

**10.** (a) $x = 6$

(b) $6y = x + 42$

(c) $3x + 2y = 14$

(d) $\sqrt{117} = 3\sqrt{13}$

**11.** (a) $y = 3$

(b) $y = x + 6$

(c) $x + y + 4 = 0$

(d) $(-3, -1)$

(e) $(-1, 1)$

**12.** (a) $y = -2x + 7$

(b) $(3, 1)$

(c) $\sqrt{45} = 3\sqrt{5}$

**13.** $y = x + 2$

---

## Exercise 6.1a *page 73*

**1.** (a) $-7$ or $-2$

(b) $-8$ or $-1$

(c) 3 or 7

(d) 5 (twice)

(e) $-7$ or 2

(f) $-6$ or 5

(g) $-1$ or 9

(h) 2 or 13

(i) $-8$ or 7

(j) $-5$ or 4

(k) $-3$ or 9

(l) 5 or 6

**2.** (a) $-3$ or 4

(b) $-10$ or $-5$

(c) $-6$ or $-2$

(d) $-12$ or 2

(e) $-12$ or $-6$

(f) $-9$ or 11

**3.** (a) $-9$ or 0

(b) 0 or 8

(c) 0 or 10

(d) 0 or 1

(e) $-5$ or 0

(f) $-0.2$ or 0

**4.** (a) $-2$ or 2

(b) $-4$ or 4

(c) $-9$ or 9

(d) 0 (twice)

(e) −12 or 12

(f) −7 or 7

5. (a) 0 or $\frac{1}{3}$

(b) 0 or $\frac{3}{2}$

(c) 0 or $\frac{5}{2}$

(d) 0 or 5

(e) −1 or 10

(f) −3 or −2

6. (a) −1 or 1

(b) $-\frac{1}{5}$ or $\frac{1}{5}$

(c) −2 or 2

7. (a) $-\frac{3}{2}$ or $\frac{3}{2}$

(b) $-\frac{11}{10}$ or $\frac{11}{10}$

(c) $-\frac{7}{8}$ or $\frac{7}{8}$

(d) $-\frac{12}{5}$ or $\frac{12}{5}$

(e) $-\frac{9}{10}$ or $\frac{9}{10}$

8. (a) −7 or 1

(b) −1 or 11

(c) −1 or 5

(d) −6 or −2

(e) 1 or 5

(f) −3 or −2

(g) −1 or 4

(h) −4 or 0

## Exercise 6.1b    *page 74*

1. (a) $\frac{1}{2}$ or 1

(b) $\frac{1}{5}$ or 1

(c) $-\frac{1}{2}$ (twice)

(d) $-\frac{1}{2}$ or 1

(e) $-\frac{1}{2}$ or $\frac{1}{7}$

(f) $-\frac{1}{5}$ or $-\frac{1}{2}$

(g) $-\frac{1}{4}$ or $\frac{1}{6}$

(h) $-\frac{1}{5}$ or $-\frac{1}{6}$

(i) $-\frac{1}{4}$ or $\frac{1}{3}$

2. (a) $\frac{1}{7}$ or $\frac{1}{3}$

(b) −1 or $\frac{1}{3}$

(c) $-\frac{1}{6}$ or $\frac{1}{2}$

(d) $-\frac{1}{5}$ or $\frac{1}{12}$

(e) $-\frac{1}{2}$ or $-\frac{1}{3}$

(f) $\frac{1}{4}$ or $\frac{1}{3}$

3. (a) $\frac{1}{2}$ or 3

(b) −1 or $-\frac{2}{3}$

(c) $-\frac{7}{3}$ or 1

(d) $-\frac{1}{5}$ or 7

(e) $\frac{1}{7}$ or 5

(f) $-\frac{5}{3}$ or 1

(g) $\frac{3}{2}$ or 5

(h) −7 or $\frac{2}{3}$

(i) $-\frac{7}{3}$ or 9

(j) $-\frac{3}{2}$ or 3

(k) $-\frac{5}{2}$ or $\frac{2}{3}$

(l) $-\frac{4}{3}$ or $\frac{7}{2}$

4. (a) $\frac{1}{5}$ or 2

(b) $-\frac{11}{2}$ or 1

(c) −5 or $-\frac{1}{2}$

(d) $\frac{1}{4}$ or $\frac{2}{3}$

(e) $-\frac{5}{2}$ or 1

(f) $-\frac{1}{4}$ or $\frac{7}{2}$

(g) $-\frac{3}{5}$ or 4

(h) $-\frac{3}{5}$ (twice)

(i) $-\frac{5}{2}$ or $-\frac{2}{5}$

(j) −4 or $\frac{2}{3}$

(k) $-\frac{5}{2}$ or $\frac{4}{3}$

(l) $-\frac{4}{7}$ (twice)

5. (a) $-\frac{1}{3}$ or $\frac{1}{5}$

(b) $-\frac{1}{2}$ or $-\frac{1}{5}$

(c) $-\frac{2}{3}$ or $\frac{1}{7}$

(d) $\frac{1}{2}$ or 2

(e) −1 or $\frac{1}{4}$

(f) −4 or 1

6. (a) −1 or $\frac{1}{2}$

(b) 0.1 or 0.3

(c) $-\frac{7}{9}$ or $\frac{7}{9}$

(d) −0.5 or 0.5

(e) −0.4 or 0.2

(f) 0 or 0.72

(g) $-\frac{1}{3}$ or $\frac{1}{6}$

(h) −0.45 or 0

(i) −1.1 or 2

(j) −5 or −0.3

(k) $-\frac{3}{2}$ or $\frac{1}{2}$

(l) $-\frac{5}{3}$ or $\frac{5}{6}$

7. (a) −0.1 or −0.1

(b) −0.7 or 0.8

(c) −3 or −0.5

## Exercise 6.2    *page 76*

1. (a) −3.41 or 0.59

(b) 0.70 or 4.30

(c) −1.59 or 1.39

(d) −4.39 or −0.11

(e) −0.54 or −0.19

(f) −2.08 or −0.21

(g) −0.59 or 3.42

(h) −0.88 or 0.66

2. (a) −0.53 or 0.72

(b) −1.70 or 1.37

(c) −16.73 or −0.27

(d) −0.94 or 1.60

3. (a) −0.29 or 2.54

(b) −0.78 or 1.78

(c) −1.77 or −0.57

(d) −4.05 or 1.51

## Exercise 6.3a    *page 77*

1. (a) −5 or 1

(b) −6 or 14

(c) −10 or 0

(d) $-\frac{15}{2}$ or $\frac{3}{2}$

(e) $\frac{1}{3}$ or $\frac{5}{3}$

(f) $-\frac{7}{4}$ or $-\frac{1}{4}$

(g) −2 or −1

(h) −1 or $\frac{1}{5}$

(i) $-\frac{3}{4}$ or $\frac{1}{12}$

**2.** (a) $-3 \pm \sqrt{5}$

(b) $1 \pm \sqrt{2}$

(c) $7 \pm \sqrt{5}$

(d) $-2 \pm \sqrt{6}$

(e) $\dfrac{1 \pm \sqrt{3}}{2}$

(f) $\dfrac{5 \pm \sqrt{7}}{2}$

---

## Exercise 6.3b    *page 77*

**1.** (a) $\cos x = 0$ or $-1$

(b) $\sin x = -\frac{1}{2}$ or $\frac{1}{2}$

(c) $\cos t = 0$ or $\frac{2}{5}$

(d) $\sin t = -1$ or $\frac{1}{6}$

**2.** (a) $t = \pm 1$ or $\pm 3$

(b) $k = -2$ or $1$

(c) $y = -5$ or $11$

(d) $A = 25$ or $36$

(e) $a = 1$ or $64$

---

## Exercise 6.4    *page 78*

**1.** (a) $x = -2, y = -2$ or
$x = 4, y = 10$

(b) $x = 1, y = 6$

(c) $x = -1, y = -1$ or
$x = 1, y = 1$

(d) $x = -2, y = 2$ or
$x = 2, y = -2$

(e) $x = \frac{1}{3}, y = 3$ or
$x = 1, y = 1$

(f) $x = -6, y = -2$ or
$x = 2, y = 6$

**2.** (a) $x = -3, y = -1$ or
$x = 1, y = 3$

(b) $x = \frac{1}{3}, y = 2$

(c) $a = -\frac{5}{2}, b = \frac{7}{2}$ or
$a = 3, b = -2$

(d) $\alpha = 1, \beta = 4$ or
$\alpha = -2, \beta = -2$

(e) $x = 2, y = -3$

(f) $x = -3, y = 1$ or
$x = \frac{1}{2}, y = -\frac{3}{4}$

**3.** (a) $x = -2, y = -1$ or
$x = -1, y = 0$

(b) $x = 1, y = 3$ or
$x = -4, y = -12$

(c) $x = -1, y = 3.5$ or
$x = -2, y = 5$

(d) $f = 1, g = 4$ or
$f = 4, g = 16$

(e) $p = 0, q = -0.2$ or
$p = 4, q = 3$

(f) $v = \frac{2}{3}, w = \frac{1}{3}$ or
$v = 2, w = 1$

---

## Exercise 6.5    *page 79*

**1.** (a) $-\frac{15}{7}$ or $\frac{15}{7}$

(b) $0$ or $\frac{7}{6}$

(c) $-8$ (twice)

(d) $-8$ or $2$

(e) $-6$ or $7$

(f) $-2.35$ or $1.49$

(g) $-5$ or $1$

(h) $-0.65$ or $4.65$

(i) $-1.15$ or $0.48$

(j) $-\frac{5}{3}$ or $\frac{1}{2}$

(k) $\frac{1}{3}$ or $1$

(l) $-0.36$ or $0.79$

(m) $-\frac{13}{15}$ or $\frac{13}{15}$

(n) $-\frac{1}{7}$ or $\frac{1}{5}$

(o) $-\frac{1}{2}$ or $\frac{10}{17}$

(p) $-1.5$ or $4$

(q) $-2$ or $1$

**2.** (a) $x = -4, y = -2$ or
$x = 4, y = 2$

(b) $x = -\frac{3}{2}, y = -\frac{1}{2}$ or
$x = 1, y = 2$

(c) $x = -1, y = -5$ or
$x = 4, y = 0$

(d) $x = -3, y = 2$ or
$x = 3, y = -4$

---

## Exercise 7.1a    *page 80*

**1.** (a)
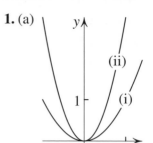

(b)
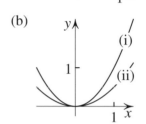

(c)
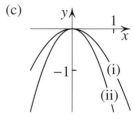

(d)
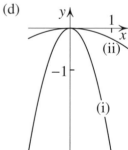

**2.** (a)
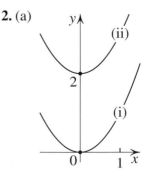

(b)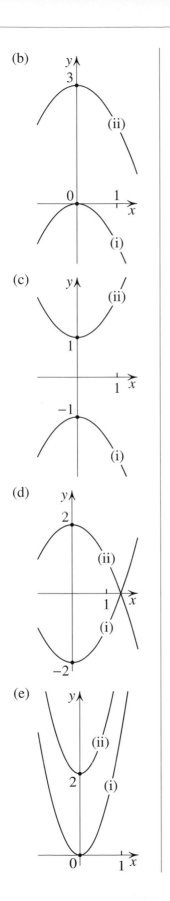

(c)

(d)

(e)

(f)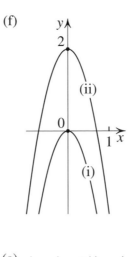

3. (a)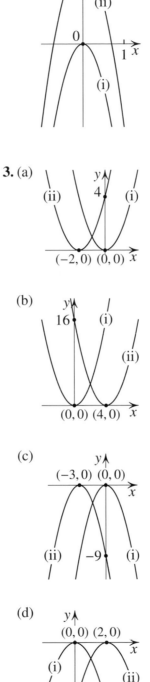

(b)

(c)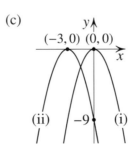

(d)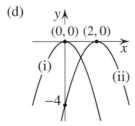

(e)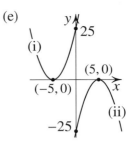

(f)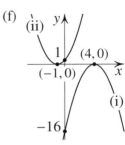

(g)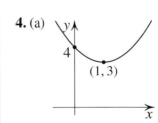

4. (a)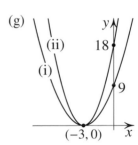

(b)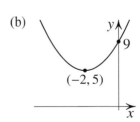

(c)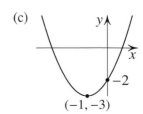

(d)

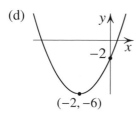

(e)

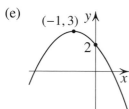

(f)

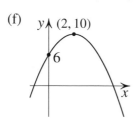

(g)

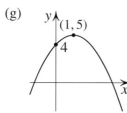

(h)

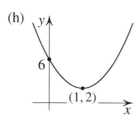

(i)

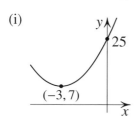

(j)

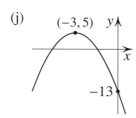

(k)

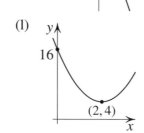

(l)

5. (a) $(3, -4)$
   (b) $(0, 5)$
   (c) $(6, 5)$

6. (a) $(2, 12)$
   (b) $(0, 8)$
   (c) $(4, 8)$

7. (a) $(-4, 2)$
   (b) $(0, 18)$
   (c) $(-8, 18)$

8. (a) $(1, 7)$
   (b) $-2$
   (c) $(-2, -2)$

9. (a) $(3, 8)$
   (b) $(-3, 8)$
   (c) $y = 8 - (x + 3)^2$

10. (a) $(4, 2)$
    (b) $y = 2 - (x - 4)^2$

11. (a) $(0, 3)$
    (b) $y = 7 - (x - 2)^2$

12. (a) $8$
    (b) $y = (x + 15)^2 - 17$,
        $y = (x + 5)^2 - 17$

---

**Exercise 7.1b** *page 83*

1. (a) $y = 3x^2$
   (b) $y = 6x^2$
   (c) $y = 4x^2$

(d) $y = -5x^2$
(e) $y = -6x^2$
(f) $y = 7x^2$
(g) $y = 8x^2$
(h) $y = -2x^2$
(i) $y = 4x^2$
(j) $y = -3x^2$
(k) $y = \frac{3}{2}x^2$
(l) $y = -\frac{4}{3}x^2$

2. (a) $y = 8x^2 + 3$
   (b) $y = 7x^2 - 1$
   (c) $y = -2x^2 + 4$
   (d) $y = x^2 - 3$
   (e) $y = 2x^2 + 5$
   (f) $y = -3x^2 + 4$
   (g) $y = 5x^2 + 8$
   (h) $y = x^2 + 2$
   (i) $y = -4x^2 - 50$
   (j) $y = -x^2 + 6$
   (k) $y = \frac{5}{2}x^2 - 4$
   (l) $y = -\frac{4}{3}x^2 + 11$

---

**Exercise 7.2a** *page 85*

1. (a) $(-2, 0), (4, 0)$
   (b) $(0, -8)$
   (c) $(1, -9)$

2. (a) $(2, 0), (6, 0)$
   (b) $(0, 12)$
   (c) $(4, -4)$

3. (a) $0$ and $-6$
   (b) $(-3, -9)$

4. (a) $4$ and $-8$
   (b) $(-2, 36)$

5. (a) $0$ and $8$
   (b) $(4, 16)$

6. (a) $(-5, 0), (-1, 0)$
   (b) $(0, 5)$
   (c) $(-3, -4)$

7. $(5, -25)$

**8.** (a) $(-8, 0)$, $(4, 0)$

(b) $(-2, 36)$

**9.** (a)

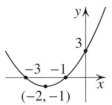

(b)

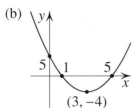

(c)

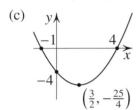

(d)

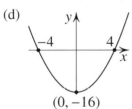

(e)

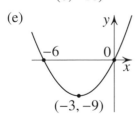

(f)

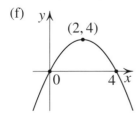

(g)

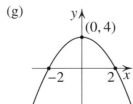

(h)

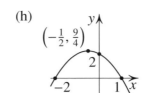

(i)

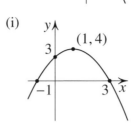

**10.** (a)

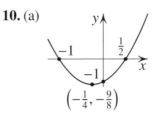

(b)

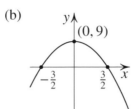

(c)

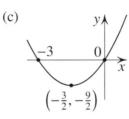

(d)

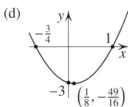

(e)

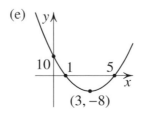

(f)

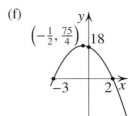

**11.** (a)

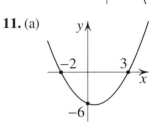

(b) 6

(c) $-4$ or $5$

**12.** (a)

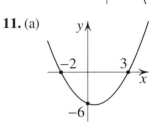

(b) 63

(c) $-4$ or $2$

**13.** (a)

(b) $-9$

(c) $-1$ or $3$

**Exercise 7.2b**     *page 87*

**1.** (a) $y = (x - 3)(x - 6)$

(b) $y = (x + 2)(x - 7)$

(c) $y = (x + 4)(x + 10)$

(d) $y = (x - 1)(x + 8)$

(e) $y = x(x - 4)$

(f) $y = x(x + 5)$

(g) $y = (x - 3)^2$

(h) $y = (x + 6)^2$

**2.** (a) $y = -(x - 1)(x - 4)$

(b) $y = -(x + 3)(x - 5)$

(c) $y = -(x + 1)(x + 7)$

(d) $y = -(x - 2)(x + 4)$

(e) $y = -x(x - 6)$

(f) $y = -x(x + 3)$

(g) $y = -(x + 1)^2$

(h) $y = -(x - 8)^2$

3. (a) $y = 3(x - 1)(x - 4)$

(b) $y = -3(x + 2)(x - 5)$

(c) $y = -\frac{1}{3}(x + 6)^2$

(d) $y = \frac{1}{2}(x - 2)(x - 4)$

(e) $y = x(x - 5)$

(f) $y = -(x + 3)(x - 2)$

(g) $y = -2(x + 2)(x + 3)$

(h) $y = 4(x + 5)(x - 6)$

## Exercise 7.3        *page 89*

1. (a) $(-3, 0), (-2, 0),$
        $(1, 0)$

   (b) $(0, -6)$

2. (a) $x(1 + x)(2 - x)$

   (b) $(-1, 0), (0, 0), (2, 0)$

3. (a) $(2, 0)$

   (b) $(0, 6)$

4. (a)
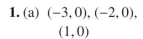

   (b)
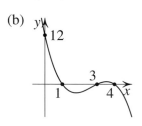

(c)
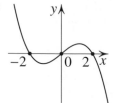

(d)
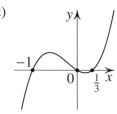

(e)
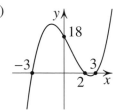

(f)
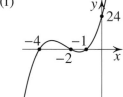

## Exercise 7.4        *page 90*

1. $(-4, 8), (4, 8)$

2.
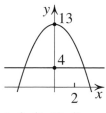

   $(-3, 4), (3, 4)$

3. (a) $y = 8$

   (b) $(-1, 8), (5, 8)$

4. (a) $y = 3$

   (b) $(0, 3), (2, 3)$

5. (a) $y = -4$

   (b) $(-3, -4)$

6. $(-3, 14), (5, 6)$

7. $(-2, -7), (5, 0)$

8. $\left(-\frac{1}{2}, \frac{1}{2}\right), (1, 2)$

9. $(1, -3)$

10. $(3, 12), (5, 20)$

11. $(-1, -2), (8, 25)$

12.
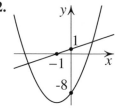

   $(-3, -2), \left(\frac{3}{2}, \frac{5}{2}\right)$

13. (a) $y = (x - 2)(x - 3)$

   (b) $y = -2x + 10$

   (c) $(-1, 12), (4, 2)$

14. (a) $y = (x - 3)^2 + 1$

   (b) $y = x$

   (c) $(2, 2), (5, 5)$

15. $(3, 9)$ (twice), the line
    is a tangent to the
    curve

## Exercise 7.5        *page 93*

1. $(-2, 4), (2, 4)$

2.
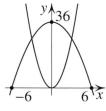

   $(-3, 27), (3, 27)$

3. $(-5, -25), (5, -25)$

4. $(0, 0), (2, 4)$

5. $(-2, 8), (2, 8)$

6. $(0, 0), (4, -16)$

**7.**

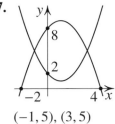

$(-1, 5), (3, 5)$

**8.** $(3, 3), (5, 3)$

**9.** $(-1, 5), (2, 8)$

**10.** $(1, 0), (4, 3)$

**11.** $(0, 3), (5, -2)$

**12.** $(1, 9), (4, 0)$

---

**Exercise 7.6** *page 95*

**1.** (a) $(-5, 0), (5, 0)$

   (b) $(0, -5), (0, 5)$

   (c) $(-3, 4), (3, 4)$

**2.** $(-5, -12), (-5, 12)$

**3.** (a) $(-6, 0), (6, 0)$

   (b) $(0, -9), (0, 9)$

**4.** $\left(-4, -\frac{9}{5}\right), \left(-4, \frac{9}{5}\right)$

**5.** $(16, -4), (16, 4)$

**6.** $\left(\frac{1}{4}, 8\right)$

**7.** $\left(-3, \frac{1}{9}\right), \left(3, \frac{1}{9}\right)$

**8.** $(-12, -9), (9, 12)$

**9.** $(3, 1)$

**10.** $(9, -3), (16, 4)$

**11.** $(-5, 3), (0, 3), (2, 3)$

**12.** $(-2, -4), (0, -4),$
   $(2, -4)$

**13.** $(-2, -2), (2, 2)$

**14.** $\left(-\frac{3}{5}, \frac{8}{5}\right), (1, 0)$

**15.** $(9, -3), (16, 4)$

**16.** $(-2, -2), (0, 2), (5, 12)$

**17.** $(-1, 7), (0, 5), (1, 3)$

---

**Exercise 7.7** *page 99*

**1.**

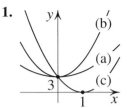

**2.** (a)

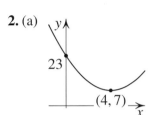

   (b)

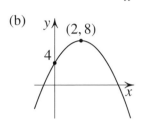

**3.** (a) $a = 3, b = -12$

   (b) $(0, -3)$

   (c) $(-6, -3)$

**4.** (a) $y = (x - 1)(x + 2)$

   (b) $y = \frac{1}{4}x^2$

   (c) $y = 6 - (x - 2)^2$

   (d) $y = -3(x - 2)(x + 6)$

   (e) $y = -2(x + 3)^2$

   (f) $y = 3 - 4x^2$

**5.** $(-2, -9)$

**6.** (a) $(-3, 0), (2, 0)$

   (b) $(0, 6)$

   (c) $\left(-\frac{1}{2}, \frac{25}{4}\right)$

**7.** (a) $y = (x - 3)^2$

   (b) $(0, 9)$

   (c) $y = 9 - 2x$

   (d) $(4, 1)$

**8.** $(-5, -6), (2, 8)$

**9.**

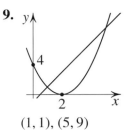

$(1, 1), (5, 9)$

**10.**

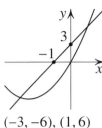

$(-3, -6), (1, 6)$

**11.** $(0, 2), (5, -3)$

**12.** $(-3, -5), (3, -5)$

**13.** $(4, 10), (1, 7)$

**14.** $\left(2, \frac{1}{2}\right), \left(-2, -\frac{1}{2}\right)$

**15.** $(2, 4), (-2, 4)$

**16.** (a) $y^2 = 4x$

   (b) $(9, 6)$

---

**Exercise 8.1a** *page 102*

**1.** (a) $64$

   (b) $32$

   (c) $243$

   (d) $1$

   (e) $1.331$

   (f) $\frac{1}{128}$

   (g) $\frac{1}{81}$

   (h) $\frac{1}{216}$

**2.** (a) $\frac{1}{8}$

   (b) $\frac{1}{16}$

   (c) $\frac{1}{5}$

   (d) $-32$

   (e) $10$

   (f) $1$

   (g) $9$

   (h) $625$

**3.** (a) $-\frac{8}{125}$

(b) $\frac{4}{3}$

(c) $0.216$

(d) $625$

**4.** (a) $2$

(b) $-5$

(c) $20$

(d) $0.8$

(e) $16$

(f) $27$

(g) $125$

(h) $8$

**5.** (a) $\frac{1}{2}$

(b) $\frac{1}{3}$

(c) $\frac{1}{10}$

(d) $\frac{1}{5}$

(e) $\frac{1}{8}$

(f) $\frac{1}{25}$

(g) $\frac{1}{4}$

(h) $\frac{1}{400}$

**6.** (a) $\frac{4}{9}$

(b) $\frac{8}{7}$

(c) $0.6$

(d) $0.343$

(e) $\frac{125}{216}$

(f) $20$

(g) $2500$

(h) $\frac{10}{13}$

**7.** (a) $13$

(b) $4$

(c) $\frac{1}{4}$

(d) $\frac{1}{25}$

(e) $1$

(f) $243$

(g) $12$

---

### Exercise 8.1b    *page 103*

**1.** (a) $5^7$

(b) $7^2$

(c) $1$

(d) $1.4^{-7}$

(e) $0.4^{-2}$

(f) $1$

**2.** (a) $6$

(b) $1.5^{12}$

(c) $5^3$

(d) $217^7$

(e) $0.9^{-3}$

(f) $4^8$

**3.** (a) $14^{10}$

(b) $0.3^{14}$

(c) $\left(\frac{1}{2}\right)^7$

**4.** (a) $2^6$

(b) $5^2$

(c) $3^{-6}$

(d) $0.1^4$

(e) $\left(\frac{2}{3}\right)^8$

(f) $1$

(g) $\left(\frac{3}{2}\right)^3$

(h) $5^2$

---

### Exercise 8.1c    *page 104*

**1.** (a) $v^9$

(b) $7y^6$

(c) $12m^8$

(d) $10t^{10}$

(e) $\frac{1}{2}\rho^6$

(f) $3\omega^4$

(g) $24$

(h) $2j^{\frac{3}{5}}$

(i) $150u^{\frac{5}{6}}$

**2.** (a) $\frac{1}{2}x^5$

(b) $4\alpha^4$

(c) $3p^{-1}$

---

(d) $\frac{3a^3}{b}$

(e) $\frac{9p^2q^4}{4}$

(f) $\frac{3y^2}{x}$

**3.** (a) $a^5$

(b) $\frac{1}{7}$

(c) $3\gamma^{-2}$

(d) $\frac{1}{8}r^{-1}$

(e) $100t^4$

(f) $\frac{9}{2}e^{-4}$

**4.** (a) $\frac{d}{c}$

(b) $\frac{d^2}{15p^3}$

(c) $\frac{b^5}{10a}$

**5.** (a) $a$

(b) $b$

(c) $3x$

(d) $1$

(e) $p^5$

(f) $\frac{1}{3}\sigma$

**6.** (a) $n^{30}$

(b) $c^4$

(c) $z^{-1}$

(d) $b^{-10}$

(e) $\tau^6$

(f) $d^{-4}$

(g) $1$

(h) $w^{-1}$

**7.** (a) $h^4j^{12}$

(b) $u^2v^{12}$

(c) $\frac{x^{10}}{y^{25}}$

(d) $\frac{125\alpha^9}{8\beta^3}$

**8.** (a) $\frac{b^6}{a^2}$

(b) $\dfrac{q^6}{p^9}$

(c) $\dfrac{3}{f^2 g^7}$

(d) $\dfrac{81 s^{16}}{16 r^2 t^{12}}$

**9.** (a) $\dfrac{t}{s^2}$

(b) $\dfrac{y^4}{z^6}$

(c) $\dfrac{h^6}{k^{15}}$

(d) $\dfrac{p^5}{q^{10}}$

(e) $\dfrac{7c^2}{2ab^5}$

(f) $\dfrac{27v^9}{1000\mu^6}$

**10.** (a) $\frac{2}{3}n^2$

(b) $2r$

(c) $3.2 f^3 g^{14}$

(d) $10a^{-3}$

---

**Exercise 8.1d**   *page 105*

**1.** (a) $x^{-2}$

(b) $2x^{-1}$

(c) $\frac{1}{3}x^{-2}$

(d) $\frac{2}{5}x^{-1}$

(e) $x^{\frac{1}{2}}$

(f) $x^{\frac{3}{2}}$

(g) $5x^{\frac{3}{2}}$

(h) $x^{\frac{3}{2}}$

(i) $\frac{1}{2}x^{-\frac{1}{2}}$

(j) $4x^{\frac{1}{3}}$

(k) $2x^{\frac{1}{3}}$

(l) $\frac{5}{3}x^{-\frac{2}{3}}$

**2.** (a) $d^6 - 2d^2$

(b) $4r^4 - 4r^5 + 20r^7$

(c) $3z^5 + 21z^7 - 6z^{10}$

(d) $2a^{\frac{3}{2}} + a^3$

(e) $2 + b$

(f) $5x^{\frac{3}{2}} - x^{\frac{7}{2}}$

(g) $u^{\frac{1}{2}} + 3u^2$

(h) $e^{\frac{1}{2}} + 1$

(i) $\rho^{-\frac{3}{2}} + 3\rho^{\frac{1}{2}}$

**3.** (a) $x^2 - 4x + 5$

(b) $3c - 1 + c^{-1}$

(c) $2z^{-3} + 3z^{-4}$

(d) $t^{-2} - 5t^{-1} + t$

(e) $4p - 20 + 25p^{-1}$

(f) $m^2 - 4 + 4m^{-2}$

(g) $y^{\frac{1}{2}} + 2y^{-\frac{1}{2}}$

(h) $\sigma^{\frac{1}{2}} + 3\sigma^{-\frac{1}{2}}$

(i) $2 + t^{\frac{5}{2}}$

**4.** (a) $d^2 - \frac{1}{2}$

(b) $1 - \frac{1}{5}r^3$

(c) $\frac{1}{2}h^2 + 2h$

(d) $x^5 - \frac{1}{3}x^3 + \frac{5}{3}x$

(e) $\frac{1}{3} - \frac{1}{3}c^{-2} - \frac{7}{3}c^{-3}$

(f) $\frac{5}{2}v - 3v^{-1} + \frac{1}{2}v^{-3}$

(g) $\frac{1}{2} + 4\alpha^{-1} + 8\alpha^{-2}$

(h) $\frac{4}{5}z - \frac{12}{5} + \frac{9}{5}z^{-1}$

(i) $\frac{1}{3}p^3 - \frac{4}{3}p + \frac{4}{3}p^{-1}$

---

**Exercise 8.2**   *page 107*

**1.** (a) $-5$

(b) 1 or 9

(c) 5

(d) $-\frac{3}{2}$ or 1

(e) 3

(f) $-1$

(g) 2

(h) $-\frac{5}{2}$ or 3

(i) $-2$ or 3

**2.** (a) $a = 4000, r = \frac{1}{2}$ or
   $a = -4000,$
   $r = -\frac{1}{2}$

(b) $a = 81, r = \frac{1}{3}$

(c) $a = 0.1, r = 10$

(d) $a = 14, r = 2$

(e) $a = 80, r = \frac{1}{10}$

(f) $a = \frac{1}{3}, r = 3$ or
   $a = -\frac{1}{3}, r = -3$

(g) $x = -32, y = -\frac{1}{2}$ or
   $x = 32, y = \frac{1}{2}$

(h) $\alpha = 7, \beta = 2$

**3.** (a) 4

(b) 7

(c) $\frac{1}{2}$

(d) $-2$

(e) 0

(f) 3

(g) $-1$

(h) $\frac{3}{2}$

(i) $\frac{3}{5}$

---

**Exercise 8.3a**   *page 108*

**1.** (a) $\dfrac{1}{2x^2}$

(b) $\dfrac{4}{p^8}$

(c) $4a^3$

(d) $\dfrac{3}{8t^7}$

(e) $\dfrac{3}{2b}$

(f) $\dfrac{3u^5}{2}$

(g) $3e^5$

(h) $\dfrac{1}{2\alpha}$

**2.** (a) $\frac{2}{3}(a + b)$

(b) $\dfrac{3}{x - 3}$

(c) $\dfrac{5}{3(x + 4t)^4}$

(d) $\dfrac{1}{4(8h + j)}$

**3.** (a) $-1$

---

(b) $-\frac{2}{5}$

(c) $-1$

(d) $-7$

(e) $-\frac{1}{2}$

(f) $-\frac{4}{5}$

## Exercise 8.3b    *page 108*

1. (a) $\dfrac{4x - 7}{5}$

(b) $\dfrac{3 + a + 2b^2}{5}$

(c) $\dfrac{t + 2s}{4}$

(d) $\dfrac{4}{3b - 2c + 5}$

(e) $\dfrac{9}{7 - 3y^2}$

(f) $\dfrac{10e + 7f}{3}$

2. (a) $\dfrac{w}{2w + 3x}$

(b) $\dfrac{2 - y}{4z}$

(c) $\dfrac{\pi r}{1 + \pi + r}$

(d) $\dfrac{3k^2}{k + 1 - l^2}$

(e) $\dfrac{5q + 1}{3}$

(f) $\dfrac{4r - 1}{7}$

3. (a) $x\left(1 + x^2\right)$

(b) $a^3\left(a^3 - 1\right)$

(c) $6 + 2y^2 + y^4$

(d) $x + 6$

(e) $\dfrac{3}{5 + 2k^4}$

(f) $\dfrac{2}{u\left(4 - u^4\right)}$

4. (a) $\dfrac{x + 2}{2x - 3}$

(b) $\dfrac{a + 2b + 3c}{4a - 5b}$

(c) $\dfrac{3 - 2k}{4k + 1}$

(d) $\dfrac{a + 1}{6 + b}$

(e) $\dfrac{1 + x}{1 + x^2 + x^4}$

(f) $\dfrac{a + 2a^2b + 3}{4a^2 - 7}$

5. (a) $x$

(b) $\dfrac{1}{v^2}$

(c) $\frac{1}{2}$

(d) $\frac{3}{5}$

(e) $s$

(f) $2$

(g) $\gamma$

(h) $\dfrac{1}{a}$

(i) $\dfrac{\alpha}{2}$

6. (a) $-2$

(b) $-\frac{3}{4}$

(c) $-\frac{4}{3}x$

(d) $-\frac{5}{2}$

(e) $-\dfrac{a}{7}$

7. (a) $\dfrac{x - 1}{2}$

(b) $\dfrac{2}{z - 2}$

(c) $\dfrac{x + 2}{4}$

(d) $\dfrac{g - 1}{5}$

(e) $\dfrac{5}{a + 5}$

(f) $\dfrac{h - 4}{6}$

(g) $\dfrac{3}{p + 4}$

(h) $\dfrac{2x + 1}{4}$

(i) $\frac{1}{4}b$

8. (a) $\dfrac{x - 1}{x + 2}$

(b) $\dfrac{a + 3}{a - 1}$

(c) $\dfrac{e - 1}{e + 2}$

(d) $\dfrac{\beta - 5}{\beta + 1}$

(e) $\dfrac{n + 4}{n + 5}$

(f) $\dfrac{m + 2}{m - 7}$

9. (a) $\dfrac{y + 2}{y + 3}$

(b) $\dfrac{5 - x}{x + 8}$

(c) $\dfrac{k + 2}{9 - k}$

(d) $\dfrac{3 - c}{c + 8}$

(e) $\dfrac{5 + h}{1 + h}$

(f) $\dfrac{z + 11}{z - 9}$

## Exercise 8.3c    *page 110*

1. (a) $\dfrac{15t^3}{4b^4}$

(b) $\dfrac{6k^6}{7m}$

(c) $\dfrac{2v^5}{3w^3}$

(d) $\dfrac{7p^5}{5q^2}$

(e) $\dfrac{8a^5}{9b^5}$

(f) $\dfrac{8y^3}{x^4}$

(g) $\dfrac{10k^4}{m^8}$

(h) $\dfrac{25a^2b^3c^2}{d^3}$

(i) $\dfrac{f^4}{g^9}$

2. (a) $\dfrac{p}{3q}$

(b) $\dfrac{5b^2t}{12}$

(c) $12r$

(d) $\dfrac{1}{5d^2}$

(e) $\dfrac{49m}{k^4}$

(f) $\dfrac{5}{7d^3e^2}$

(g) $\dfrac{1}{2k^3nm^2}$

(h) $\dfrac{9}{2v^2w^4z}$

(i) $1$

3. (a) $\dfrac{(2\beta + 5)^2}{28}$

(b) $\dfrac{15z^2}{(z+2)(z+3)}$

(c) $\dfrac{(x+2)(x-2)}{12}$

(d) $\dfrac{p^3}{2p-5}$

(e) $\dfrac{3}{c}$

(f) $\dfrac{x^2}{x+y}$

4. (a) $\dfrac{15r}{2}$

(b) $18y$

(c) $50t^7$

(d) $\dfrac{1}{4s^3}$

(e) $9x^4$

(f) $\dfrac{1}{24p^2}$

5. (a) $12a$

(b) $21h^4$

(c) $\dfrac{2}{25k^3}$

(d) $\dfrac{3}{20p^3}$

(e) $25\alpha^5$

(f) $\dfrac{5}{27x^5}$

6. (a) $2y$

(b) $\dfrac{1}{3a}$

(c) $\dfrac{4}{p^3}$

(d) $\dfrac{w}{3}$

(e) $6t^2$

(f) $\dfrac{j}{2}$

7. (a) $4 + \dfrac{4}{x} + \dfrac{1}{x^2}$

(b) $p^2 - 2 + \dfrac{1}{p^2}$

(c) $k^4 + 2k + \dfrac{1}{k^2}$

(d) $x^2 - \dfrac{25}{x^2}$

(e) $2t^2 - 3 - \dfrac{2}{t^2}$

(f) $2a + 13 + \dfrac{15}{a}$

---

## Exercise 8.3d    page 112

1. (a) $\dfrac{2t+3}{1-4t}$

(b) $\dfrac{x+1}{3x-1}$

(c) $\dfrac{2r-3}{4r+1}$

(d) $\dfrac{1}{a^2-5}$

2. (a) $\dfrac{1+\tan x}{\tan x - 1}$

(b) $\dfrac{5n^2-2}{3}$

(c) $\dfrac{3-8y^2}{10y^2-7}$

(d) $\dfrac{2a^2+5}{4a^2+5}$

3. (a) $\dfrac{7x}{2x+1}$

(b) $\dfrac{8z-1}{6z}$

(c) $\dfrac{12y}{1-6y}$

(d) $\dfrac{1-14t}{35t}$

4. (a) $\dfrac{g\left(2+g^2\right)}{3g-1}$

(b) $\dfrac{\cos x(7+\sin x)}{5\cos x - \sin x}$

(c) $\dfrac{b(8+a)}{a}$

(d) $\dfrac{\sin C(\sin C - 4)}{\cos C}$

5. (a) $\dfrac{1-2e^2}{e(1+4e)}$

(b) $\dfrac{v(2v+1)}{2+5v^2}$

(c) $\dfrac{5-3b^3}{b^2(6+7b)}$

(d) $\dfrac{a(a+3)}{a^2+1}$

6. (a) $\dfrac{t(s+2)}{s(7+t)}$

(b) $\dfrac{m(4mn+1)}{n(mn+1)}$

(c) $\dfrac{\sin t}{\cos t}$

(d) $\dfrac{g(2f^2+1)}{f^2(2g+1)}$

7. (a) $\dfrac{12+t}{2t-3}$

(b) $\dfrac{20+3a}{a-8}$

(c) $\dfrac{2\omega-5}{15+4\omega}$

**8.** (a) $\dfrac{2-p}{9p+4}$

(b) $\dfrac{5a-2}{a-3}$

(c) $\dfrac{\cos\theta - 3\sin\theta}{2\sin\theta + 5\cos\theta}$

---

### Exercise 8.3e  *page 113*

**1.** (a) $\dfrac{4}{x}$

(b) $\dfrac{3}{b}$

(c) $\dfrac{-1}{w+5}$

(d) $\dfrac{1}{2p-1}$

(e) $\dfrac{8}{3y}$

(f) $\dfrac{-1}{t+7}$

**2.** (a) $\dfrac{10k}{9}$

(b) $\dfrac{s}{4}$

(c) $\dfrac{r}{5}$

(d) $\dfrac{4a}{3}$

**3.** (a) $\dfrac{2-x}{x}$

(b) $\dfrac{2+mn}{m}$

(c) $\dfrac{pq-2}{q}$

(d) $\dfrac{a-6b}{2b}$

(e) $\dfrac{3\beta^2 - 2}{\beta}$

(f) $\dfrac{a+4b^2}{b}$

**4.** (a) $\dfrac{19x-5}{6}$

(b) $\dfrac{23a+5}{10}$

(c) $-\dfrac{15}{4}$

(d) $\dfrac{11b+6}{42}$

(e) $\dfrac{13s-8}{30}$

(f) $\dfrac{225-2d}{60}$

**5.** (a) $\dfrac{2x+y}{xy}$

(b) $\dfrac{35q-6p}{21pq}$

(c) $\dfrac{3s+4t}{3st}$

(d) $\dfrac{7z-2xy}{xyz}$

**6.** (a) $\dfrac{2n-3}{n^2}$

(b) $\dfrac{x+3}{x^2}$

(c) $\dfrac{5-2m^2}{m^3}$

(d) $\dfrac{2+9v^3}{v^8}$

(e) $\dfrac{p^2+2p-5}{p^3}$

(f) $\dfrac{3-4r+r^3-9r^4}{r^5}$

**7.** (a) $\dfrac{3b-4}{b-2}$

(b) $\dfrac{-13d-6}{2d+1}$

(c) $\dfrac{11p+2}{2p+1}$

(d) $\dfrac{3}{a^2-1}$

(e) $\dfrac{2\sin x - \cos x}{\sin x}$

(f) $\dfrac{1+\tan\theta}{\tan\theta}$

(g) $\dfrac{\cos A + 2}{\cos A}$

(h) $\dfrac{\sin t \cos t - 1}{\sin t}$

**8.** (a) $\dfrac{4x-3}{x(x+3)}$

(b) $\dfrac{6s-7}{s(s-7)}$

(c) $\dfrac{5w+11}{(w+1)(w+3)}$

(d) $\dfrac{9t+35}{t(t+7)}$

(e) $\dfrac{5\alpha+11}{(\alpha-2)(\alpha+5)}$

(f) $\dfrac{v-8}{(v-4)(v+1)}$

**9.** (a) $\dfrac{x^2+4x-27}{x(x-9)}$

(b) $\dfrac{12n^2+14n-3}{(n+4)(n-3)}$

(c) $\dfrac{-5t^2+7t+14}{(t-1)(t+7)}$

(d) $\dfrac{2e^2+5}{(e-6)(e+1)}$

(e) $\dfrac{d^2-5d-3}{(d-4)(d+3)}$

(f) $\dfrac{2\rho^2-5\rho+13}{(\rho-3)(\rho+1)}$

**10.** (a) $\dfrac{x-8}{(x-7)^2}$

(b) $\dfrac{1}{m-2}$

(c) $\dfrac{3}{p-3}$

---

### Exercise 8.4a  *page 115*

**1.** (a) $\tfrac{1}{3}$

(b) $\tfrac{5}{2}$

(c) $14$

(d) $2$

(e) $\tfrac{6}{7}$

(f) $-6$

(g) $-\tfrac{9}{2}$

(h) $2$

(i) 4

**2.** (a) $-\frac{8}{5}$

(b) $\frac{17}{4}$

(c) 0.3

(d) 2

(e) $\frac{13}{8}$

(f) $-2$

(g) $-6$

(h) 9

(i) $\frac{4}{3}$

**3.** (a) $\frac{2}{3}$

(b) $\frac{1}{12}$

(c) $-\frac{1}{6}$

(d) $-6$

(e) 2

(f) $\frac{1}{2}$

---

**Exercise 8.4b**　　*page 115*

**1.** (a) $-1$ or 5

(b) $-3$ or $-1$

(c) $-3$ or 4

(d) $-5$ or 12

(e) 7 or 10

(f) 2 or 3

**2.** (a) $-\frac{3}{2}$ or 1

(b) $\frac{1}{5}$ or $\frac{1}{3}$

(c) $-\frac{2}{3}$ or 5

(d) $\frac{1}{2}$ or 3

(e) $-\frac{1}{5}$ or 1

(f) 5 or $\dfrac{17}{2}$

---

**Exercise 8.4c**　　*page 116*

**1.** (a) $m = \frac{1}{2}, n = 2$

(b) $g = 4, h = 2$

(c) $p = 5, q = -1$

**2.** (a) $x = 10, y = 2$ or
$x = -10, y = -2$

(b) $x = 6, y = 3$ or
$x = 6, y = -3$

(c) $x = -3, y = 11$ or
$x = 3, y = -13$

**3.** (a) $a = -3, r = 4$ or
$a = 4, r = -3$

(b) $a = 6, r = \frac{1}{3}$ or
$a = 3, r = \frac{2}{3}$

(c) $a = -\frac{4}{3}, r = \frac{3}{2}$ or
$a = 4, r = -\frac{1}{2}$

(d) $a = -10, r = -1$ or
$a = 5, r = 2$

(e) $a = \frac{1}{2}, r = \frac{1}{2}$

---

**Exercise 8.5**　　*page 117*

**1.** (a) $2\sqrt{2}$

(b) $2\sqrt{6}$

(c) $2\sqrt{7}$

(d) $5\sqrt{2}$

(e) $7\sqrt{2}$

(f) $5\sqrt{3}$

(g) $10\sqrt{2}$

(h) $3\sqrt{10}$

(i) $4\sqrt{3}$

(j) $5\sqrt{5}$

**2.** (a) $2\sqrt{3}$

(b) $2\sqrt{6}$

(c) $6\sqrt{3}$

(d) 8

(e) $3\sqrt{2}$

(f) $6\sqrt{2}$

(g) 18

(h) 18

(i) $90\sqrt{2}$

(j) 100

(k) $36\sqrt{2}$

(l) 42

(m) $24\sqrt{2}$

(n) 72

(o) 56

**3.** (a) $3\sqrt{5} + 3\sqrt{2}$

(b) $6\sqrt{3} + 5\sqrt{2}$

(c) $5\sqrt{2} - \sqrt{5}$

(d) $8\sqrt{3} + 3\sqrt{7}$

(e) $20\sqrt{3} - 4\sqrt{2}$

(f) $10\sqrt{5} - \sqrt{7}$

**4.** (a) $5\sqrt{3}$

(b) $7\sqrt{5}$

(c) $2\sqrt{2}$

(d) $5\sqrt{5}$

(e) $2\sqrt{7}$

(f) $9\sqrt{2}$

(g) $3\sqrt{3}$

(h) $5\sqrt{2}$

(i) $3\sqrt{5}$

**5.** (a) $2\sqrt{3} - \sqrt{2}$

(b) $2\sqrt{3} + 2\sqrt{2}$

(c) $4\sqrt{5} + 2\sqrt{3}$

(d) $5\sqrt{3} + \sqrt{2}$

(e) $6\sqrt{2} - 2\sqrt{7}$

(f) $5\sqrt{2} - 4\sqrt{3}$

**6.** (a) $\dfrac{1}{8\sqrt{2}}$

(b) $\dfrac{2\sqrt{2}}{7}$

(c) $\dfrac{3\sqrt{2}}{5\sqrt{5}}$

(d) $\dfrac{7\sqrt{3}}{5\sqrt{2}}$

(e) $\dfrac{10}{11}\sqrt{2}$

**7.** (a) $2 - \sqrt{2}$

(b) $3\sqrt{5} - 5$

(c) $12 - 5\sqrt{3}$

(d) $7\sqrt{2} - 21$

**8.** (a) 1

(b) 4

(c) 13

(d) $-1$

(e) $2$

(f) $5$

9. (a) $2\sqrt{2} - 1$

(b) $7 - 2\sqrt{5}$

(c) $7 - 2\sqrt{2}$

(d) $7 + 4\sqrt{5}$

10. (a) $8\sqrt{2}$

(b) $5\sqrt{5}$

(c) $\frac{1}{2}\sqrt{7}$

(d) $\frac{4}{3}\sqrt{3}$

(e) $1$

(f) $5$

(g) $\frac{6}{5}\sqrt{2}$

(h) $\dfrac{3\sqrt{5}}{\sqrt{2}}$

11. (a) $\sqrt{2}$

(b) $2\sqrt{5}$

(c) $2\sqrt{3}$

(d) $3\sqrt{7}$

(e) $4\sqrt{3}$

(f) $9\sqrt{2}$

(g) $\sqrt{2} + 1$

(h) $3 + \sqrt{5}$

(i) $5 + \sqrt{2}$

(j) $1 + 2\sqrt{7}$

(k) $\dfrac{5\sqrt{3}}{3} + \sqrt{2}$

(l) $\dfrac{1}{5} + \dfrac{2\sqrt{2}}{5}$

---

**Exercise 8.6**     *page 119*

1. (a) $125\,000$

(b) $\dfrac{36}{25}$

(c) $\dfrac{27}{64}$

(d) $2$

2. (a) $0.2^4$

(b) $6\alpha^4$

(c) $3j^5$

(d) $d^3$

(e) $1.6t^{-2}$

(f) $480x^9$

3. (a) $\frac{1}{2}x - 1 + 2x^{-2} + 3x^{\frac{5}{2}}$

(b) $2t^{\frac{3}{2}} + 2t^{\frac{5}{2}} + 8t^{\frac{11}{2}}$

(c) $x^{\frac{5}{2}} - 4x^{\frac{1}{2}}$

4. (a) $-4$

(b) $6$

(c) $\frac{3}{5}$

5. (a) $\dfrac{3c^2}{16}$

(b) $\dfrac{5}{2z}$

(c) $7(x + 4)^4$

(d) $\dfrac{\alpha\beta^4}{1 + \beta + \alpha\beta}$

(e) $-\frac{2}{3}$

(f) $\dfrac{1}{t + 2}$

(g) $\dfrac{s + 6}{s + 1}$

(h) $\dfrac{w - 1}{2w + 1}$

(i) $\dfrac{2(r + 5)}{3(3 - r)}$

6. (a) $\dfrac{3 + b}{6b}$

(b) $\dfrac{10e^2}{10e^2 - 3}$

(c) $\dfrac{\sin^2\theta}{\sin\theta + \cos\theta}$

(d) $\dfrac{y + 3}{y - 2}$

7. (a) $\dfrac{10}{p}$

(b) $\dfrac{\pi(3x - 2)}{12x^2}$

(c) $\dfrac{6e + 1}{e + 2}$

(d) $\dfrac{3\sin\psi\cos\psi + 2}{\cos\psi}$

(e) $\dfrac{2x + 5y - 3xy}{xy}$

(f) $\dfrac{5 - qs + rs}{s^2}$

(g) $\dfrac{6q - 19}{(2q + 1)(q - 5)}$

(h) $\dfrac{\alpha^2 - 6}{(\alpha + 1)(\alpha + 2)}$

(i) $\dfrac{3}{b - a}$

8. (a) $\frac{2}{5}$

(b) $\frac{7}{8}$

(c) $-84$

(d) $\dfrac{1}{15}$

(e) $-\dfrac{31}{5}$

(f) $\frac{2}{11}$

9. (a) $-\frac{6}{5}$ or $1$

(b) $2$ or $9$

(c) $1$ or $9$

(d) $-\frac{4}{3}$ or $6$

10. (a) $x = \frac{1}{2}, y = -\frac{1}{2}$

(b) $a = 4000, r = -\frac{1}{2}$

(c) $a = -2, b = \frac{1}{3}$

(d) $s = \frac{1}{3}, t = \frac{1}{6}$

(e) $a = 7, r = 2$

(f) $c = -4, d = -0.2$
or $c = 4, d = 0.2$

11. (a) $x = -2, y = 2$ or
$x = 4, y = -1$

(b) $x = \frac{5}{2}, y = \frac{11}{2}$ or
$x = 4, y = 4$

12. (a) $8\sqrt{2}$

(b) $3\sqrt{5}$

(c) $10\sqrt{6}$

(d) $100\sqrt{6}$

(e) $2\sqrt{3}$

(f) $\sqrt{5}$

(g) $9\sqrt{3}$

(h) $\frac{3}{5}\sqrt{10}$

13. (a) $6\sqrt{3} - \sqrt{7}$

(b) $4\sqrt{10} - 3\sqrt{11}$

(c) $8\sqrt{3}$

(d) $12\sqrt{2}$

14. (a) $\sqrt{5} + 35$

(b) $2 + 3\sqrt{6}$

(c) $6 + 30\sqrt{2}$

(d) $4$

(e) $8 - 2\sqrt{7}$

(f) $7 - 4\sqrt{6}$

15. (a) $21\sqrt{2}, 6\sqrt{7} + 2\sqrt{14}$

(b) $31, 24$

(c) $8, \dfrac{4\left(a^2b^2 + 18\right)}{3ab}$

16. $x = \sqrt{2}, y = 2$

17. (a) $\sqrt{2}$

(b) $(\sqrt{2}, 0)$

(c) $2\left(\sqrt{2} - 1\right)$

---

**Exercise 9.1a**　　*page 122*

1. $x(x + 6)\,\text{cm}^2$

2. (a) $(28 - l)\,\text{cm}$

(b) $l(28 - l)\,\text{cm}^2$

3. $34 - n$

4. $4s^2$

5. (a) $50 - 2s$

(b) $s^2(50 - 2s)$

6. (a) $p = n + 3$

(b) $\dfrac{89}{n(n + 3)}$

7. (a) $2b$

(b) $2b^2$

(c) $\dfrac{5}{b^2}$

(d) $4b^2 + \dfrac{30}{b}$

8. $(30 - 3w)\,\text{cm}$

---

9. (a) $2 - a^2$

(b) $2a(2 - a^2)$

10. $\sqrt{2\,(x^2 - 4x + 8)}$

11. (a) $x\,\text{cm}$

(b) $(30 - 2x)\,\text{cm}$

(c) $(24 - 2x)\,\text{cm}$

(d) $4x(12 - x)(15 - x)\,\text{cm}^3$

(e) $4\left(180 - x^2\right)\,\text{cm}^2$

12. (a) $3w\,\text{cm}$

(b) $3w^2\,\text{cm}^2$

(c) $\dfrac{17 - 3w^2}{4w}\,\text{cm}$

(d) $\frac{3}{4}w\left(17 - 3w^2\right)\,\text{cm}^3$

13. (a) $\dfrac{100}{v}\,\text{hours}$

(b) $\left(2v^2 + \dfrac{700}{v}\right)\,\text{litres}$

---

**Exercise 9.1b**　　*page 124*

1. (a) $7$

(b) $5$

(c) $4$

2. $7$

3. $8$

4. $70\,\text{p}$

5. $3$

6. $110\,\text{cm}, 120\,\text{cm},$
$130\,\text{cm}, 140\,\text{cm}$

7. $4\,\text{litres}$

8. $32$

9. $3\text{ and }5$

10. $9$

11. $3$

12. $2$

13. $5\,\text{m} \times 12\,\text{m}$

14. $660\,\text{cm}^3$

15. (a) $2l\,\text{m}$

---

(b) $3$

16. $8$

---

**Exercise 9.2**　　*page 127*

1. (a) $x = 3b - a$

(b) $x = 11t$

(c) $x = \frac{1}{2}c$

(d) $x = -\frac{1}{4}t$

(e) $x = as$

(f) $x = 2r^2$

(g) $x = \dfrac{h}{h - 2}$

(h) $x = \frac{1}{5}(c - k)$

(i) $x = \dfrac{b - 6}{a}$

(j) $x = 2 - m$

(k) $x = -\frac{2}{5}\pi$

(l) $x = c - 6g$

2. (a) $x = 8kn$

(b) $x = gh^2$

(c) $x = \dfrac{3}{h}$

(d) $x = \dfrac{g}{9}$

(e) $x = \dfrac{a}{c^2}$

(f) $x = \dfrac{\pi}{4}$

(g) $x = -y$

(h) $x = -\dfrac{\pi}{2}$

(i) $x = \dfrac{2\pi}{5}$

(j) $x = \dfrac{ab}{4}$

(k) $x = \dfrac{1}{2p}$

(l) $x = \dfrac{1}{5pq}$

3. (a) $x = y^2$

(b) $x = (p - 2)^2$

(c) $x = (b + c)^2$

(d) $x = \dfrac{t^2}{s}$

---

163

(e) $x = g^2h^2$

(f) $x = \dfrac{1}{q^2}$

(g) $x = j^2 + f$

(h) $x = u(v^2 - 1)$

(i) $x = b^2(c + d)^2$

4. (a) $x = \pm\sqrt{m}$

(b) $x = \pm\sqrt{\dfrac{s}{\pi}}$

(c) $x = \sqrt[3]{\dfrac{a}{b}}$

(d) $2\sqrt[3]{k}$

(e) $x = \pm\sqrt{6 - gh}$

(f) $x = \pm\sqrt[4]{\dfrac{f + 5}{b}}$

(g) $x = g(4 - h)$

(h) $x = \pm\sqrt{k} - j$

(i) $x = b^3d + c$

(j) $x = \pm\dfrac{2}{\sqrt{p + 2q}}$

(k) $x = \dfrac{f}{2f + g}$

(l) $x = \sqrt[3]{d} + e$

(m) $x = n^2(n - m)$

(n) $x = \dfrac{t}{s^2} - 1$

(o) $x = v(\pm\sqrt{w} - u)$

5. (a) $x = \dfrac{y^2}{a}$

(b) $x = k(m + n)$

(c) $x = \dfrac{7}{2 + p}$

(d) $x = \dfrac{p - y}{q}$

(e) $x = y^2 + 4$

(f) $x = \dfrac{qr}{p}$

(g) $x = \pm d\sqrt{h}$

(h) $x = \left(a^2 - 1\right)^2$

(i) $x = \dfrac{1}{y} - 2$

(j) $x = b(p - a)$

(k) $x = 3 \pm \sqrt{m}$

(l) $x = 3(8 - k)$

6. (a) $x = \dfrac{k}{1 - k}$

(b) $x = \dfrac{u^2}{u - 1}$

(c) $x = \dfrac{c + d}{1 + c}$

(d) $x = \dfrac{b}{1 - a}$

(e) $x = \dfrac{p}{1 - r}$

(f) $x = \dfrac{p}{p - 1}$

(g) $x = \dfrac{d - b}{a - c}$

(h) $x = \dfrac{2g}{h - 1}$

(i) $x = \dfrac{c + d}{c - d}$

(j) $x = \dfrac{c}{a - b + d}$

(k) $x = \dfrac{3}{2 - p - q}$

(l) $x = \dfrac{a + g}{u^2 - v^2}$

(m) $x = \dfrac{a}{b - 6}$

(n) $x = \dfrac{2d - b}{a - 2c}$

(o) $x = \dfrac{3p + 4q}{3q - 4p}$

7. (a) $r = \dfrac{C}{2\pi}$

(b) $u = v - at$

(c) $\cos\theta = a - b$

(d) $l = \dfrac{V}{bh}$

(e) $t = \dfrac{d}{V}$

(f) $i = \dfrac{V}{R}$

(g) $r = \sqrt{\dfrac{A}{\pi}}$

(h) $b = \tfrac{1}{2}P - l$

(i) $h = \dfrac{2A}{b}$

(j) $I = \sqrt{\dfrac{P}{R}}$

(k) $t = \dfrac{v - u}{a}$

(l) $r = \sqrt{\dfrac{V}{\pi h}}$

(m) $u = \sqrt{v^2 - 2as}$

(n) $h = \dfrac{S - 5x^2}{6x}$

(o) $d = \sqrt{\dfrac{k}{s}}$

(p) $m = \dfrac{Fr^2}{GM}$

(q) $v = \sqrt{\dfrac{2E}{m}}$

(r) $\sin B = \dfrac{b\sin 40°}{a}$

(s) $m = k - dt$

(t) $R = \sqrt{\dfrac{A}{\pi} + r^2}$

(u) $\rho = \dfrac{D - 6\alpha}{2\pi + 3}$

(v) $l = \left(\dfrac{T}{2\pi}\right)^2 g$

(w) $a = \dfrac{n(P - n)}{1 - p}$

(x) $e = \dfrac{l - r}{r\cos\theta}$

## Exercise 9.3    page 129

1. (a) $(x + 3)^2 - 9$

(b) $(x - 6)^2 - 36$

(c) $(x + 5)^2 - 25$

(d) $(x - 2)^2 - 4$

(e) $\left(x - \tfrac{1}{2}\right)^2 - \tfrac{1}{4}$

(f) $\left(x + \tfrac{11}{2}\right)^2 - \tfrac{121}{4}$

(g) $(x - 4)^2 - 11$

(h) $(x - 1)^2 - 7$

(i) $(x + 8)^2 + 6$

(j) $(x - 7)^2 + 1$

(k) $(x - 5)^2 - 13$

(l) $(x + 2)^2 - 7$

(m) $\left(x + \frac{3}{2}\right)^2 - \frac{5}{4}$

(n) $\left(x - \frac{7}{2}\right)^2 - \frac{33}{4}$

(o) $\left(x + \frac{5}{2}\right)^2 - \frac{29}{4}$

2. (a) $4 - (x - 2)^2$

(b) $9 - (x - 3)^2$

(c) $36 - (x + 6)^2$

(d) $17 - (x - 4)^2$

(e) $21 - (x + 1)^2$

(f) $\frac{25}{4} - \left(x + \frac{1}{2}\right)^2$

3. (a) $2(x + 3)^2 - 18$

(b) $5(x + 2)^2 - 20$

(c) $7(x - 4)^2 - 112$

(d) $4(x - 3)^2 - 41$

(e) $5(x + 1)^2 + 1$

(f) $3(x + 10)^2 + 100$

(g) $2\left(x + \frac{5}{2}\right)^2 - \frac{19}{2}$

(h) $7\left(x - \frac{3}{2}\right)^2 - \frac{47}{4}$

(i) $3\left(x + \frac{1}{6}\right)^2 - \frac{37}{12}$

4. (a) $8 - 2(x - 2)^2$

(b) $75 - 3(x - 5)^2$

(c) $42 - 2(x + 4)^2$

(d) $1 - 4(x - 1)^2$

(e) $63 - 7(x - 3)^2$

(f) $\frac{5}{4} - \left(x + \frac{1}{2}\right)^2$

5. (a) $2(x - 3)^2 - 17$

(b) $8(x + 1)^2 - 11$

(c) $-5(x + 4)^2 + 84$

(d) $2(x + 0.4)^2 + 0.68$

(e) $0.1(x + 3)^2 + 1.1$

(f) $-(x - 6)^2 + 36$

6. (a) $-2 \pm \sqrt{3}$

(b) $3 \pm \sqrt{7}$

(c) $-\frac{1}{2} \pm \frac{1}{2}\sqrt{5}$

(d) $-1 \pm \sqrt{\frac{7}{2}}$

(e) $2 \pm \sqrt{\frac{17}{3}}$

(f) $-1 \pm \sqrt{\frac{6}{5}}$

7. (a) $2 \pm \sqrt{3}$

(b) $-4 \pm \sqrt{21}$

(c) $-5 \pm \sqrt{6}$

(d) $3 \pm 2\sqrt{2}$

(e) $-2 \pm \sqrt{5}$

(f) $-\frac{2}{3} \pm \frac{1}{3}\sqrt{10}$

---

**Exercise 9.4a**   *page 131*

1. (a) $22, -3, 7, 7.5$

(b) 4

2. (a) $\frac{1}{2}, -\dfrac{19}{4}, 0.8,$
$-1.375$

(b) $-12$

3. (a) $49, 17, -1, 1.42$

(b) $-3$ or $3$

4. (a) $64, 1, \frac{1}{4}, 2$

(b) 2

(c) $-2$

5. (a) $23, 7$

(b) $-4$ or $4$

(c) $a^2 - 2, t^2 - 2, r^2 - 2$

6. (a) $-1$

(b) $-5$ or $3$

(c) $a^2 + 2a, m^2 + 2m$

7. (a) $3m - 2$

(b) $6t - 2$

(c) $3a - 3$

8. (a) $2a^2 + 7$

(b) $18t^2 + 7$

(c) $2m^2 + 12m + 25$

9. (a) $t(t + 3)$

(b) $2a(2a + 3)$

(c) $(3m - 1)(3m + 2)$

10. (a) $x(4 - x)$

(b) $x^2\left(4 - x^2\right)$

(c) $x^3\left(4 - x^3\right)$

11. (a) $3a + 2, 5 - 3a$

(b) 1

12. (a) $\sqrt{2a + 9}, \sqrt{4b + 3}$

(b) 8

(c) $-\frac{1}{2}$

13. (a) $-3$ or $1$

(b) $-1$ or $1$

14. 2 or 5

15. (a) $-1$ or $\frac{5}{4}$

(b) 2 or $\frac{9}{2}$

---

**Exercise 9.4b**   *page 133*

1. $8, -9$

2. $3, 2$

3. $\frac{1}{2}, 0$

4. $\frac{1}{3}, 2, 7$

5. $-2, -7$

6. $-2, 3$ or $3, -2$

7. $5, 6, 0$

---

**Exercise 9.5**   *page 134*

1. $n(14 - n)$

2. $a\sqrt{20 - a^2}$

3. $16 - \sqrt{3}s^2$

4. 2

5. 4

6. 4

7. (a) $h = \dfrac{S - 8r^2}{5r}$

(b) $u = \dfrac{2vt}{3 - t}$

(c) $v = 3u$

(d) $p = a + b$

(e) $k = \pm\sqrt{m + 4}$

(f) $\gamma = \dfrac{1}{(\beta^2 - \alpha)^2}$

(g) $x = \pm\dfrac{a}{b}\sqrt{b^2 - y^2}$

(h) $\theta = \alpha + \sin^{-1}\dfrac{r}{h}$

**8.** $\sin A = \dfrac{a \sin B}{b}$

**9.** $\cos A = \dfrac{b^2 + c^2 - a^2}{2bc}$

**10.** (a) $(x + 3)^2 - 8$

    (b) $-(x - 4)^2 + 17$

    (c) $3(x + 2)^2 - 14$

    (d) $5\left(x + \frac{1}{5}\right)^2 - \frac{1}{5}$

(e) $-2\left(x + \frac{3}{4}\right)^2 + \frac{25}{8}$

(f) $7\left(x + \frac{3}{2}\right)^2 + \frac{1}{4}$

**11.** (a) $-3 \pm \sqrt{7}$

    (b) $5 \pm 4\sqrt{2}$

    (c) $-1 \pm \frac{1}{2}\sqrt{2}$

**12.** (a) 33

(b) 3

**13.** $-\frac{1}{5}, 0$

**14.** $5, -7$

**15.** (a) $(p - 9)(p + 2)$

    (b) $3 + 11\sqrt{3}$

**16.** (a) $-7$ or $-2$

    (b) $-2$ or $2$

# Index